In the Eye

of the Typhoon

*Recollections of the M.C.C.
tour of Australia 1954/55*

Frank 'Typhoon' Tyson

Foreword by David Frith

The Parrs Wood Press
Manchester

First Published 2004

THE PARRS WOOD PRESS
St Wilfrid's Enterprise Centre
Royce Road, Manchester, M15 5BJ
www.parrswoodpress.com

© **Frank H. Tyson 2004**

ISBN: 1 903158 57 5

Printed and bound in Spain

CONTENTS

ACKNOWLEDGEMENTS

This book owes everything to my colleagues in the M.C.C. touring party of 1954/55 and our Australian opponents. They are its very essence - more especially to the survivors from those distant days: Keith Andrew, Reg Simpson, Vic Wilson, Bob Appleyard, Trevor Bailey, Alec Bedser, Tom Graveney, Peter Loader, Arthur Morris, Neil Harvey, Keith Miller, Richie Benaud, Alan Davidson, Bill Johnston, Ron Archer, and Colin McDonald. Memories of the fifties came aplenty - and still do, from them and from my still extant Northamptonshire colleagues, especially George Tribe, Denis Brookes, Peter Arnold and Lewis McGibbon. The hard yards were done by the Kay family, especially Fanny and her daughter Margaret, who, 50 years ago, compiled the scrapbooks which provide the factual record on which this story of the tour is based. Edwin Kay supported me in my younger days at Middleton - his brother John of the Manchester Evening News was just one of the many journalists who backed me in print: Alf Gover, Alan Ross, John Arlott, Frank Rostron, Charles Fortune, Charles Bray, et alia. To my wife Ursula and my family my thanks for their encouragement to write about times which predated them. I shall forever be indebted to Margaret, Alan and Rita Jenkins, Stan and Rosemary Bentley, the Warren and Forsaith families, whose acquaintance enriched this period of my life. As regards the production of this book, special thanks to my friend David Frith, for his advice and guidance whilst compiling this book and for providing the Foreword, and to Andy Searle and his staff at The Parrs Wood Press, who have worked so assiduously in putting together the finished product. Finally, a big thankyou to the country which provided the setting for this story and subsequently made me one of their own.

FOREWORD

by David Frith

IMAGINE A BOY FROM London sitting on a wooden bench at the Sydney Cricket Ground amidst 49,317 throaty Australian cricket fans. England toil all day under a hot sun and Neil Harvey, Keith Miller and Ian Johnson stack the runs, taking the home side well into the lead and setting up an innings victory on the morrow, when Jack Iverson's baffling spinners would dispatch six Englishmen for 27 runs. That made it three-nil to Australia after three Tests and the deflated immigrant lad sloped off back to school, where the mocking was intense.

Imagine this boy, two years later, staying up half the night, shivering in darkness by the crackling wireless during the 1953 series over in England, and imagine his joy when his hero, Len Hutton, at long last led England to victory at The Oval in the final Test, recapturing the little urn which had been lost to Australia nineteen years previously. Notwithstanding his freshly-minted affection for Ray Lindwall and Neil Harvey, the teenager quietly shed a tear or two of ecstasy at the historic success of Hutton, Edrich, May, Compton, Graveney, Bailey, Evans, Laker, Lock, Trueman and Bedser, immortals all. What a golden age for English cricket had unfolded.

Next, imagine the 17-year old, now hopelessly beguiled by cricket, racing out to the SCG to see the newest England/MCC side play in Australia during the 1954/55 season. Local (St George) batsman Billy Watson dominated that Saturday's play with a patient and unexpected century, but this new English fast bowler, Frank Tyson, caught the eye by virtue of three things: his run-up, which started from near the sightscreen; the lightning speed of his deliveries, powered by a strapping physique and a rugged, explosive action; and his receding hairline. We asked ourselves how old he might be. The NSWCA souvenir handbook revealed that Tyson was only 24. We'd heard about the early shocks he'd inflicted in Northamptonshire's match against the 1953 Australians, so the man soon to be universally known as "Typhoon" was already right up there on the top shelf of expectations among the new faces, as was young Cowdrey. By contrast, and ominously, there were coarse cries drifting from the masses on the Hill of "Old man!" whenever Alec Bedser lumbered after the ball. Among my eager notes on the match is the further observation that Bob Appleyard was saturated in sweat as he plugged away at medium-pace.

So what happens in the opening Test match a fortnight later? Mr Tyson comes away with the blush-making figures of 1 for 160 and England plunge to an innings defeat.

Frank Tyson: a rugged, explosive action.

Imagine, therefore, that hopeful young spectator back at the SCG four years on from the 1950-51 humiliation suffered by Freddie Brown's Poms. He had wriggled out of the difficulties generated by England's sorry showing at the Gabba in the first Test by congratulating all the tellers at the bank where he was employed. In fact, he went on and on with the congratulations, quite undermining any attempt at mockery. And now he sat among the semi-gentry in the Sheridan Stand at the Randwick end, with a wonderful view of the 19th Century architecture of the ground. History oozed from every timber and every section of the intricate lace ironwork.

There was a problem, however. As Hutton and Bailey walked out to face Lindwall on a bowler-friendly pitch, I had serious difficulty breathing. My hands trembled. I hadn't known such tension since German bombers had groaned across the dark skies of north-west London a dozen years earlier. Only when my Len had a few runs on the board did I start to feel normal again.

It was not merely a memorable match. For me it remains, hundreds of Test matches later, the match of my life, and it survives as a package of incidents preserved in full colour, more vivid than much that I saw just last year. There was a back-cut off Lindwall which Hutton executed on tiptoe. There was Trevor Bailey's flying middle stump, courtesy of Lindwall, and Alan Davidson's incredible full-length dive at leg slip to send Hutton back. There was some hilarious swishing and swatting by Johnny Wardle to give the almost-dead England innings a late lift, with Bill Johnston giggling as his bowling was squirted and carted. And in England's second innings there was a thrilling pull by Peter May off Ron Archer, and the sickening spectacle of Frank Tyson being laid out by a Lindwall bouncer. An egg-like bump ballooned on the back of his head, and he was a long time coming round. A British sailor near me was stirred to white anger.

What I didn't know at the time - it's revealed in this book - was that Tyson had bowled bouncers at Ray in the first Test and in the first innings here at Sydney. Further, Bill Edrich turned to the bowler and spluttered, "My God, Lindy, you've killed him!" That's what we all thought.

But Frank resumed his innings later. I recall how Appleyard was hoisted onto the scoreboard, but when the crowd recognised the slightly stooped incoming figure as that of Tyson, they gave him a loud and sympathetic reception. So what did he do? He scored eight more runs before Lindwall bowled him again. Then, valiant soul, he made the ball fly and blew Australia away with 6 for 85 in the second innings, when they had needed only 223 to win.

A fortnight later he capitalised on a suspect Melbourne pitch with 7 for 27, and by the end of the series he had whooshed his way to 28 cheap wickets and acquired a *nom de guerre* for all time - "Typhoon" - with England retaining the Ashes, sending Len Hutton off gloriously into retirement.

The final Test, back in Sydney, was ruined by rain that delayed the start until the fourth day. Yet still there was fun and games, a last-wicket muddle causing Australia to follow on with a couple of hours still remaining. To save time, Tyson bowled off only a few paces - and still almost knocked the bat out of Keith Miller's hands. Physio Harold Dalton was the hidden (until now) influence. He put Frank on a lunchtime "liquid lunch" of raw eggs in milk or orange juice, with a dash of sherry, a more sophisticated intake than Harold Larwood's pint of beer in pre-war days.

The 1954/55 tour was considered the best of all by everyone who took part, including the journalists, but with the obvious exception of Alec Bedser, who was bluntly sidelined after the first Test. We are all especially impressionable as teenagers, and I count myself fortunate to have been witness to so much of the action during that Australian summer. The Tests I could not see I tasted at the newsreel cinema in those pre-television days, and in later years I was privileged to see the 16mm films taken by several of the English players. Happily for me, the 1954-55 Englishmen played four times in Sydney, which was then my hometown.

It is the personal sights that remain vividly ingrained: Peter May's mastery in a match-winning Sydney century and his stand - Cambridge with Oxford - with Colin Cowdrey. When patience finally gave way and Cowdrey was caught in the deep off Benaud, the match was still in the balance. Frank Tyson reveals here that Cowdrey wept upon reaching the dressing-room. Those of us peering from the Hill, of course, had no knowledge of that. Nor did the authors of the half-dozen or so books on the series.

So much else is revealed in this book by a key insider. The author paints pictures of the long-forgotten innocence of Australia half-a-century ago, displaying also a sensitivity for the glorious scenery that the cricketers often encountered, which might come as a surprise to those who thought he was merely a ruthless, ferocious fast bowler.

There is stern frankness here too. One example: when the Ashes were almost within England's grasp at Adelaide, Miller ripped out the first three in his opening three overs, then dived at cover to remove May with a dubious catch. That, says Frank Tyson, was the "most unworthy thing that I ever saw Keith do on the cricket field".

There are insights into the usually impenetrable Len Hutton, like this beauty: "Len always looks askance at rubicund players like Tom [Graveney]. They seem to enjoy the game too much." Tom certainly enjoyed the last Test. They took drinks when he was on 85, and when he removed his cap, you could see how beetroot red was his face from his exertions. Had he enough strength left to get his hundred? An old chap next to me on the benches had been comparing Graveney to Wally Hammond and Charlie Barnett, Gloucestershire batsmen of the previous generation. As if he had heard this, Tom drove and swept Miller for four fours in the (eight-ball) over upon resumption. How disappointed the batsman and all his admirers would have been that evening had they known that this was to be his only hundred ever against Australia.

Foreword

So many images flicker still in the mind's eye: there is young Cowdrey, his crumpled flannels much in need of a good ironing; the last-ever sight of Compton in Test combat, cramped, inhibited - until he tossed his cap to the umpire and began to play some shots; Bailey nobly giving Lindwall his 100th England wicket; John Arlott's unique tenor voice suddenly coming through on my portable radio; Yorkshire singsong - "Coom on ye broad acres!" - as Wardle teased with his left-arm wrist-spin. The skipper had made it plain at the start of the tour that certain players, Tyson among them, were expected to be the supporting cast and nothing more, barring injuries to the principals. That's one aspect which renders the story so romantic. Soon Hutton was placing almost all his faith in Tyson and Brian Statham, that superb and tireless and skilful into-the-wind bowler. The slow over rate upset the Australians, but in this book Frank Tyson defends the strategy with an intellectual logic that brooks little argument.

Diaries filled copiously with contemporary thoughts and observations are wonderful things, and here, when the Englishmen reach New Zealand, not only do we revisit what is still the lowest Test score ever made (26), but at last some light is thrown on the slightly amusing speed test in which Tyson and Statham took part, letting rip with metal-coated balls on a cold, damp day, without any warm-up, and still recording speeds on a par with all the top quickies. If it is tempting to cast doubt on the sonic-beam machine's accuracy, just consult some of those Australian and New Zealand batsmen who were caught with their bats still aloft as the Typhoon blew their houses over.

As the English cricketers left the SCG for the last time on that emotional day in early March 1955, I was captivated by Len Hutton's pale-blue suit, and for days afterwards I searched Sydney for something similar: but in vain. It must have been a Bradford special. I also caught a close-up glimpse of F.H.Tyson. Just after the match he and Graveney had stood by the window of the dressing-room, both with only towels around their waists, and I marvelled at the express bowler's meaty shoulders and back muscles. It seemed he could have taken on many of the world's top cruiserweights. One thing I knew there and then: with my relatively light physique I could forget about blinding batsmen with speed. Henceforth, Lindwall would be the centre of aspiration.

Now here came Tyson himself, strolling down the pathway towards the members' gate. And, dreamy lad that I was, I froze until he was about 22 yards away, when I experienced some sort of phantasmagoric flash. I was the batsman. Here he comes. Go on, let it go. Fast as you like. Then I think I blushed, turned and hurried away from the Sydney Cricket Ground, returning only to watch Sheffield Shield cricket for the next three seasons before the Englishmen came back, Tyson this time a yard or two less fast and England helpless before the rejuvenated Australia. Frank probably didn't bother keeping a diary on that tour. Thank goodness, though, he kept one on the fabulous 1954/55 tour, and got it out of the bottom drawer in time for the 50th anniversary.

Imagine, then, the pleasure of that isolated young admirer of so long ago when he became an acquaintance, and then a part-time neighbour in Queensland, and then a friend of the Typhoon, and was honoured with the chance to pen a foreword to the book on that exciting summer of so long ago.

In 1955 the Northants committee, in their inexplicable meanness, voted against backing a civic reception for Frank Tyson and Keith Andrew. Perhaps that doesn't matter, for the entire country - and expatriates faraway - gave Len's Men a tender vote of thanks in their hearts which lasted for days into years.

David Frith
March 10th, 2004

INTRODUCTION

Shipboard photograph of the M.C.C. touring team
to Australia & New Zealand 1954/55.

FRANCIS BACON wrote that 'he that travelleth into a country before he hath some entrance into the language, goeth to school and not to travel. Let diaries therefore be brought into use.' When I embarked on my journey to Australasia with the M.C.C. side of 1954/55 I went, as Bacon wrote, to school; indeed it was the greatest educational experience of my life. Thus I make no excuse for re-living the events of those memorable few months. I kept a diary of the trip, which I am now expanding and reproducing - just to show that a cricketer never stops remembering and learning.

No doubt there are those who baulk at living in the past; and certainly nothing is worse than listening to former cricketers moaning about things not being what they used to be 'in the old days'. Forgive me, however, if I think that Len Hutton's touring side to Australia fifty years ago was unique. It must have been special to have inspired so many books on it from authors such as 'Johnny' Moyes, Alan Ross, John Arlott, Keith Miller, and Dick Whitington.

In the first instance, it was one of an elite half dozen of 23 England sides to have won a Test series Down Under in the twentieth century. One of those six teams triumphed 5-1 simply because its Australian opposition was decimated by mass desertions to the Packer Camp in the dark days of the 1977 schism. In 1932/33 Douglas Jardine's team pummelled its way to a 4-1 victory over Woodfull's eleven - but used suspect 'Bodyline' tactics. Hutton's Yorkshire acolyte, Ray Illingworth, managed to imitate his master's example by winning in 1970/71 - but not by the same 3-1 margin as Hutton's men. Chapman's 1928/29 combination, alone, was of the same stature as the 1954/55 side. And what a side Chapman's was, containing, as it did, Hobbs, Sutcliffe, Hammond, Hendren, Chapman, Larwood, Tate and White!

Let us compare and equate such talent with that of Hutton's side: the Skipper himself, the irrepressible Denis Compton and the gutsy Bill Edrich - all admittedly past their best; the two batting prodigies, Peter May and Colin Cowdrey: and the variegated attack of the metronomic Statham, and the guileful Wardle and Appleyard. There is not much to choose between the two teams.

The cruel depredations of mortality have prompted me into writing this diary, fifty years on from 1954. I felt that I had to record the great qualities - human and sporting- embodied in the eighteen people who shared those halcyon months in Australia so long ago. I simply cannot let them fade from memory without their just reward and recognition. Eventually we all have to admit that Death cares nothing of keeping a team together. So it was that baggage-man, 'Admiral', George Duckworth packed his bags first for his final trip. Then the joker Wardle laughed his last on his farm tractor, to be followed by Bill Edrich - who else could get into Cricket's Valhalla by falling DOWN a flight of stairs on his seventieth birthday? Bill never went anywhere without his Middlesex twin - so the ebullient Compo accompanied him to his maker. Then, in quick succession, followed Peter May, Sir Len Hutton - did he ever bat so low? - Lord Colin Cowdrey and Brian Statham. Godfrey Evans, who always cheered us up on hot days in the field with calls of 'Come on lads, they can't stop the clock' - finally found his clock had wound down. Then Jim McConnon spun his last ball and the gentleman manager, Geoffrey Howard, after making sure that everything was in order, got on the team coach.

The passage of 50 years has given me the opportunity to reflect on the individual cricketing abilities and human qualities of those men who played alongside me in 1954/55, to compare them with others who have passed across the international stage since, and assess how they might have responded to the game's changing background. How might they have developed? What heights might they have reached? Certainly the fielding skills of the fifties bear no comparison to the modern player's mastery of this department of the game. Today's cricketers are much fitter, much bigger, much stronger, eat and drink more sensibly, prepare game plans much more methodically, use more psychology, travel less stressfully, are better coached and are generally much better prepared than their counterparts of half a century ago. In this respect it is worth remembering that when we embarked on the 'Orsova' on September 15th 1954, many commodities in England - food, fuel, clothes - were still rationed ten years after the end of the war! The first lunch I ate on board was the most food I had seen in my life! The support team of the M.C.C. team was a manager and baggage man. Harold Dalton was the first qualified masseur appointed to tour with the side, who normally relied on locally recruited supernumeraries. Coaching was done by the senior professionals in the side. There were no bowling, batting, fielding coaches, media and operations managers, warm-ups and warm downs. Fitness was in the hands of the physiotherapist, who was often just a 'slap and tickle merchant' - fortunately not in our case. Flying replacements out for injured players was an expensive rarity. Touring teams economised and were expected to return a profit to headquarters. Gate money was expected to fund the tour - there was no television or sponsorship income. Nor did teams always stay at the best hotels - their cost was a factor to be considered. Geoffrey Howard was not even provided with a touring account to pay expenses. He had to open a personal bank overdraft to pay the early touring costs.

The one constant of Test teams of the fifties and those of the third millennium is skill. Players of the 1900s had to have a natural talent which was the equivalent of their modern counterparts. Indeed, I contend that the many advantages which today's players enjoy in the areas of fitness, tactical and mental preparation, support personnel, equipment, travel, accommodation, pitch and outfield quality, lessen the skill demands on them. Denis Compton hooked better than any modern player - yet he never wore a helmet. He just depended on the Compton flair. Hutton's technique enabled him to score an unbeaten 62 out of an England total of 122 on a Brisbane 'sticky' in 1950. The old timers at the 'Gabba still speak of it in reverend, hushed tones. I doubt whether there is one modern player in the world capable of emulating Hutton's feat.

Thus the question I ask when judging the merits of my 1954/55 team-mates is: 'How well would they have played if they had all the advantages of the X Generation?' How prolific a scorer would the innovative Denis Compton have been in One-Day Cricket? How effective a bowler would the deadly accurate Brian Statham or Bob Appleyard have been in Limited-Overs Internationals? How many more Test wickets would Johnny Wardle have taken in today's opportunity-rich era? Even without such match bonuses, Johnny - in his dual capacity as an orthodox or wrist spinner - must have added to his career tally of 102 victims had he not been sacked by the Yorkshire Establishment and demoted from the 1958/59 M.C.C.side - just for writing unacceptable articles about Headingley politics! He had a wonderful tour of South Africa in 1956/57 - could he have repeated it the following year and helped England come closer to beating Benaud's Australians? How many more Test runs would the iron-willed May and fluent Cowdrey have scored in today's helter-skelter international programme - and, in May's case, with the help of better health. After all, Cowdrey was able to stage a comeback at the age of 40 and score 41 against the pace of Jeff Thomson and Denis Lillee on the lightning fast Perth pitch. With the help of modern sports injury management could I have avoided the minor but persistent injury of the bruised heel which kept me out of Tests for so long in the mid-fifties? I often wonder how much better players of my time would have been if they had known as much and had the same benefits as today's cricketers?

We should be happy that we played with and against giants. Could we have aspired to higher ambitions? God might have drawn the line there!!

Frank Tyson
September 15th, 2004

Chapter One

The Departure

CERTAIN DAYS IN ONE'S LIFE, BE they rosy or grey, are forever recorded in one's memory. One such day - or rather the evening of one such day - was that on which I was told that the dream which I had dreamt all my cricketing youth had come true. I was chosen in an England side sent to win the 1954/55 Ashes series in Australia! This intoxicating moment set off a whizz-bang firework display in my imagination of the possible. I visualised mowing down the stumps of Arthur Morris, bouncing Neil Harvey into submission, and rattling the wickets of Graeme Hole. Suddenly the sober drabness of the Northants dressing room was transformed into the brilliance of cricket's seventh heaven.

Northamptonshire's home game against Middlesex on July 27th 1954 had just ended. We were sipping our end-of-match drinks. A battered Vidor portable radio lay on the plank table of the team's spartan dressing room: the transmitter of joy or disappointment. We were waiting for the announcement of the names of the 18 English cricketers chosen to tour Australia, news which usually preceded the County Championship close-of-play scores. It was all well and good for Keith Andrew. The party was broadcast in alphabetical order, immediately after

CAP FOR TYSON— AND A REQUEST

FRANK TYSON, the Northants fast bowler, was to-day awarded his county cap, and it was also announced that he had received a request from M.C.C. to say whether he would be available for the Australian tour if selected. This is Tyson's first full season for Northants. He is 24, a native of Bolton, and played league cricket with Middleton.

Len Hutton was named England's captain. Thus, within five seconds of the newscaster beginning to read out the names of the selected players, Keith knew that he was to be the reserve keeper to Godfrey Evans; what

Tyson is hot tip for Australia

THE only thing in circulation among the waters of Old Trafford yesterday was the story that Frank Tyson, Northants speed man, rated the fastest bowler in the world, would be named this evening as a member of England's party in Australia this winter.

M.C.C. have asked Northants if Tyson will be available to make the trip. Queries as to the availability of nearly 40 players have been sent out, but I now believe that Tyson will be No. 1 support to Statham and Trueman.

This Lancashire - born very fast for half a dozen overs, and quite likely to get a quick couple of wickets at low cost.

But Tyson, lacking the movement in the air and off the pitch of some of our more mature speed bowlers, has

FRANK TYSON

Says TONY STEVENS

attacker is a shock bowler— not quite the same explosive effect in any later spells.

That observation is judged by his performances so far on English wickets. The firmer conditions in Australia will make him even faster, but a too-soon introduction to Australian batting can upset his career.

FOR EXPERIENCE

There is no doubt that a number of post-war young tourists have had their cricket careers set back by their introduction too soon to Test cricket.

Tyson will probably play only in up-country games.

He could be a dynamic success right away, and force his way into the Tests, but I think M.C.C. will be satisfied to use him for experience on this tour.

Play in the Test at Manchester yesterday was called off for the day at two o'clock after four hours' solid rain.

WATERLOGGED

Soon after the downpour the wicket was waterlogged, and at 1.30 stretches between the covers were completely under water.

Any more rain to-night may force the abandonment to-day of this match, because the ground has taken a soaking on every one of these first four days.

So the tourists have so far in this Test series managed to play only eight days out of a scheduled 14.

followed was thirty seconds of agony for someone whose name started with 'T'!

The wait was worth it! The words 'Frank Tyson, Northamptonshire' provoked a chorus of cheers, cries of 'well done', 'congratulations' and slaps on the back from my team-mates. Keith and I were literally dragged out of the dressing room into a jubilant members' bar, down the pavilion steps and on to the ground. There we posed for photographs for the local 'rag'- the *Northampton Chronicle and Echo* - hoisted high on the shoulders of our fellow players. We posed shaking hands, standing with our arms around one another's shoulders, as even the Aussies in the Northants side - 'Jock' Livingston, Ray Hogan and George Tribe - wished us 'Good luck'. The

dressing room phone began to ring and ring - and ring - never stopping. As I quit the ground and headed for my lodgings, people in the street stopped me to shake me by the hand. The following day, a never-ending stream of telegraph boys delivered hundreds of congratulatory telegrams and letters to the County Ground! I have kept them all to this day. They came from my Middleton and Knypersley Club team-mates, from University teachers and friends, from the Providence Congregationalist Church, from men who played with me in the Army, from girl friend, from festival organisers, from the Durham University Fives Club and the Colleges Hockey team, my former headmaster and ex-history teacher, my army sergeant-major, young, old, some dear friends and others but casually met! The messages were all precious. I replied to them through the media and I tried my best not to disappoint their writers. I wonder if I succeeded?

The adrenaline may have been flowing at Wantage Road in July 1954, but a year later 'Cricket's Bible', *Wisden*, reported the selection of Keith and I in matter-of-fact terms: 'For the first time in the history of the club two Northamptonshire professionals were selected for the M.C.C. Australian tour, Andrew and Tyson gaining this honour in their first full season of county cricket.'

'K.V.' and I had come a long way since we joined the Midland county and shared digs at Emily Birrell's terraced house on Roseholme Road only twelve months earlier. After August 1954 and our selection for Australia, it seemed that there would be no more having to exist on £400 a year; no more arguing with the county committee about £100 raises. We were to receive a handsome £800 for England's six-month tour, stay in the best hotels, get £8 a week spending money and travel first-class. No more fixing up 'lazy' switches from string, so that we could turn off the lights of our shared bedroom from the comfort of our beds on cold nights. No more salad dinners waiting for us on the dining-room table when we returned late from Club and Ground and Second Eleven matches at Peterborough, Rushden and Wellingborough and other far-flung corners of the county; no more being woken at some ungodly hour of the morning by 'Arry Farrer' and his 'barrer' rumbling over the cobble-stones of the back lane. We would be on easy street. So confident of their future were Keith and his new wife, Joyce, that, on K.V.'s return from Australia they decided to buy their first house in the Northampton suburb of Westone. Still the bachelor, I moved into a flat.

There was much to do before we left for Down Under, and very little time to do it in. Amidst the publicity, the glamour and the rush of a touring team's embarkation, it was easy, in 1954, to lose sight of the many housekeeping tasks which had to be done before eighteen cricketers could leave on a six-month trip. My first-class ticket arrived; it cost £163 one way!

Selected! Keith Andrew and I congratulate each other.

Enclosed in same envelope were two booklets, one containing the passenger list of the ship in which we were to sail, the 'Orsova'. In the other were colourful M.C.C. luggage labels and a handbook of information about every detail of the ship and the voyage. Nowadays touring cricket teams carry all their baggage with them. Fifty years ago, equipment and personal gear not needed on the ship were locked into steamer trunks, labelled and sent off by British Rail a fortnight before sailing day. This heavy baggage was decorated with stickers stating it was 'Wanted Fremantle' and despatched to the shipping agents - Anderson Green and Co. Ltd., Tilbury dock, Essex.

On board Orsova, cabin 402 was to be my home for the four weeks of our sea voyage and my cabin luggage was marked accordingly. At Tilbury - the port of embarkation - the previously completed custom documents were processed, and the trunks were stowed in the ship's baggage room, only to be accessed and dragged out on urgent occasions, prefaced by a couple of days notification to the baggage steward. The members of the touring party were urged to avoid such inconvenient forays to the baggage room - except just before arrival at Colombo where we were scheduled to play two games against Ceylon, a week before landing in Western Australia.

Our two-day stay in Ceylon occasioned a visit to the North-amptonshire County Club's doctor for injections against several tropical diseases. Then, of course, there was another trip to the medico for him to run the rule over us to ensure that we were fully fit and injury-free. I did not have to bother about a new passport; I acquired one the previous year when Dick Hansell, Colin Danskin - a couple of student friends from Durham University - and I holidayed on the continent. But there was still the matter of checking for any irregularities in documentation and visas. And then there was the important detail of the M.C.C. contracts to be signed - how unsophisticated the carbon copies of those agreements, with the names of the individual players typed in, look to modern eyes accustomed to computerised documents!

Cricket in the fifties did not bother too much about external trappings. The England uniform was plain white, plus a navy-blue M.C.C. blazer with its distinctive pocket badge of St. George slaying the dragon and its garish 'bacon and egg' taped lapels. To get this distinctive and treasured jacket, every team member had to visit London and Simpson's in Piccadilly, to be measured individually and collect two sleeveless and one long-sleeved M.C.C. sweaters, a couple of caps, shirts and two or three pairs of flannels. This visit to the tailor was an awe-inspiring experience for someone like me who had never before moved in Saville Row circles.

Other sporting companies gave freely - but not lavishly - of white flannel shirts, thick, grey woollen socks, batting pads, and batting gloves. Stuart Surridge, the bat manufacturers, sent a couple of their blades along for each member of the side. In one respect, I was extremely lucky. Northamptonshire is not only the county which gave me my start in international cricket. It is also the boot and shoe manufacturing capital of England and, as such, could hardly allow me to leave for Australia inadequately shod. As soon as they learned of my selection in the touring party, the Lotus Shoe Company gave me half a dozen pairs of cricket boots and several pairs of dress shoes. The cricketing boots were custom-made to withstand the extreme demands of fast bowling on Australian grounds. Thick-soled, with a substantial heel and accompanying support, they fitted the pattern which, I had read, was favoured by my teenage idol, Harold Larwood, the match-winning fast-bowler of the 'Bodyline' years. They were heavy - true - but they were the Rolls-Royce of boots: strong and suited to my purpose. Later, when I discussed fast-bowling boots with 'Lol' in Sydney, he restated his opinion that one should not sacrifice boot strength and shock absorption for the sake of lightness. His judgement, of course, was formed before the discovery of modern lightweight footwear material which combined all three qualities.

The backing of the Lotus, the C.W.S. Footwear Companies and later the Shoes and Allied Trade Research Association, in Kettering, stayed with me throughout my career. One year later, when stone bruises to my left heel kept me out of the England side, men were set to work walking up and down the hard pavements outside SATRA's Rockingham House to discover the cause of those injuries. After two years the problem was diagnosed. The blood blister was not impact bruising, but was caused by friction created by the rotation of the heel inside the boot. A close-fitting heel glove made of seamless horse-hide eliminated that friction and the bruising never reappeared! Sadly my heel problem was not solved until it had caused me to miss at least a full season and a half of home Test matches.

It came as a shock to discover that I had to buy a dinner suit. Never before had I moved in the social circles which necessitated such formal gear; but on board Orient liners, first-class passengers dressed to dine. Moreover, in the fifties, the management of touring teams did not restrict the number of formal events which the side were obliged to attend. Quite the opposite. In their role as the ambassadors of English cricket, it was not unusual for M.C.C. team members to have to attend half-a-dozen official civic functions in each of the capital cities and the major country centres of the Australian States. So it was off to Northampton's premier tailor, Montague Jeffries, for a 'penguin suit' - with a few shirts, and a couple of sports jackets thrown in! Was I to be a fast bowler or a fashion plate?

The French have a saying: *Mieux voyager, qu'arriver* - "Better to travel than to arrive". As far as the beginning of an old-fashioned M.C.C. overseas tour was concerned, the axiom would be better expressed as *Mieux voyager, que partir* - "Better to travel than to leave". The departure of Hutton's '54 side was pure pandemonium. North-

SPORTING PERSONALITIES in the News

Frank Tyson (Northampton)

WHETHER Frank Tyson the 24 years old genuinely fast bowler from Northants proves as great a menace to the Australian batsmen as " Lol " Larwood did before the war remains to be seen.

Already some of the more caustic critics " down under " have been inclined to be sceptical of the England new boy. Be that as it may you can quote his former skipper, Freddie Brown, any time, as saying " Frank is the fastest I have seen since Larwood ". And Mr. Brown should know!

Tyson, a Bolton born lad whose pace through the air has been estimated as devastating as 95 miles per hour, has been in first class cricket only two years.

A meteoric rise, almost as comet-like as his bowling, but he remains un-affected by his sudden climb to fame. He is a studious type and had he not gone to Australia would have pursued his studies for an Arts degree at Durham University this winter.

amptonshire played the last day of its final championship match against Nottinghamshire at Trent Bridge on August 31st. We lost by six wickets. But even that late fixture did not write *finis* to the English domestic season. In the seaside resorts of Scarborough, Hastings and Torquay, composite teams played light-hearted festival games to entertain cricket-loving holiday-makers for a further ten days. The last ball of those encounters was not bowled until September 10th.

Four days after that ball was delivered, Hutton's touring team to Australia had to attend an eve-of-departure dinner in the Tavern at Lord's: a function at which Lord Cobham, the former Governor-General of New Zealand and the President Designate of the M.C.C., proposed the toast of 'Success to the Team' - to which the team's captain, Len Hutton, replied. The tenor of Lord Cobham's address was that we were the identifiable face of English cricket and we should never disgrace the responsibility of that image - even at the cost of losing the approaching Test rubber. Some of us in the touring party, however, held other opinions about polite behaviour taking precedence over victory!

As the departure date approached, social commitments came thick and fast. The evening before the Cobham dinner saw us don our 'best bib and tucker' once more to partake of *Filet de sole au vin blanc, Poulet rôti au Cresson* and *Pêche Frâiche Melba* at

Berner's Hotel. The occasion was the farewell dinner to the first Pakistan team to tour England. It was a notable occasion celebrating as it did, Pakistan sharing its inaugural 1954 Test series with England. It was rendered even more notable by a wonderful speech from England selector Harry Altham.

On the last day of the Torquay Festival, I took stock of the social scenario for the week of September 10th to the 15th. I awoke to the fact that I had exactly three days in which to quit Devon, pack and take my leave of Northampton and betake myself to London for the two mandatory dinners. Luckily, my departure from Northampton on Monday, September 13th was uncomplicated. There was no house to leave tenanted; I did not possess one. There was no car to put up on blocks; I could not afford one. Nor was there any of the local hysteria now typical of the leave-taking of international sporting teams. There were few farewell functions. My home town of Middleton and its cricket club had bid me goodbye and presented me with a travelling case a month earlier.

Northampton had no mayoral farewells for me, no presentation evenings, no band of well-wishers from the county club, and no representatives of the county committee. Neither the secretary nor assistant secretary came to the station to see me off - nothing, no-one, zero, zilch. As *Wisden* reported 'a heavy financial loss caused the club serious concern at the end of the season.' That anxiety far outweighed any beneficent thoughts about its players bound for Australia. I therefore decided to assert my individuality and set out in style. Casting aside all considerations of expense, I splurged on a taxi to take me the five or six miles from my digs to Northampton's Castle Station. I rang for my transport, carried my labelled suitcases to the cab, loaded them into it and I was off on the first step of a journey of 14,000 miles. And as Chairman Mao said, 'The longest journey begins with the first step.'

In 1954 Northamptonshire cricket supporters were apparently very busy or very blasé about their cricketers being chosen for M.C.C. touring teams. But blasé or busy - whatever the reason for the absence of well-wishers at the station - they stayed away in their droves! I have a photograph of my last few moments in Northampton, taken by one enthusiastic photographer of the local rag, the *Chronicle and Echo*. There I am on platform one, Castle Station, about to begin my great adventure; dressed in a double-breasted grey suit, wearing a trilby pulled well down over my eyes and, like any true cynical Mancunian, carrying a raincoat neatly folded over my forearm. A couple of metres down the platform and in front of the waiting room door, a scruffy teenager looks away as though fearful that I was having my photograph taken for the police gazette! Close by a flat-capped, pipe-smoking old gaffer sitting on a luggage trolley shares his cynicism. Total number of people on the platform - 12, tops!

Goodbye Northampton. Hello Australia!

Goodbye Northampton.
Hello Australia!

I was rapidly becoming addicted to taxi travel. An hour down the line, after rattling through Newport Pagnell, Bletchley, Leighton Buzzard and Watford Junction stations - my train rumbled into the semicircular cavern of Euston station. Without giving another thought to the expense, I tossed my cases into the luggage compartment alongside the driver and ensconced myself on the back seat of a London cab, at the same time calling out to the cabbie, "Great Western Hotel. Paddington, please!"

Philosophically! That was how I had to approach my trip Down Under. I decided this as the cab crawled along Marylebone Road towards the Paddington station hotel. In choosing me for the team ahead of Yorkshire's Freddie Trueman and Middlesex's Alan Moss, Harry Altham and his co-selectors had displayed a brave and imaginative faith in my pace and youth: a confidence which was not shared by most of the 54-strong press party who were accompanying the England side Down Under. Probably Harry Altham and fellow-selector Gubby Allen had been convinced of my outstanding speed - and my possible usefulness in Australia - by my beating England and Middlesex opener Bill Edrich to the hook during a county game at Lord's - and consigning him overnight to a hospital bed with a broken cheek bone. Quite a feat, when one considers that Bill in the fifties was regarded as the best hooker in first-class cricket.

As yet I was an ingénue in county circles. My confidence and enthusiasm were high and I was unaffected by the media's negative influences. Deep within my mental processes, I determined to commit myself wholly to the success of Hutton's side and to try with a synergy which would far exceed the limits of the totality of my efforts. Whatever happened, I made up my mind to enjoy the Australian experience to the full and at least learn from it.

The cab pulled into the forecourt of the hotel. Identifying the vehicle's occupant by the colourful M.C.C. labels on his luggage, uniformed porters materialised and bore off my cases, consigning them to the ever growing pile of bags in the hotel foyer - and into the care of the team's baggage master, George Duckworth. George kept wicket for Lancashire for many years. He kept to Larwood on the 'Bodyline' tour. In his own right he was an experienced manager of Commonwealth Eleven tours. What better guru could the side have? His main role, however, was that of the successor to that legendary scorer/luggage man, 'Fergie'. The tour had begun!

In the Eye of the Typhoon

Wednesday September 15th.

This morning, at nine o'clock, the touring party and their families assembled in the Great Western Hotel's lounge. The fifties was the era when players' wives were not allowed to accompany their cricketing husbands on an overseas tour, even if they travelled at their own expense. Nor were they permitted to stay in the same hotels as their spouse. They simply had to stay at home and 'keep the home fires burning'. The wives, parents and children, who farewelled their husbands, fathers and sons this morning, will not see them again for six months. This arrangement does nothing to foster lasting marriages; and I find it quite understandable that such separations exact a terrible cost in terms of broken marriages amongst cricketers.

Mother came from Middleton to see me off. It was the first time in her life she had been to London. Chaperoning her on her adventure were two dear friends, Fanny Kay and her daughter Margaret. Fanny's mother, Mrs. Helliwell, is mother's closest companion; Fanny herself is the wife of the man who shaped my formative years with the Middleton Central Lancashire League club; Edwin Kay. Edwin was a fine opening batsman for Middleton for many years and might have played for Lancashire - possibly England - had not his job as head compositor of the *Manchester Evening News* prevented him. He would have liked to come to London to

say goodbye - but again his job stopped him and wife and daughter, Margaret, deputised for him. Margaret is a trainee teacher at Matlock College: a lovely girl who many think is intended to be my future wife. Edwin's brother, John, is the chief cricket writer for the Manchester Evening News and is accompanying the touring team to Australia.

The boat train was scheduled to leave St. Pancras Station at twenty to twelve. So at nine we piled into cabs and off we went, chugging from west to east across London. By the time the families, the M.C.C. and British Rail officials, the Station Master in his gold-braided suit and top hat, the press, the photographers and the players' friends assembled on the boat train's departure platform, the scene was somewhat reminiscent of a Cup Final crowd. I could not help reflecting on the contrast between my departures from St. Pancras and Castle Stations! Keith Andrew and I intend filming the highlights of the tour on a 16mm camera - so we bought one specifically for the purpose. But such was the jostling crowd at St Pancras that our shots of the train departure came out as though they were taken by someone suffering from an attack of Berri-Berri! Everyone on the platform seemed to want to defer their last farewells to the dockside at Tilbury - so everyone crammed into the train. The guard blew his whistle and the green flag fell. We were off!

The train rattled through London's straggling East End, emerging from the city into the monotony of flat suburban Essex. On many of the fences and walls of the terraced houses backing on to the railway track, people had scrawled or painted messages of goodwill. 'Bring back the Ashes'; 'Good luck Len'; 'Stick to it Boil'. Slowly the train bore the men defending cricket's Holy Grail through Purfleet and Grays to emerge at the dock city of Tilbury. It clanked to a halt at the rail terminal next to a wharf, alongside which was moored the gleaming white, yellow-funnelled 28,000-ton Orient Line Steamship, the Orsova. I recalled that it was at this same town of Tilbury in 1588 that Elizabeth I 'Gloriana' made the speech which rallied her troops at the approach of the Spanish Armada. Could it be that with Bannister's running the four minute mile, the Conquest of Everest, the Coronation - and possibly the retention of the 'Ashes' - England was about to enter a second Golden Elizabethan era?

The team's emigration and custom formalities were fast-tracked by the man who in modern day E.C.B.-speak would be called 'Operations Manager'. In 1954 he was just the baggage-man, alias George Duckworth, a.k.a. 'The Admiral', since he was now i/c maritime movements. He gathered all of our tickets, passports and customs declarations - handing them to Customs and Emigration officers seated at a trestle table in one of the quayside sheds. The team members had only to make their way through the mountains of trunks, crates and cases being hoisted aboard in nets, stroll up the gangway to examine their cabins and then take their guests and families to a lunch in the air-conditioned first-class saloon.

A luxurious world, completely new to a working-class Middleton lad, unfolded before my eyes: a scene which blazed white with snowy tablecloths and

S.S. Orsova

swan-shaped napery and gleamed with highly polished crystal and silver cutlery: a restaurant in which the starched white ghosts of stewards shimmered noiselessly between galley and table to the tinkling accompaniment of silver on china. The lunch was hosted by the M.C.C. at the princely expense of 7s/6d per head! And what a lunch it proved to be! The ornate parchment menu was a double foolscap-size folio and detailed five courses each with innumerable choices. The memory of it still makes me salivate today.

It should not be forgotten that in 1954 the United Kingdom was still in the grip of stringent post-war rationing. Everything was in short supply: meat, butter, sugar, bacon, eggs, petrol - even fuel and clothes, which had to be purchased with coupons. The jokes of the time described how the meat ration could be wrapped in a tram-ticket; and if one was not careful, it might slip out through the punch hole!

That 27-day voyage to Australia in 1954 was literally manna from heaven for the slim-line M.C.C. team and several of us quickly acquired the reputations of being good trenchermen. From 1945 to 1954 it had been impossible for nutritionists to advocate a good diet for English athletes; at least, they could advocate, but not provide it! I state unashamedly that in the course of the 1954/55 tour my weight increased from eleven and a half to thirteen stone. Thankfully most of it was muscle, attributable to exercise and an increased intake of good body-building food. None of it was unhealthy flab.

The cost of first-class fares to Australia in those days must make amusing reading to modern eyes. My number 402 berth, in a cabin shared with my Northamptonshire team-mate Keith Andrew, cost £163 one way! Admittedly, the cabin was not a state-room and did not even overlook a promenade deck. Nor was it on the port side, as required for the P.O.S.H cabins on the ship, but it had its own facilities; its port-hole was equipped with an air scoop to maintain a constant flow of cool air into the cabin; it was well above the water line, and it was only a couple of decks down from the public rooms. These were the days of cheap sea travel; a twelve-year-old child could travel first-class to Australia for £82! For a mere £7 a day, one lived in the equivalent of a five-star hotel, enjoyed four meals of gourmet food at fish-and-chip shop prices - mid-morning beef tea and afternoon snacks thrown in - and travelled an average of 500 miles. Cabaret entertainment was provided, plus film evenings, race-nights, dances, fancy dress balls, and, during the day, there was no shortage of organised deck sports and other *petits divertissements*. When in port, shore trips were organised; in short, shipboard life gave one a very good idea of what life must have been like in one of the Great Houses of aristocratic England!

King of this floating palace is Captain Whinfield: a stocky no-nonsense mariner who gives the impression that he runs a tight ship. He exercises a velvet-gloved control of 850 passengers and 500 crew yet retains a flair for public relations, carrying out his serious duties with a well-developed sense of humour. Throughout the voyage, each and every first-class passenger visited his table in the saloon for at least one meal. Nor were the passengers in Tourist B Class neglected. 'The Skipper' often shared their meals and social activities.

Captain Whinfield is assisted in his benevolent despotism by his Staff Commander Mr. Stretford, his Chief Officer Mr. Murray and his First Officer Mr Blois. Indeed every officer on board has the obligation of hosting one table in the dining-room; but the Captain's is the major responsibility. In reality, the Orsova has two skippers: Len Hutton and Captain Whinfield. It is a duality which was to lead to humorous confusion later during the voyage, when a couple of our lads misbehaved and were ordered to 'report to the Skipper!'

After gawking our way through the ship's oak-panelled, air-conditioned public rooms, the touring party was summoned to its last press conference on English soil - correction - on the Orsova's sports deck! The 54-strong media contingent who are accompanying the M.C.C. team are an eclectic lot: a contrasting amalgam of hardened professional journalists and former players. Amongst the former are 'Lord Jim' Swanton of the *Daily Telegraph*, 'Splinter' Johnny Woodcock of *The Times*, 'Chalky' Crawford White of the *News Chronicle*, Frank Rostron of the *Daily Express*, Alex Bannister of *The Daily Mail*, Len Bailey and E.M.

Captain Whinfield welcomes the tourists.

Wellings of the London evenings, Alan Ross of *The Guardian*, John Kay, Jim Kilburn and Bill Bowes representing the *Manchester Evening News* and the *Yorkshire Posts*, and Ron Roberts, Harry Gee and Reg Hayter who file for the agencies. Charles Bray and Denys Rowbotham are veteran scribblers but Freddie Brown, the skipper of the previous touring side to Australia, and my former county captain, is a new-comer to the press box. Also on the boat is the England leg-spinner of the thirties, Ian Peebles, and Alec Bedser's twin brother, Eric, who opens the innings and bowls off-spin for Surrey. Everywhere that Alec goes on tour, Eric is sure to go, paying his way with press work or drumming up business for the twins' office supplies company.

As the team posed for final photo-graphs, the manager answered the usual platitudinous questions and Len Hutton delighted the media by appropriating Captain Whinfield's gold-braided cap and assuming command of the vessel. To one side of this horseplay, the youngster of the party, Colin Cowdrey, was in earnest conversation with a spare, stooped old man, dressed immaculately in a blue pin-stripe suit. Standing next to the pair, I overheard a scrap of their conversation, which consisted of some advice from the city gent to the young Kentish batsman: "When you get to Ceylon, Cowdrey, have a hit and get your eye in. Then when you reach Australia, just remember one thing - Hate the Bastards!"

The vehemence with which he spat out the later phrase took me aback. Retiring from the scene of the exchange, I asked George Duckworth,

The two "skippers": Orsova and England.

who the old gent was. "That," said the 'Admiral', "is Douglas Jardine, my former captain in Australia during the Bodyline series in 1932/33. He's come down specially to see Cowdrey off. It's the least he can do for a fellow Oxford man."

As three o'clock and sailing time approached, gongs rang throughout the ship and passengers not travelling were repeatedly advised to go ashore. One last hug for mother and the Kays, then they too descended the gangway. Wives Joyce Andrew, Jo Loader, Dorothy Hutton, Jean Evans and Greta Bailey - then the M.C.C. officials, Harry Altham and Ronnie Aird - one by one they left the ship. Keith Andrew, Vic Wilson and Trevor Bailey busied themselves filming the last farewells. Those on the quay threw streamers to be caught by their friends on board. Within minutes ship and land were connected by a multitude of rainbow-hued umbilical cords.

Denis Compton stood next to mother on the jetty, leaning on a wooden bulwark; he looked disconsolate and unhappy. 'Compo' was staying behind for a month for some remedial surgery on his gammie knee. After surgeon Bill Tucker has finished with him, he will fly out to join us in Adelaide.

All the gangways save one were withdrawn to shore as the Orsova slipped her lines for'ard and aft. The shore crew retract the last gangway. The Orsova's siren sounds three deep baritone blasts, as the tugs on the river side of the ship take the strain, slowly manoeuvring the huge liner into mid-stream. The gap between ship and wharf widens until the boat and land are connected by nothing but paper streamers, slowly slipping through the fingers of those leaving and those staying behind. They cling to their tactile connections, reluctant to part. Finally they too sever and the ship is free. Its engines begin to throb as it moves forward and slightly to starboard, still at dead slow speed.

A party of the New Zealand Boy's Brigade are sailing with us down aft, in the tourist accommodation. As the Orsova begins its trip down the Thames, they chant a Maori haka and then, with the distance between ship and shore ever expanding, burst into song with the haunting farewell melody of the native Kiwi: 'Now Is The Hour For Us To Say Goodbye'. When the last strains of their boy soprano voices die away, it leaves an ache in the chest. We can no longer pick out the individuals on the banks of the Thames. They are just smudges of pale faces in the distance - and will remain just pictures in the memory for the next six months. I wonder where those lads of the Kiwi Boys' Brigade are today? Or indeed if they are still alive?

The bow wave of the Orient liner rose as the ship increased speed, ploughing through the brown muddy waters of Old Father Thames, rolling, like us, down to the mighty sea. On the port bow, Canvey Island came and went and we could distinguish the low outline of the buildings of Southend-on-Sea and Westcliffe. Trevor Bailey could have stayed an extra day at home then joined us by row boat, just like the convict fugitive in *Great Expectations.* On the starboard side of the ship, Sheerness and the Isle of Sheppey slip past. Then, on the same quarter, the town of Whitstable reminds us that in a few weeks, we may be eating Sydney oysters: the equal if not better than those found on the Kentish coast. Passing Herne Bay and Margate, we round the North Foreland before heading south down the Dover Straits, past Ramsgate, Deal and Dover.

It being the first night of the voyage, we were not required to dress for dinner, which we ate as we skirted the south coast. Through the portholes we could see the lights of Hastings, Bexhill and Eastbourne, adorning the Sussex coast like the gleaming reflections of some gigantic necklace. As we drew abreast of Eastbourne's lights, I was standing alongside Keith Andrew as he hung disconsolately over the rails of the promenade deck. He and his new bride, Joyce, spent their honeymoon there a few short weeks before.

The ship turned south and, picking up speed, left the Sussex coast in its wake, striking out into the English Channel and setting a course which took it to the west of the Cherbourg Peninsula where it breasted the reputedly stormy waters of the Bay of Biscay. I faced the prospect with equanimity; a University friend, Lewis Gordon, had written just before we sailed, assuring me that the Orsova was the pride of the Orient fleet, equipped with stabilisers to eliminate rolling and prevent its passengers from becoming sea-sick!

From time to time we passed ships of all shapes, sizes and nationalities, inward or outward bound for European ports. The Channel certainly lived up to its reputation for being the busiest waterway in the world. Watching the lights of the English coastline sink below the horizon in the wake of the Orsova, I suddenly felt what the French call *dépaysé*. We were going to be away from home for a long time. Now there was a sense of semi-permanence about our departure. We could not just climb into an aeroplane and be back in Heathrow in a matter of hours.

Chapter Two

Outward Bound

Thursday, September 16th

A SHORT, CHOPPY SEA DID NOT make for a healthy appetite and I gave breakfast a miss. However, the cutting salt-sea air and a morning of deck quoits, tennis and paddle ball revived me, and I was able to eat a substantial lunch. My table mates got a great deal of enjoyment of seeing me work my way through the lengthy menu.

The Bay of Biscay let me down. I expected gales and a rough sea; instead I got a dead calm with little or no breeze. Socially, this was a time of getting to know one's fellow passengers and to expedite matters, the Skipper - nautical not cricket - put on a cocktail party before dinner and the Gala Dance which followed. I met two pleasant Australian families, Mr. and Mrs Cohen of South Australia and the Gregorys of Sydney.

Friday September 17th.

As the novelettes have it, 'the morning dawned hazy with the promise of a brilliant day to follow'. As the temperature climbed into the seventies Fahrenheit, that promise was fulfilled. There was fog during the night, but in spite of this, the Orsova logged 480 miles. Part of the ship's daily routine was the sweepstake on the distance covered each day in the twenty-four hours between noon and noon. Conducted by the purser's department and supported by most of the passengers, who each wagered a 'bob' or two, the first prize amounted to a tidy little sum. Needless to say, I never won it during the entire voyage!

Barely visible fifty miles away off the port bow was the lighthouse atop the cliffs of Cape Finisterre, a promontory of north-western Spain. The Ship's Sports Committee was by now up and running, manned by experienced volunteers - hardened, clubbable Indian Civil Servants and planters who had made the trip many times and were familiar with ship-board routine. Each and every morning, their fellow-travellers tossed deck quoits, shuttle-boarded and played cards according to their programme, printed and posted on the notice boards in the lounges.

The Portuguese coast slipped by as we lunched. Then we emerged from the dining saloon to do nothing but simply lie in the sun. This was a pastime beloved of Reg Simpson, our Nottinghamshire opening bat - who, during the voyage, spent so many hours sunbaking and acquiring such a deep tan that we nicknamed him 'The Native'.

K.V. playing deck quoits.

By mid-afternoon we were abreast of the mouth of the River Tagus on the banks of which stood the Portuguese capital Lisbon. From its estuary in the fifteenth century the celebrated navigators, Magellan and Vasco da Gama, set out to explore and sail beyond the as-yet-undiscovered Australia, eventually circumnavigating the globe. Now there was a trip and a half that made our little sea-jaunt look almost insignificant! The ship's tannoy disturbed our post-prandial sleep, recording our progress and informing us that Lord Nelson had won the Battle of Trafalgar quite close to our present location, way back in 1805. At eleven that night, we shared Robert Browning's *Home Thoughts from the Sea*, as 'Nobly, Nobly Cape St. Vincent to the North-west died away'. But, as we were in the ship's cinema, watching David Niven in the film *Happy Ever After*, the poetic geography went unnoticed.

Today was a day of meetings. Freddie Brown treated Keith Andrew and I to a beer and congratulated us on our selection. I think that he, too, was surprised by our inclusion in the team. He volunteered any advice and help that lay within his power. Just before dinner, Len Hutton called a players' meeting in one of the smaller lounges for'ard. We were handed some shirts and trousers and arrangements were made to hold a Saturday Evening Club get-together - starting tomorrow. Colin Cowdrey was appointed treasurer. What goes on at these meetings, I shudder to think!

What an enjoyable day this has been! I am beginning to bond with the other team members and what I see of them, I like. All are affable and helpful towards Keith and I, the juniors in the party. The vice-captain, Peter May - 'P.B.H.' - seems to be on a tightly wound spring. He and I have met head-to-head in a couple of games - once in an Army v Navy match at Lord's and once at Kettering. He is a compulsive perfectionist and an individual with great powers of self-discipline: an asset which, unfortunately, he seems to have difficulty in transmitting to those he is destined to command. From our previous encounters I have found P.B.H. to be a natural player, well-organised in his movements, extremely straight and orthodox and a totally ferocious punisher of the minimally bad ball. The heavy power of his favourite drives - on and, strangely, off - emanate from the controlling influence of his bottom hand, 'the old guide and master'. In his rare moments of relaxation, he exhibits a great sense of humour which he often expresses in a rising, high-pitched giggling laugh, which he chokes off at birth, as if it were not allowed, with an expression of simulated indignation: "Do you mind?" Perfectly proper in his behaviour, he strikes me as being the archetypal public schoolboy, wonderfully coached and always under control. If he ever loses mastery over himself, his remorse amounts almost to psychological self-flagellation..

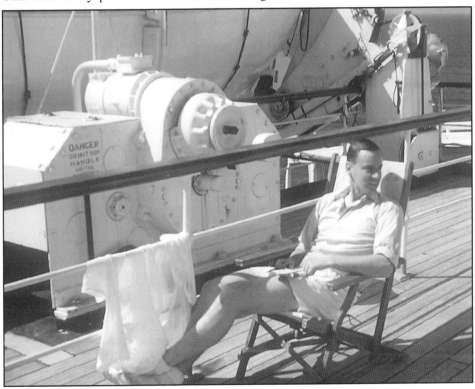

**P.B.H., of Charterhouse and Cambridge,
relaxes on the deck of the Orsova.**

Bill Edrich is a totally different kettle of fish. Two years short of his fortieth birthday 'W.J.' is Middlesex skipper and a veteran of pre-W.W.2 Tests, having scored a double hundred against South Africa in 1938 and two centuries against Australia at Leeds and Sydney in 1948 and 1946/47. More significant than these scores, however, is the nature of the man himself. Never have I met a more courageous individual. He appears almost indifferent to his own safety. No bowler is too fast to hook; no score too large to defy challenge. During the war, Bill flew Beaufighters. He never talks of those days, but his subsequent way of life witnesses an immense relief that he survived. Although deep down in his psyche he is a serious and dedicated cricketer, he is also a man who believes in *Carpe Diem*. He loves a party and needs little prompting to demonstrate his favourite trick of launching himself at a horizontal tray supported on a glass of water. On the tray a raw egg rests in an egg cup. The trick is to knock the tray from underneath the egg cup so that the egg drops into the glass of water on which the tray is balanced. Bill's exhibition occasions a lot of laughter - but it also results in a lot of broken eggs, spilt water and wall-stains!

Bill was a wonderful morale-booster, ever willing to contribute his signature tune to Saturday night team meetings. The volume was pianissimo and the tempo adagio:

Ginger, Ginger, they all know
Captain Ginger.
Jolly old Sot, O-T hot,
Ninety-Nine in the shade What! What!

He loves the ladies,
But none of them would he injure.
All the girls are fond of Gin.
Gin, Gin, Gin, Gin Ginger!

The other song in Bill's limited repertoire involves a duet with the 'Skipper', Len Hutton:

Susie, Susie, sitting in a shoe-shine shop
All day long she sits and shines.
All day long she shines and sits.
Susie, Susie, sitting in a shoe-shine shop.

Try singing that after a couple of beers!

W.J. was the life and soul of the party.

W.J. has rarely missed a major M.C.C. tour or a Middlesex season in his 24 years on the first-class scene. But his 39 Tests necessitated frequent absences from home and his international success came at a heavy marital cost. He was married five times and such was the frequency of his commitment to holy matrimony that when asked for his invitation to Bill's fifth wedding, his Middlesex team-mate and well-known wag, John Warr, declared he had 'a Season's Pass'.

Aside from his personal peccadillos, Bill Edrich was a team man right down to his boot-straps. He proved to be a great prop for Len Hutton on the 1954/55 tour. He never shirked the onerous responsibility of opening the innings in spite of scant success; he served the selection committee and on the occasion when Hutton wanted to opt out of the crucial Melbourne Test because of his fibrositis, he helped Geoffrey Howard and the senior members of the side to convince Len that he had to play. When victory in the Ashes series arrived in Adelaide's Fourth Test, no-one celebrated the win more wholeheartedly than Bill. At 10 o'clock on the night of that notable triumph, Bill was to be found at the top of a polished marble colonnade in the foyer of Glenelg's Pier Hotel, singing *Ginger*. How he shimmied up there no-one knew. More importantly, how he got down remains a secret to this day!

Saturday, September 18th.

Gibraltar! So this is the Historic Rock. My team-mate in the Northamptonshire side, the left-handed paceman, Bob 'Nobby' Clarke, often spoke of Gib. Few knew of it, but Nobby and his Royal Navy mate Armstrong, a duet forever in strife with authority, sailed in two Malta convoys during W.W.2. Nobby's survival was recognised with a 'gong' - but this he never mentioned. Those were the Real Voyages of No Return. The ships which made them were under constant air attack from the Italian island of Pantelleria and forever dodging the torpedos of U-Boat packs. It was only the bravery of men like Nobby which brought a life-saving few of the ships which left 'The Rock' safely into Valetta harbour with the desperately needed supplies for the George Cross Island.

Apparently Nobby was on an escort frigate which, during one of the hellish trips, sank a U-Boat. The German submariners abandoned ship and floundered towards the English warship's scramble nets. One Nazi appeared to be in trouble. Nobby turned smartly towards an officer standing nearby. 'Permission to go overboard, sir,' he snapped out. 'Permission granted!' Over the side he went, hauled the drowning man to the side of the frigate and hoisted him on board. No sooner had the German set foot on the English deck, than he sprang to attention, clicked his heels and gave the Nazi salute: 'Heil Hitler!' Flabbergasted at such ingratitude, Nobby promptly pushed Fritz back over the side and into the 'oggin'. Result - a week's 'jankers'!

Surprise! Surprise! Who is that lovely lady in one of the first launches to come out from Gibraltar harbour to greet the Orsova? Surely it can't be Josy Loader, Peter's wife! But it was! Jo farewelled us at Tilbury, then flew out to stay with her parents who were stationed and lived on the English outpost! It certainly is a small world!

We saw little of the colony. A white tablecloth of cloud covered the crest of the Rock and prevented any successful photography. Nor had we the time to climb to the peak to see the apes, whose desertion, it was rumoured, would forecast the loss of Gib to the former British Empire. We just had time to do a little bartering with the bum-boats which materialise out of nowhere as soon as a ship such as the Orsova drops anchor, and then take on more passengers, supplies, fuel and mail. Then we weighed anchor, passed through the Pillars of Hercules which formerly marked the limits of Known Ancient World, and were soon ploughing eastwards in the Mediterranean.

Tonight marked the first meeting of the Saturday Night Club. In later years, touring England sides dispensed with the weekly get-together, accusing it of being a mere excuse to booze. In reality it was a harmless hour of conviviality which never went beyond its allocated sixty minutes. It was also a means of raising funds for the team's kitty, to be spent if and when the need arose. Individuals were fined for a variety of transgressions including drinking with the right hand, unseemly behaviour, bad language and, if one was a steward, failing to keep members' drinks topped up. Funny and embarrassing moments were dredged up, and the ragging was merciless. All in all, it was a good bonding catalyst.

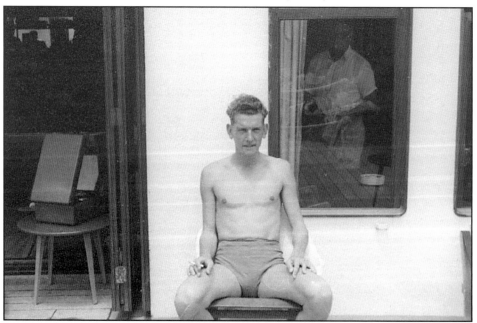

Peter 'Muscles' Loader - the body of a fast bowler!

Sunday September 19th.

The skipper, Len Hutton, today had a confidential word with the junior members of the party: Peter Loader, Colin Cowdrey, Jim McConnon, Keith Andrew and myself. The gist of his pep-talk un-pepped us, so to speak. It seems that, as the lesser lights of the team, we cannot expect to play a major role in the coming series. We are more of a supporting cast. 'Scrubs' Loader is incensed at being condemned without a fair trial. Scrubs - so nicknamed because of his distinctive crew-cut hair-do - is a bit of a fiery character. For his part, Keith Andrew was more philosophical, since he knew from the outset that he was no more than Godfrey Evans's understudy. Personally, I am committed to England winning the series and resolved to give of my best so that, if I take wickets, no power in Australia would keep me out of the eleven. I have prepared for this challenge in body and mind and I will give of my best. No man can do more. I will keep my own counsel and pay no attention to the Skipper's premature advice. Len seems too wrapped up in his own head. I have come this far in cricket, I will go further.

Keeping fit on the deck of the Orsova.

We ploughed on through moderate seas passing close to the barren Cape Spotivento on the southern tip of the island of Sardinia. Church services for protestant and catholic were held on board and quite a few of the team and the press attended. Throughout the tour Colin Cowdrey, E.W. Swanton and Peter May were punctilious in their observance of the Sabbath and it was not unusual for Colin, in particular, to read the lesson or take part in the service. Jim Swanton is High Anglican and, I think, shares the almost catholic beliefs of the Oxford Movement.

Mount Vesuvius - Naples.

Monday September 20th.

I awoke to find that, during the night, the Orsova had berthed alongside, in the Italian port of Naples. Through the portholes of our cabin came the clamour and smells of a southern Italian city. Even at this early hour, radios blared from harbour-side cafes, and on looking out from our floating hotel, we discovered a colourful tangle of narrow streets, pile upon pile of white buildings climbing out of the ocean up the mountainous flanks of the nearby hills. An endless, colourfully-dressed, procession of chattering humanity climbed or descended the ship's gangways. The already hot rays of the sun bounced off the whitewashed walls of ageless buildings, illuminating our cabin better than any human agency, and making it a breathless sauna of a place.

Planned for today are two trips ashore: one to the former Roman resort of Pompeii and the other a more sentimental journey. Turning first to our sightseeing expedition: Pompeii was built on the slopes of the still active volcano of Vesuvius. It was originally a fashionable retreat for Roman nobles who built their villas and established their vineyards there. On August 24th AD79 a massive eruption of Vesuvius engulfed the town, burying the buildings in thick stratum of cinders, stone and ashes and hiding the very site of Pompeii for fifteen centuries. It was not until 1763 that archaeologists began its systematic excavation and un-covered temples, amphitheatres seating 20,000 people, rich mosaics, baths, amphorae, cauldrons with liquid still in them and even the petrified or carbonised remains of some 85 people and their pets transfixed in time by the suddenness of the eruption. We visited the museums which housed these relics and paused awhile at a cameo factory. The concave peak of Vesuvius was hidden by a thick haze and the thick heat was rendered more unbearable by the choking volcanic dust kicked up by the feet of the many tourists tramping the narrow alleyways of the Roman city.

The haze cleared as the sun rose higher and we could now discern very clearly the striations of the lava formations down the side of the mountain. The top of Vesuvius had been completely blown off by an eruption in the early part of the twentieth century. Alec Bedser told us that he visited Naples during W.W.2, just after the eruption of 1944. Ten years later he ended his visit ashore by accompanying Vic Wilson, George Duckworth, Len Hutton, Johnny Wardle and Bob Appleyard on a visit to the grave of Hedley Verity at Casserta. The famous Yorkshire and England left-handed spinner of the thirties was a major in the Green Howards and took part in the invasion of Italy late in the Second World War. He was wounded in the stomach and captured at Casino. There, a German surgeon operated on him, without the benefit of an anaesthetic, and dressed the wound. The custodian of the war cemetery told the M.C.C. party that the doctor's instructions were that Hedley's dressings should not be touched for 24 hours, but the Italian nursing staff ignored his directions, dressed the wound again - and Verity died. His loyal batman, who chose to be captured with Hedley, stayed with him until the end. In memory of the great left-handed spinner - and, incidentally, a former Middleton player - the Skipper and the rest of the Yorkshire contingent left a floral tribute tied with a county tie on his grave and Alec arranged with the custodian to plant a perennial white rose bush on it.

Back on board, the team left sad memories behind them and enjoyed a cocktail party given by the parents of Heather Jenkins. The day ended with a dance.

Tuesday September 21st.

The first day out of Naples. We passed to landward of the Isle of Capri and then down the Italian coast to the Straits of Messina, lit up like the Blackpool Illuminations. The Orsova sped through the straits at an alarming speed and reached the open Adriatic Sea in the early hours of the morning.

Today I began preparing for the work ahead. I started the daily routine of skipping and running a few miles each day around the ship's promenade decks. If I am to believe everything that Godfrey Evans says about the heat in the Red Sea, I shall probably have to relax that regimen a little as we sail further south. But that's in the future. I would like to work in the ship's gym as well - but the atmosphere in the weight room deep in the bowels of the ship is unbearably stuffy. The ocean is now flat calm and with the temperature still rising, the swimming pool is becoming the main attraction of those inclined to physical exercise. In the evening I went with several of the boys to the Purser's party down on the Tourist deck.

Not a day goes by without our press companions trying to invent news about us. Today they really outdid themselves by drumming up a fabricated story about a romantic attachment between the Bedsers and the McDonald twins: two attractive sisters travelling first-class with us. True they have spent time in each other's company. But romantic liaison? That will be the day when any girls come between Alec and Eric!!!

Big Al - inseparable from brother Eric.

Wednesday September 22nd.

We must be approaching the Egyptian coast and the Nile Estuary, for the sea has turned a dark brown - heavy with the silt drawn from a thousand miles away in the heart of the Dark Continent. Whoever named the two Niles 'White' and 'Blue'? He or she must have been colour blind! The swimming pool had been completely filled with this liquid mud before the crew awoke to its dirty presence and turned off the pumps. It looks as if there will be no dipping to keep cool for some time to come. We crept into the roads of Port Said in the early evening, crossing paths with "The Empire Ken"; a grey-painted troopship, homeward bound with a cargo of "squaddies", returning to England home and beauty after a spell of duty guarding the Suez Canal. Frenzied Cossack music blared from a Russian ship as it steamed past us, heading for the Dardanelles and the Black Sea. We hove to for a couple of hours; and immediately the flanks of the Orsova were engulfed by a multitudinous fleet of clinging bum-boats.

"Hey Johnny, you want to buy a leather handbag for missus? Only a quid"

"You like this wallet? Make it five bob."

"How about this stool? This brassware?"

"Hey Joe, you like this ebony elephant?"

Goods whizzed up to the ships rails in baskets hoisted at the end of long cords. Money passed down by the same route. But we impecunious players decided that bartering for such goods was too risky - too much a case of 'Never mind the quality, feel the width'. Instead, we decided to go ashore for an hour and make our purchases at the more reliable emporium of Simon Artz. I would like to boast that we did not get bilked; but I can't! I bought a leather stool, an inlaid cigarette box and some black elephants - I hesitate to call them ebony. Still, it was another experience to put down in the diary. And so back to the ship which sailed an hour before midnight.

Thursday September 23rd.

Awoke this morning to find the Orsova anchored in the Great Bitter Lakes, half-way down the Suez Canal. It is here that the south-bound convoy meets and has the room to pass its north-bound counterpart. This means that ships can pass in both directions in the course of a single day. I completed my daily run of a couple of miles, breakfasted with the team as usual and then mounted to the promenade deck where I peered over the rail and found

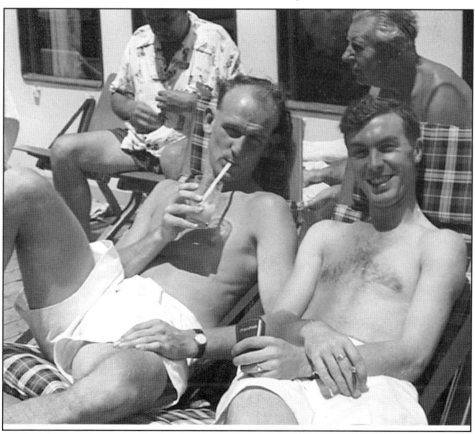

KV and I sipping through a straw.

The MCC are piped through the Suez Canal.

an animated shouting-match taking place at the gangway hatch, below and to my right. Apparently some enterprising English troops had commandeered two launches off the locals and had sailed out, intending to board the ship and meet the M.C.C. players. They were now demanding that we should at least show ourselves and shake their hands. How could we refuse such initiative? Sensing a story Frank Rostron, of the *Daily Express*, sent below for some ice-cream - and the ship's photographer! Soon the latter was busy clicking as the England team passed or threw rapidly melting Wall's ice cream blocks down to the servicemen. In a very short space of time, everyone - throwers and catchers both - were splattered with the sticky, creamy mess.

But no sooner had the last northbound ship passed us than the Orsova's propellers began turn and we were on our way again, this time to Suez at the southern end of the Canal. The liner's speed was dead slow, since any pace above that would cause a bow wave which could erode the banks of the narrow canal. The sun's glare bounced off the sands of the surrounding and apparently boundless Egyptian desert with a blinding intensity. I did not envy the lot of the English troops stationed along the canal. What was there to do during the endless hours spent in hostile surrounds, amidst unfriendly locals? When the Orsova glided through the desert, they could at least break the boredom by turning out to wave their cricketers *bon voyage*. But then it was back to the N.A.A.F.I. and the same monotonous routine. As we passed through Suez, at the southern extremity of the canal, we were piped on our way by the band of a Scottish regiment stationed there. Drawn up to attention on the wooden wharf erected where canal met the Red Sea, they gave us a right royal send-off. Len and the rest of us climbed to the right hand side of the Orsova's bridge to take the salute as we slid from the canal into the Red Sea! It was the least we could do. It must have been hot, hot, hot, underneath those busbies and uniforms! We cannot let such supporters down in Aussie. We must give them something to cheer about!

Friday September 24th.

The Red Sea! Even Moses had trouble with this expanse of water! Small wonder then that it gave me a bit of bother! I could not upstage the Bearer of the Ten Commandments! Even night-time did not bring relief from the blistering, following wind which blew the desert into our cabins. Below decks one could almost grasp handfuls of the torrid heat and taste the sand in it. Stepping out on to the deck was like entering an oven. The crew told us that in the days before air-conditioned ships, every evening, the skipper would reverse the ship into the breeze to cool it down. To me it seemed like a fruitless exercise.

Cooling off in the ship's pool.

Saturday September 25th.

We are steaming down the Red Sea with the timeless desert of the Middle East to our left and right. Flying fish cross the bow in front of the ship. It is much too hot to contemplate any physical activity. After the meeting of the Saturday Night Club, the team spent the evening in the Scrap Book Room: a kind of night club - importantly, a kind of air-conditioned night club! As Keith Andrew and I returned to our cabin, I was suddenly seized with a gut-wrenching spasm of pain which kept me up all night. The following day, the ship's doctor diagnosed colic and confined me to hospital for two uncomfortable, foodless and dehydrating days. It was little consolation to me that both Len Hutton and Keith Andrew had been struck down by the same mystery illness.

Sunday September 26th.

A day of Sabbatical rest - thank goodness. But it was not too pleasant to spend it in the ship's sick bay.

Monday, September 27th.

Up and about again, I am eight pounds lighter and feeling as weak as a kitten. Obviously my physical condition has deteriorated, as I have not been able to exercise for three days. We have now passed the arid crater outpost of Aden, refuelled and entered the Indian Ocean.

In Aden, a few of the boys took advantage of the opportunity to stretch their legs, do a bit of shopping, and spend a few hours on shore. Keith Andrew was sufficiently over his colic to venture out and take advantage of the duty free opportunities to be found in the shops in the crater. He came back with two cameras: one for himself and one for me. They were Zeiss Icons and at £32 they were real snips.

Most of the boys were entertained at the R.A.F officer's mess. It was a great to bring a little pleasure into the lives of the service men, who must have been bored out of their skulls having to spend day after day on alert in the torrid heat of Yemen - sitting on their bums on an extinct volcano at the tip of the Red Sea. George and Scrubs really enjoyed themselves. So much so that, trapped in the mess bar, they completely lost track of time. They were only awakened to the lateness of the hour by three blasts on the Orsova's siren: the signal for its immediate departure. Racing down to the jetty they discovered that the last lighter to the ship had left! They had to jump aboard the tug charged with the job of guiding the liner out to sea. They pursued and just caught the departing ship, clambering aboard at the very last moment. The officer of the watch played along with the rest of the lads when we requested that he should tell Brian and Peter that "the skipper wanted to see them in his cabin"! Since the order came from a ship's officer, the two late-comers presumed that it was the captain of the ship who wanted to interview them. They took themselves off to Captain Whinfield's day cabin and waited an hour for him to come down from the bridge! Captain

Whinfield, of course, was completely mystified by their presenting themselves for what they thought was going to be a real dressing down!

As soon as we entered the Indian Ocean, the Orsova encountered the tail end of a monsoon: a masterpiece of Nature's mistiming and misfortune which did absolutely nothing for my gastric juices.

Tuesday September 28th.

I am back in training, running and fully recovered. It is now much cooler than the 94 degree heat in the Red Sea. I learned today that a signal from a passing ship had informed Colin Cowdrey that his father, a tea planter and a legal officer in the Indian Civil Service, had passed away. Poor Colin! It seems like only yesterday that Kipper was having lunch with his parents on the day we sailed from Tilbury.

The team has raided the baggage room for bats and balls - and is now preparing for the serious cricket business which lies ahead. The Bedsers, Tom Graveney and Bill Edrich are still in the ship's deck quoits competition. They are doing quite a bit of running around, both on the quoit courts and the promenade decks. The Skipper spends more time on the scientific subtlety of shuffle board. But with the shipboard activities slowly winding down, we

Pool tennis.

have more time and space available for us on the sports deck - now enclosed by nets - for slip and fielding practice. This is now on every order of the day. The bowlers are turning their arms over, but we quickies can do little at full pace in such a confined area. Johnny Wardle, however, is a different kettle of fish. Three hours a day he is on deck, bowling against the bulwarks, practicing - not the orthodox spinners one would expect - but over-the-wrist stuff! K.V. practices with him, getting acquainted with the Yorkshireman's 'flipper', 'wrong 'un' and other variations.

Johnny Wardle aboard the Orsova.

Thursday September 30th.

Early this morning the Orsova anchored in the roads off the Ceylonese capital of Colombo. Here we said farewell to those passengers returning to positions on tea plantations or in the Indian government service. As for us, we are to spend the day playing a game against an island team. In Ceylon we are almost

on the Equator and whilst it is hot, it is the humidity which is energy-sapping. We went ashore by tender to be greeted on the jetty by a huge mob of Singhalese and the darker-skinned Tamil natives, all wanting to touch clothes of the visiting English cricketers or slap them on the back.

Cricket is a religion on this island and its practitioners are revered as gods. The crowds around the jetty and our cars were so numerous that we had to have a police escort to the Tamil Cricket Ground, where our game against the locals is to take place. It is not going to be a walk-over for us. We have played with and against Ceylonese cricketers in England - players like Gamini Gooneseena - and we know their capabilities. It must also be remembered that we have been at sea for a fortnight and it will take a little while to find our land legs.

Colombo is a straggling city of low, white colonial buildings and broad untidy avenues which leaves one with an impression of overgrown neglect. The cricket oval is a pretty little ground, surrounded, save on the popular side, with low shady stands. The wicket seems well grassed and could be quite fast and bouncy.

Peter May tossed, won, and decided to bat first. The M.C.C. began the tour, the match and the innings in very disappointing fashion, losing Bill Edrich, Reg Simpson and Tom Graveney with very few runs on the board. The topee-hatted locals had us in trouble, but a brilliant innings from Colin Cowdrey - who followed Douglas Jardine's instructions to a tee -

The Orsova in Colombo roads.

enabled May to declare with 180 runs on the board for the loss of nine wickets. Colin remained 65 not out in spite of being handicapped by an injury to his knee, which was bruised during the pre-match knock-up.

Playing in Ceylon is a bizarre - even unsettling - experience. Each time the England team walked out on to the field, the crowd greeted their appearance with strange hoots, shouts, screams and, occasionally, applause. The M.C.C. batsmen, when they stepped from the pavilion to make their way out to bat, suffered stinging slaps on the back from young spectators who abandoned their positions near the pavilion to run on to the field and virtually assault the visiting players - albeit in a well-meaning fashion. Vic Wilson got a good slapping and suffered most from their friendly fire. His back was quite marked. The humidity was so high that we thought we were playing in an open-air sauna bath. Perspiration trickled from one's forehead into the eyes, stinging them closed. It streamed down the hollow of one's spine. I became so dehydrated before the match ended that I cramped, even while I was running up to the wicket.

Another strange aspect of the spectators' behaviour was their continuous attempts to draw the players' attention with strange snake-like hisses and requests for identification: "Pssst! Pssst!… Pssst!… name plees?" When I began my long run-up the crowd's din was ear-splitting. During the lunch and tea intervals, skinny, dark bodies were everywhere: hanging from ledges, palm trees and every projecting cornice of the refreshment room. They peered in through glassless windows and every crack and crevice. After the game the natives pressed their faces against the dressing room windows, before pelting the changing rooms with stones. One could sense that violence was only just around the corner; we learned later that before the game a policeman had been stoned and sent to hospital.

When the home team batted, Brian Statham was the only English bowler to strike a length and line; he finished with 2/15. Loader took 1/15 and I conceded 30 runs without taking a wicket. I did not realise how weak the colic attack had left me and, for the first time in my life, I was extremely glad to leave a cricket field. From the Tamil Club, we went on to the Colombo Cricket Club for a little socialising with the local cricket association officials. Then it was off to do a bit of shopping - I bought some moonstone cuff-links - before we finally made our way to a reception at the Great Orient Hotel, where we received gifts of rubber, tea and ebony elephants - just the sort of useless things we need in our luggage for the next five months! Eventually we were escorted back to the jetty and the launches which took us back to the ship. Our return was delayed by an unscheduled encounter with a drunken Scandinavian sailor and a Tamil porter, who failed to see the humour in the Skipper pretending to pinch his official uniform cap. The Orsova sailed at midnight and as we hung over the aft rails, we saw the lights of Colombo shine, grow dim and finally fade to disappear over the horizon.

Friday October 1st

As we began the final seven days of our shipboard journey, the tedium of our month-long Odyssey began to tell. This stimulated the Purser and his staff into a fresh bout of inventive activity to keep the passengers amused. On the first day out of Colombo, King Neptune and his Court came aboard to welcome those travellers who had never before 'Crossed the Line'. These ingénues were duly shaved, drenched and beautified by the Monarch of the Sea and his attendants. One afternoon was taken up with a 'Test Match' contested by the Press Corps and the crew on the sports deck. The 'Oval' was enclosed by nets and the implements were reduced in size proportionately to the smallness of the ground. The bats were shaved down to half the width of a normal blade and the ball was smaller than regulation size and made of plaited rope. The journalists were more skilled than their opponents - but the sailors had the local knowledge and a closer acquaintance with their tools. They were too good.

One evening after dinner, we were introduced to the nautical version of horse-racing. This involved lady 'jockeys', dressed in racing silks, winding wooden horse shapes painted in the same colour as their silks by means of windlasses and ropes along tracks laid the length of the sports deck. These devices are not easy to handle, and many a rider came a cropper before reaching the end of the straight! The fun of race-night, however, came in the betting on the 'horses'. Normally, all wagers were laid through a tote operated by the crew: a system which ensured that all the gambling proceeds were returned - albeit redistributed - to those who laid them. Because the M.C.C. was on board, however, Captain Whinfield relaxed this policy and permitted the team to field its own 'bookie'. This was none other than Godfrey Evans, who had brought along an outrageously loud check suit and bowler hat specifically for the meeting. I acted as his 'pencil man'. During dinner Godfrey and I moved amongst the tables in the first-class saloon, accepting the money and the horsey hopes of our fellow passengers. Thanks to some judicious manipulation of the odds, we managed to make a small profit on the evening - for the team's kitty of course!

The high point of this final week's social programme was the Fancy Dress Ball - and the climax to this spectacular evening was again the performance of 'Godders', who made a dazzling entry to the ballroom, dressed as the South American 'bombshell', Carmen Miranda. Beautifully corseted, his figure was voluptuously curved and encased in a clinging gown, decorated with a vivid floral design. On his turbaned head and above his coiffed wig, Godfrey balanced a veritable fruit bowl - a mini-mountain of tropical fruit - and he danced in on elevated platform slippers. He rumba-ed into the saloon to the accompaniment of the ship's orchestra, playing *Aye, Aye, Aye, I Love You Very Much*. How he kept his Covent Garden headgear balanced as he danced to the rhythm of

the castanets, I shall never know! The fancy dress competition was 'no contest.' Godfrey walked away with the first prize!

Godders is a unique character. I have never met a more ebullient and optimistic extrovert. On and off the field he is a one-man show: 'keeper, entertainer and athlete. Forever a ball of energy, he simply cannot resist the

'Godders'
- a unique character.

temptation of exhibitionism. He throws himself body and soul into everything he attempts - and tells everyone about it! Enthusiasm pervades everything Evans does. There are no half measures. In England he works for a manufacturing jeweller and part of his luggage on the tour is a showcase full of marcasite specimens, which he hawks tirelessly around the jewellers of the major cities we visit. Later in life he tried his hand at poultry farming, setting up holiday resorts and pub-keeping. Whatever he did, however, seemed dogged by bad luck. His partner in the farming venture deserted him; he chose to develop a Billy Butlin-type of holiday camp in an area which was so exclusive that it refused access to the railway; his career as a publican flopped because there was too much of the 'Jolly' and too little of the 'Drover' in his efforts!

For all that, the glass is always half-full for Godders and never half-empty! At the Saturday Night Club, he is the life and soul of the party, and the meeting is never complete without his rendition of *The German Band*.

"I am the Music Man."
I come from down you way,"
"And I can play!"
"Vat can you play?"
'I can play the big, bass drum."
"Boom di-di- Boom, Boom di-di Boom!"

The song, bawled out with a thick German accent, goes through the various instruments of the band and is accompanied by Godfrey marching up and down, pretending to play them and imitating the sounds they give off: the trumpet, piccolo, euphonium, saxophone, the trombone.... The rendition finishes with the strange instrument of 'the telephone'. Godfrey plays this by pretending to grab receivers to his left and right, and to answer them singing "Allo, allo, allo". Puerile - yes! But it bonded!

Gala Dances and Hampstead Heaths added to the nightly entertainment and the ship's passengers were, by and large, right royally entertained for the remainder of the trip. By this stage I had returned to full training and was skipping and running a few miles a day around the decks, in addition to remaining fairly active in the deck games and swimming departments. As the days before our arrival in Australia passed, one of our daily chores was to spend an hour signing autographed sheets for distribution at the various games we were to play around Australia. It was a boring duty and some of the team's more independent spirits did not take to it too kindly. 'The Boil' - Trevor Bailey to the uninitiated - was one such. The autograph sheets were lodged in the manager's cabin and we used to go there in groups to carry out our chore, usually in late afternoon. On one occasion Trevor's usually ice-cool self-control snapped. He rose languidly from the signing table, holding his cigarette delicately and affectedly in his finger tips - a mannerism of his. "I've had it," he announced. "I'll just put the sheets in the safe!" He scooped up a bundle of a few hundred, opened the port-hole and stuffed them through the window; and as far as I know, there are still hundreds of autographed sheets of the 1954/55 M.C.C. side floating around the Indian Ocean to this day! Indeed there might be more, since 'the Boil' might have done the same thing on other occasions.

'The Boil'
- an independent spirit.

Chapter Three

Arrival and Western Australia

The party await the Press on their arrival at Fremantle.

Thursday October 7th.

KEITH AND I WERE UP AT DAWN today, to catch our first glimpse of 'Terra Australis'. At 4a.m. the Orsova, slipped between Rottness Island and the Western Australian mainland and moved at dead slow pace up the Swan River to berth at Fremantle's Victoria Quay. Early birds though we were, the Australian press were even earlier. Their launches met the ship while it was still in the Indian Ocean. We have been led to believe that the Aussie media are a ferocious lot, but the natives appeared, at least outwardly, to be less hostile than we have been led to believe. One can only presume that we have been misinformed - or that we have not yet provoked them!

After obliging the local photographers with innumerable shots, and taking our leave of the passengers who have shared their last 27 days with us - some of whom have become very dear friends, we went ashore. I have become very attached to a good-looking Sydney girl called Margaret, whom I met on our second day out of Tilbury. Our parting on the last evening on board was very emotional. By coincidence, we met again, walking along the streets of Perth just before the Orsova headed for Adelaide. It strikes me that I am looking forward, perhaps more eagerly than normal, to seeing her again in Sydney.

Our very first Holden cars - the General Motors all-Aussie product - whisked us from dockside to the Palace Hotel in central Perth, stopping for half an hour to admire the wild flowers and view from King's Park. There we saw 'the Kangaroo Paw', a delicate little bloom which is the Western Australian state flower. Its shyness is that of Wordsworth's little celandine.

Our first impressions of Australia were not very favourable. The port of Fremantle is like a shabby ghost town.

On reflection this is not surprising, since it is made up mostly of docks, run-down warehouses and ancient, but not historic, maritime buildings. Few of its citizens walked the streets in the early hours of the day of our arrival. Our hotel - The Palace - is 'nineteenth-century comfortable', right in the centre of town and decorated with the nuances of a Parisian bordello - not that I have been in one - more's the pity! At every meal, it provides such a varied and plentiful menu that we wonder whether the good citizens of Australia have ever experienced war-time rationing. The rooms are extremely comfortable in a rich plush kind of fashion. It is great to stretch out after our cramped shipboard quarters. We have also been introduced to a typical Aussie public bar, which, in the case of the Palace, is hidden away around the corner from the portico-ed,

Perth from King's Park on the morning of our arrival.

marble-stepped and brass-bannistered entrance to the residential part of the hotel. No easy chairs in the bar - just upright stools, a long counter, beer taps, and various bottles of short drinks set on glass shelves against a backdrop mirror.

After unloading our personal luggage, sending our cricket bags off to the cricket ground and unpacking, we were given the rest of the day off. We took advantage of this compassionate leave to chase away the stress, relax and play golf - very badly!

Perth is a peaceful city, with buildings which seldom exceed three or four storeys. It is situated on a broad sweep of the River Swan, which, as it flows towards the port of Fremantle, some ten miles downriver, curves left under the hilly bank and nature reserve of King's Park. The city fathers laid their city out on a symmetrical grid system. It is as clean as a new pin and deserves its reputation as one of the most beautiful cities in the world.

Friday October 8th.

My first taste of Australian cricket conditions. This morning we rode our Holdens just a mile down Hay Street, Perth's main road skirting the Swan, to have our initial practice session in the Western Australian Cricket Ground nets. I think that I am going to like Oz! If I am to judge from my first morning at the nets, the pitches are lightning fast. The groundsmen here do not spare the roller. They employ a hand-guided, electric monster a metre and a half high, which they parade - ever so slowly - not just up and down the wicket, but, in the early stages of the pitch preparation, across and from corner to corner of the square. As they complete the finishing touches to their work, they swing the roller from side to side, imparting a shine to the surface. In all the matches we played in Perth, the pitches were of local black clay rolled iron-hard - until they were depressed, sometimes about an inch below the level of the square! The result is a wicket fast and bouncy enough to make any pace bowler salivate!

A row of practice nets lies to the left of the pavilion alongside the enormous W.A.C.A. oval, which is so large that the boundary immediately in front of the players' changing rooms has to be brought in 30 metres - presumably to eliminate the possibility of running six! The off-the-ground practice facilities at the W.A.C.A. Oval mean that the batting team and players not involved in the game can practice or warm-up while a match is in progress on the main arena. The Perth ground leaves one with an overwhelming impression of space. It possesses one grandstand, which faces a scoreboard which details every run scored - every ball bowled - every wicket taken - every catch accepted - by every individual player in both teams. Beyond the outer spectator area on the river side of the ground looms the state police headquarters, several storeys high and built on the banks of the Swan River. The sounds of bat on ball at the ground are punctuated several times a day by the wail of sirens, as police cars exit the building at speed.

Its flat roof also provides off-duty policemen with an unrivalled view of matches on the nearby oval - just one of the perks of the job!

At our first practice, the temperatures climbed into the seventies and we had soon worked up a healthy sweat. What a contrast to Bradford or Old Trafford! The beauty of the Perth weather is that whilst the sun is fierce, its warmth is tempered by a cool breeze which comes off the River Swan and arrives early in the afternoon. This is the famed 'Fremantle Doctor': not just a cooling agency, but also a moving boon to outswing bowlers operating from the city end!

Taking a lunch-time break from the nets, the team headed for the Perth City Council Chambers for a civic reception. There the mana-'Ger', Geoffrey Howard, spoke very well and introduced each member of the team to the Australian public. Geoffrey is an outstanding manager. He does not seek the limelight, but works industriously and competently in the background, ensuring that all the housekeeping details of the tour are in place. In Perth, however, he was floored by an unanticipated problem which came out of right field and demanded a response which was well above and beyond what even he would recognise as the call of normal duty. He discovered that the Nabobs at Lord's had omitted to provide him with an expense float with which to pay the team's initial tour expenses until the gate-takings began to flow! He had, therefore, to take on the role of a theatrical 'Angel' and negotiate a personal bank loan of £10,000! - just to get the tour under way! What a remarkable lack of organisational foresight! Needless to say Geoffrey never mentioned his financial initiative to any of the team! At least not until well after his retirement.

After the civic reception and lunch, we repaired once more to the nets for an enjoyable work-out in beautiful weather and on flawless pitches. 'Kipper' Cowdrey looks to be in wonderful touch and full of confidence. There cannot be a better striker of the

'Kipper' Cowdrey.

P.B.H. and I leave the sea at Scarborough beach in Perth.

ball in the modern game. The Kent man makes batting look so easy. His flat feet and ungainly, rotund build hide a gifted ball player. At Tonbridge School he was an outstanding schoolboy racquets player of national representative calibre.

In Australia he keeps himself fit by taking his indefatigable Kent colleague, Godfrey Evans, onto the squash court, where he runs the 'keeper ragged. Godders is very fit and never gives Colin best, but chases the ball to every corner of the court. Kipper, for his part, moves minimally around a central strategic position, coaxing the ball into unreachable corners - and squeezing torrents of sweat out of his opponent.

Kipper earned his strange nickname from his love of taking a 'kip' or sleep. His future father-in-law, and President of the Kent County Club, is Stuart Chiesman, who controls a few retail emporiums in South-East London. He fostered Colin's Rip Van Winkle image by appointing him manager of the bedding department in one of them!

The admirable secretary of the W.A.C.A., Les Truman, has ensured a warm welcome for every member of the touring team in just about every club in Perth. He has arranged that we are honorary members of the Celtic Club, The Commercial Travellers' Club, the Naval, Military and Air Force Club, Tattersall's, and The Royal Perth, Cottesloe and Mount Yokine Golf Clubs.

Saturday October 9th.

Another excellent work-out at the nets, organised by the 'Admiral' and the 'Ger', and supervised by the skipper and P.B.H. It is a joy to bowl on Aussie wickets. The ball bounces and zips through at a rewarding pace for fast bowlers. One minus, however, is the fact that the 'Kookaburra' balls quickly lose their hardness and shine. The concrete-hard pitches simply rip the surface leather off them. Fielding is also a bit of a problem. In Perth catches carry further in the dry, warm air and are more difficult to judge. The out-fields are lightning fast and do not give the fieldsmen a second 'bite of the cherry' once the ball is past them. Batting-wise, the ball comes on to the bat and favours stroke-making; but the batsman has to beware of the bounce; the lunging front foot defensive stroke is a 'no-no'. The lift off the pitch quite often finds the ball hitting the shoulder rather than the meat-edge of the bat, and producing a slip catch.

Today is the third consecutive warm day. We lunched at the Palace Hotel and then we did what we would be doing back home in England on a Saturday afternoon in winter. We went to a football match! An Australian Rules football match! This is very different to watching Manchester City at Maine Road, the Latics at Boundary Park or Northampton Town at the County Ground. No soggy turf underfoot, no rain, no snow and no wrapping up in winter clothes! The match was the Grand Final of the Western Australian league. To start the game, the State

Governor, Sir Charles Gairdiner, bounced what appeared to be a thin rugby ball in a centre circle. The game was played on an enormous oval which measured at least 250 by 200 yards. Nicknamed 'aerial ping-pong', the skill of Aussie Rules lies in players leaping high into the air to catch the ball kicked to them by team-mates often 60 yards away. To score a goal the contestants have to propel the ball - by any means possible - between two posts about 15 yards apart. For this their team receives six points; for near misses passing between two outer posts 25 yards apart, sides get one point. Goals are plentiful and three-figure scores are not unusual. It is a fast, open and, I think, dangerous game, in which players are 'shepherded' away from the ball by opponents who are not playing it. Running with the ball is permitted provided that the player bounces the ball on its point once every ten steps. Rather tricky!

I was told that the game was devised by a couple of Victorian cricketers, Tommy Wills and H.C.A. Harrison, to keep cricket teams fit during the winter months! I was also informed that the sport has some of its origins in Gaelic Football. Why was it, I wonder, that this Irish ancestry did not surprise me? What did give me a great deal of satisfaction from this otherwise mysterious game was the fact that, when the most outstanding player of the match was named and rewarded, the judges' choice fell on a certain 'Charlie TYSON'!

Later this evening, after the Club meeting and dinner, a few of the 'boys' were invited to the Fremantle Trots:

harness racing over several laps of an eliptical track with horses pulling sulkies and jockeys along at great pace and at a trotting gait. It was a race meeting just up Godders' street! It seemed like a Bookies' Benefit Night to me, so I gave it a miss!

Sunday, October 10th.

This afternoon the team travelled to Bunbury, a country town on the south-west coast of Western Australia. We are about to make local sporting history by becoming the first international team to play in this prosperous rural community on the banks of the Leschenault Estuary. We travelled the 120 miles in several cars along an excellent tarmac road, through extremely dry country-side and dense bush scenery covered by grey gum trees. We stopped for a snack at Pinjarra, a little town half-way to our destination. It was not a good move for it resulted in Bill Edrich and Trevor Bailey arriving a couple of hours after the main party in Bunbury. They blamed their tardiness on the 'accident' of 'running into a bar'! When we arrived at our Bunbury hotel, it seemed that the whole town had turned out to greet and meet us, especially Len Hutton. His reputation with the Aust-ralian public is phenomenal; and everyone's interest seems focussed on tomorrow's match.

Bunbury is a pleasant little seaside community with idyllic surf beaches, pounded by the incessant rollers of the Indian Ocean. Its main street of single storeyed buildings puts me in mind of those films of Wild West towns I have seen at the cinema. The eve of the match

A spin along the beach, Bunbury
- Tyson, Wardle, Edrich and Wilson.

was given over to that famous Australian institution, the barbecue - otherwise known as the 'barbie'. We were driven to the scene of the meal at the South Bunbury Hall by a taxi-driver who hailed from Horwich in Lancashire. We live in a small world! We enjoyed the 'barbie'. Never had I seen such quantities of chops, steaks, crabs and prawns, as those piled on the communal outdoor grills by our hosts. These cooking facilities are a common feature of the parks and open spaces of Australia. Of course a 'barbie' would not be a 'barbie' without beer. A couple of kegs of 'the amber fluid' were produced, broached and duly consumed, thus giving the lie - so we thought - to the much-publicised

potency of the Aussie brew. It was the first such meal I had experienced and I found it, quite literally, very hard to swallow the rumour of the strong beer - and the reality of endless quantities of meats, salads and sweets which epitomise Australian country hospitality!

Monday, October 11th.

Our opponents in the opening game of the M.C.C. tour are a Combined Country Eleven of Western Australia. They are no easy-beats. Three of them - Herbert, Outridge and James, wristspinners all - have represented the state in first-class games. Three more -

Slattery, Sampson and a youngster called Barry Shepherd - are regular performers in Perth first-grade sides (Shepherd, a burly, aggressive left-hand bat from the Donnybrook club, went on to represent the state and Australia, and later became a member of the Australian Cricket Board). The cricket oval is cheek by jowl with the beach, which is 20 metres away across a road. The ocean is so close that several times in the game I mistook the booming of the surf for thunder. The sea breeze was a delight, tempering the hot sun and making for a perfect day of cricket. The bowler's main bugbear was sand. There was sand everywhere: the outfield was all sand, the bowlers' run-ups were sandy, sand surrounded the pitch and sand constantly blew into the batsman's eyes. Considering that the narrow pitch - a slim strip of black clay soil - had only been laid twelve months previously, it played blamelessly. But the approaches to the square were deplorable, both being slightly uphill and made up, in parts, of loose sand. After the opening bowlers had each bowled one or two overs, the ground began to give way under our feet as we ran up and our spikes could not gain any purchase. It was like bowling on the beach - two steps forward and one step back!

There is no mistaking the enthusiasm of the Australian cricketing public. Six thousand spectators turned up for each of the two days' play in Bunbury. I am sure that Geoffrey Howard was relieved to receive the M.C.C.'s £500 share of the gate money! Losing the toss, Hutton found himself on the receiving end of skipper Slattery's generosity. He inserted us so that we could benefit from some much needed match practice. Bill Edrich took some time to find his timing, but once established, he hit hard through mid-wicket and over long-on. His 129 complemented half-centuries from Tom Graveney and Len. 'Long Tom' rolled out his most graceful cover drives, taking 20 from one James' over. Colin Cowdrey contributed an unbeaten 48 which included two effortless straight drives for six. An hour before close we reached the comfort zone of 5 for 344 and declared, so that our bowlers could have an hour's bowling at the local batsmen. Neither Peter Loader nor I could master the conditions and bowled very unimpressively. The Combined Eleven were 32 without loss at the close, providing both the local and English press with the ammunition to declare that 'The Typhoon Is No More Than a Gentle Zephyr'. This headline was to come back to haunt them time and time again later in the tour.

To relax Keith Andrew, Scrubs and I spent the evening crabbing and fishing, after which we went to another - this time private - barbecue. And so to bed.

Tuesday October 12th.

The country game resumed at half-past eleven, much in the same vein as it concluded on the previous evening. Neither Peter Loader nor I could make any early inroads. One word described my over-enthusiastic effort - 'wild'. But at least I did work up some pace and after I yorked Hutchinson for 37, off-spinner Jim McConnon stepped in to snaffle five wickets for 30 runs and Peter Loader mopped up the tail. All out for 116, the Combined Country Eleven followed on shortly before tea. The Skipper had apparently done his homework and his research had revealed that during his schoolboy days at Tonbridge, Colin Cowdrey had been a leg-spinning prodigy: an extremely successful Public School purveyor of over-the-wrist slow bowling. Tossed the ball, Colin obliged with four wickets for 35 runs, not a bad performance when compared with Wardle's single-wicket reward from his 19 overs! In my opinion, however, none of our bowlers came up to snuff, and the locals deserved to survive as they did, with four wickets of their second innings still intact and a further 105 runs needed to make us bat a second time. The country opener, Stephen, occupied the crease for a total of 280 minutes of the game - but only scored 53 runs!

Bunbury turned on perfect weather for us and our stay was most enjoyable. It was with regret that tonight we quit the Prince of Wales' Hotel and mine host Outridge - the father of the country eleven player. The return to Perth was through a moonless, pitch black landscape, haunted by the silhouettes of ghost gums flashing past in the beams of our car headlights. Our driver told us that many of the dead, white trees are killed by indiscriminate land clearances and bush fires. Once again we stopped at Pinjarra, for a bite to eat. Later in our stay in Perth, Vic Wilson and Bill Edrich returned to Pinjarra for a trots

meeting. We arrived back at the Palace Hotel at eleven and, after a tiring two days, went straight to bed.

Wednesday, October 13th.

With our first major match of the tour against Western Australia only two days away, we conserved some of our energies for Friday. Morning nets were optional and after a brief work-out, most of us relaxed on the golf course or the glorious ocean beach at suburban Scarborough. The beaches are magnificent. Mile upon mile of unspoiled sand stretching as far as the eye can see and washed by greenish, curling breakers six-foot high. It pays not to be careless in the surf, since tragedy lurks in every rip and every undertow of every channel. We stayed between the yellow and red flags indicating the sections patrolled by the surf life-savers.

Back at the hotel, there was just time for a brief rest before we were whisked off to Government House to meet the Western Australian Head of State, Sir Charles Gairdener, at a tea party where we were also introduced to military, parliamentary and society notables. It was one of the first of many such functions and, for protection against being button-holed by bores, we devised a *M-aidez* 'signal'; it consisted of placing the forefinger in the right ear as though clearing the wax and meant 'come to my relief, I am being ear-bashed!'

The beach had made me weary, and after dinner I was not long out of bed.

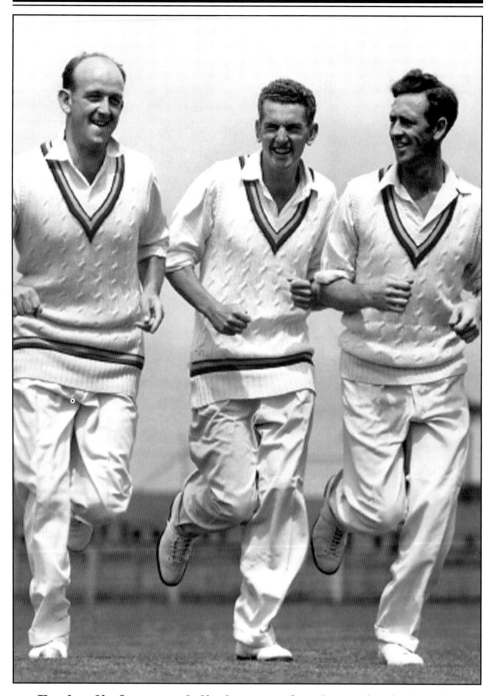

**England's fast attack limbers up for the series in Perth.
Left to right: Frank Tyson, Peter Loader and Brian Statham.**

Thursday October 14th.

No efforts spared this morning. A good hard net and fielding session aimed at attuning us to local conditions. The team for the West Australian game was announced - and I was disappointed to find myself not in it! On this sort of a wicket, it is an opportunity missed! I must work harder to become a recognised regular in the England side.

Friday October 15th.

A stiff, cool breeze and a pitch rolled hard to a level below the square made conditions ideal for pace bowling on the first morning of the match. Our selectors brought out their big guns. They played Len, most of the recognised batsmen, and an attack perfectly suited to the conditions: Brian Statham, Scrubs, Loader, the Boil and spinners Wardle and McConnon.

Len won the toss and indicated his policy on this tour would be that of the French Revolutionary, Danton - *De l' audace, toujours de l'audace* - by asking the home team to bat. This insertion tactic was to serve him well on four occasions - up to the fateful Brisbane Test! A fleeting shower just before the first ball was bowled, freshened a pitch that needed no freshening. Both of W.A.'s openers bagged 'ducks' and when Statham bowled McCarthy before another freshet of rain temporarily halted proceedings, the scoreboard read seven for three wickets. With the first ball after the interruption, the Lancashire paceman 'sconed' former Test man Ken Meuleman and he retired hurt, not to resume his knock until six wickets were down and the home side's innings in ruins. Statham's 6/23 was a very auspicious beginning to his tour and restricted the host side to a 103-run total.

Batting for half an hour before close, we began solidly and were well on our way to a first innings lead when time was called.

Saturday October 16th.

Today, the Skipper showed his class, batting for four and a half hours and plundering 145 from the local bowlers, before being compelled to retire with a pulled leg muscle. He handed over the reins to Peter May. Len's innings was like the curate's egg - good in parts. It was particularly good in the second-day, post-lunch period, when he smacked nine boundaries in scoring his last 45 runs. Colin Cowdrey and Vic Wilson lent him support with scores of 41 and 38 respectively (Coincidentally, Cowdrey was to play another much more hazardous innings of 41 at the W.A.C.A. 20 years later in a Test against the ferocious fast bowling of Dennis Lillee and Jeff Thomson).

The best of the West Australian bowlers were Strauss, who, with the aid of the 'Freemantle Doctor', swung the ball prodigiously at slow medium-pace, and spinner Herbert, one of our earlier opponents in Bunbury.

I wish I could say that I was an appreciative observer of the whole of Len's three-figure start to his tour. Alas, I was inveigled into accompanying Bill Edrich, Big Al, Keith Andrew and Bob Appleyard to the races and only saw the latter part of his knock. Not being a follower of 'The Sport of Kings', I lost eight pounds: a whole week's spending money! But the experience taught me the important lesson that rich bookies are far more common than rich punters.

Sunday October 17th.

Today was a day of rest and recuperation after attending a duty dance on the previous evening at the Cottesloe Civic Centre.

Monday October 18th.

We were at the ground early for a hard session at the nets before lunch. After the interval we divided our time between watching the cricket and more net practice. As a result we witnessed a useful recovery from the Perth side. Batting a second time, 218 runs in arrears, West Australia were indebted to Meuleman, who went to the crease half an hour before close on Saturday and then occupied the crease for the whole of Monday's play to score a chanceless century. In this, he was assisted by the W.A. skipper, Keith Carmody - of Carmody field fame - who contributed 75. The joint resistance of these two players meant that the M.C.C. bowlers had to wait until the last ball before tea for their first success: a delivery which saw Carmody fall to a fine catch by Statham at square-leg off McConnon. Jim has an excellent command of flight - which is perhaps just as well, since his chances of turning his off-spinners on this wicket are minimal.

Tuesday October 19th.

The fabian partnership of Meuleman and Carmody postponed, but could not prevent, the inevitable. Their 128-run, 230 minute partnership enabled West Australia to compile 255 in its second innings and ensured that we had to bat again. Alarmingly, we made heavy weather of the 40-run victory chase. With Len still nursing a groin injury, we lost the wickets of Reg Simpson, Vic Wilson and Colin Cowdrey before Jim McConnon made the winning hit, just before lunch. In West Australia's second innings, 'George' Statham again bowled splendidly, his three wickets bringing his match analysis to 9/91. Peter Loader and Jim McConnon added to their promising first-innings impressions by chipping in with two victims each.

Wednesday October 20th.

Our win early on Tuesday gave us until Friday to prepare for the next important appointment with a Combined Australian Eleven: a composite side of West Australians, reinforced by the talents of three eastern state players: off-spinner Ian Johnson and batsmen Graeme Hole and Neil Harvey. Ken Meuleman was originally chosen, but a knee injury ruled him out and probably eliminated him from contention for a berth in Brisbane's First Test.

Today I ventured once more on to the golf course. Let me be the first to admit that I am a hopeless golfer. I only took up the Royal and Ancient Game when I joined county cricket ranks and played to occupy the Sunday rest days. Let me make my limited abilities crystal clear. I can usually hit the golf ball; and provided my primeval desire to burst it does not cause me to lift my head, I can normally hit it a long way. But WHERE I hit it is another matter! It usually ends up in the distant regions of deep extra-cover. In Perth, I had the consolation of knowing that my partner, 'George', was a golfer of similar ilk. With the important difference that I am right and he is left-handed! Thus, whereas my tee shots normally end up miles to my right, his drives come to rest leagues away to the left! This directional divergence makes a Tyson-Statham golf round a completely anti-social experience. It consists of a Tyson drive to the right followed by a Statham drive to the left. Then comes our main spoken exchange: 'See you on the green!' And off we trudge!

After today's fiasco, shared with 'George', Johnny Wardle and Bob Appleyard at the Royal Perth Club, I resolved to abandon golf. At least… until the next time someone asks me to try my hand! I love a challenge!

In the evening several of the side attended a private barbecue organised by some nurses from the local hospital.

Thursday October 21st.

The knowledge that I had been chosen for the game against the Combined Eleven spurred me to put in a hard working day at the nets. Most of the side kept pretty close to the cricket ground and the hotel. From my observation post in the lounge of the Palace, I took careful note of the habits of the average young Australian female. Apparently they are strong believers in the segregation of the sexes. The ladies who entered the Palace Hotel were usually unescorted. The men prefer to frequent the 'drinking hole' of the public bar around the corner. There they can swop jokes, indulge in man-talk and drink, secure in the knowledge that no woman would dare to intrude into their masculine domain. And they rarely do! The ladies keep to their own lunch and tea-time hen parties. It is not unusual to see groups of 10 or more females in the Palace lounge sinking beer at a rate which would occasion admiration in their male counterparts!

Friday October 22nd.

One of the joys of playing cricket in Australia lies in the delight of knowing that when you pull back the curtains of your bedroom in the morning, you usually do so, knowing that 'the old currant bun' will be shining. So it was today, when I opened the bedroom door to the waiter bearing the morning 'cuppa' tea revivers for K.V. and me. We ate breakfast in the dining room with the team, then we were 'Holdened' down to the W.A.C.A. ground and began our pre-match net. Our inspection of the wicket suggested that the curator had learned from the Western Australian game and had 'toned down' the pitch. It was obviously going to be much slower than the last strip. In spite of this consideration, Peter May, skipper for the day, won the toss and granted the Combined Eleven the first use of the wicket. The old hands in the side groaned inwardly. It seemed that we were in for a hard day in the field.

Imagine our delight, therefore, when we went into lunch after two hours of accurate and penetrative bowling, with our opponents having only 35 runs to show for their efforts, and with Laurie Sawle, Neil Harvey and Graeme Hole all back in the 'hutch'. It took just over an hour to separate the Combined side's openers, but when they departed, so did everyone else. Jack Rutherford's 39 was the only double-figure score in a paltry total of 86. Our bowlers shared the wickets, Statham's three victims taking his 'bag' in three innings in Australia to 12. Trevor Bailey, Johnny Wardle and I each claimed two. Late in the opening day, our turn with the bat came - and we were shaken to lose three wickets for 42. But this was the last window of opportunity for the opposition bowlers.

The MANCHESTER EVENING NEWS.
From John Kay. Perth. Friday.

Australian Test players Neil Harvey, Ian Johnson and Graeme Hole failed with the bat here today, when M.C.C. shot out a Combined Eleven for 86, but lost three wickets for 60 in reply.

Johnson regained some of his lost prestige by dismissing Simpson and Graveney in his first over, but the star bowlers were the tourists. Brian Statham led the way with 3/21, but Tyson, Bailey and Wardle each had a couple of cheap victims and Godfrey Evans sparkled by dismissing five batsmen in a grand display of team-work.

Over by over.

Statham and Tyson attacked relentlessly but Lawrie Sawle, a young university student and Rutherford, although frequently in doubt, weathered the opening new ball spell. They were content with seven singles in the first half-hour and another eight runs in the next, when Bailey and Appleyard took over the attack. Statham had bowled only four overs and conceded six runs, while Tyson in one more over - eight balls, bear in mind, gave away five runs to behind the wicket shots of doubtful pedigree.

Harvey shock.

Appleyard started with a good maiden, but Rutherford off-drove him for four in his second over and it seemed that May's ambitious 'put-them-in' plan was to misfire. Then Bailey had Sawle behind the wicket at 19, after 80 minutes, and in came Harvey, first of the Test batsmen to meet up with the M.C.C. to date.

May promptly brought back Statham after three Appleyard overs at the cost of one scoring shot. Three singles to Harvey and then the Evans-Bailey combination won through again, leaving the Combined side 25/2 and Harvey going back a disconsolate figure, thoroughly ashamed of a shot which a schoolboy would have disclaimed.

Bailey's two wickets had cost him only five runs and he next attacked another Test batsman in Graeme Hole who edged his second ball to slip and was lucky to see it fall in front of Edrich.

Hole next.

Another edged shot brought Hole four lucky runs, then back came Tyson to partner Statham in the ten minutes to lunch.

The move paid off immediately and again all credit to the magnificent Evans, who took his third catch to dismiss Hole. At 35 for 3, the Combined Eleven went into lunch pondering the power of this new-look M.C.C, attack.

Carmody started with a flourish after the break, square cutting Tyson for four, but at 48 he mishit the same bowler to mid-on for Statham to take an easy catch.

Rutherford had then batted two and a quarter hours for 25 and runs were still the exception rather than the rule, when Pavy entered the fray. Appleyard was still accurate but unsuccessful. Bailey then took over from Tyson, whose direction was far better than at Bunbury.

The scoring crawl continued and all the crowd of 6,000 saw in three hours was a beggarly 70 runs, a position that flattered the M.C.C. attack on this easy-paced wicket

Then the mercurial Evans again starred by whipping off the bails as Pavy danced out to drive Wardle, who was bowling his off-breaks and 'chinamen' instead of the usual orthodox left-arm spinners. Now it was 75 for 5 with Ian Johnson, another Test 'guest' as Rutherford's next partner.

Like Harvey and Hole, he too failed, lbw victim to Statham and the Australians were well and truly in a mess when Rutherford - 3½ hours for 39 - was caught and bowled by Wardle in the next over.

Statham next accounted for Price and James with successive deliveries at 86, Evans taking his fifth victim when he caught Price.

James was bowled first ball and Gorringe was run out two balls later to end the innings at 86.

What a feeble show it had been! Full marks to all the M.C.C. bowlers for grand work in trying conditions.

Saturday October 23rd.

Today Peter May showed what the Australian bowlers would be up against in the approaching Tests. His commanding 320-minute innings of 129, together with a sound 72 from the bat of Vic Wilson, yielded a stand of 179, taking us to 4/221 just before tea: a total which was further augmented by an additional 90-run contribution from the tail.

Vic Wilson is a Yorkshire farmer: a mountain of a man with hands like hams. A left-hand batsman and a totally reliable catcher at short leg, he can hit the ball with crunching force; as a county player, year in, year out, he is one of the most consistent performers in the game. I always thought that, in view of his fairly sound start to the Australian tour, he was extremely unlucky not to be given the same Test opportunities which were afforded to Bill Edrich and Reg Simpson purely on the grounds of their seniority and greater international experience. Vic, however, was the first choice for one position in the England team: he was the automatic selection for twelfth man. In this Combined Eleven game he brought off three reflex catches on the final day. Surprisingly, the Aussies raised no objection to his fielding in his specialist short-leg position!

Monday October 25th.

Batting a second time, the Combined Eleven again failed to pass the 200 mark, being bowled out for 163 and going down to defeat by an innings and 62 runs in less than three days. This time it was the Yorkshire spin duet of Appleyard and Wardle who did the damage, claiming a joint seven wickets for 70 runs conceded in 38 miserly overs. Bailey and I helped out with three victims.

The press box universally condemned the batting in this match as 'unenterprising'. The scribes simply did not get it! The Australian batsmen were never given the chance to be 'enterprising'! Between them, the eastern reinforcements of Johnson, Harvey and Hole boosted the Combined Eleven's total by just 60 runs. Appleyard's bounce and medium-slow variations of swing and cut, plus the over-the-wrist 'funny stuff' of Wardle, completely dumbfounded them. In Yorkshire, Wardle's wrist-spinning talents are dismissed as 'an unnecessary luxury'. On softer northern

pitches more accurate finger spin probably yields more economic results. But on the evidence of this game, and at the end of this tour, there will be a lot of first-class batsmen in Australia and New Zealand who will have a different opinion of Wardle's wrist-spinning capabilities!

It was in this game that I struck a batsman on the leg and so hurt him that - in spite of all of his protective padding - his leg had instantly swollen like a balloon and forced him to leave the crease. I think that it was at this point that Len Hutton realised that he had a bowler of exceptional speed in his team - and that England's opportunity to return the previously unanswered hostile fire of Miller and Lindwall was at hand.

That was for the future. For the present we are happy that we are the first England touring team to win both of their first-class games in Perth. Hole's high backlift was carefully noted, as was Harvey's inclination to flirt outside the off-stump.

Tuesday October 26th.

Today the whole side enjoyed the bonus of a day's well-earned rest, thanks to the early finish of the Combined Eleven game. Most of us spent it with some of the many friends we have met in this most pleasant state. Jeff and Robyn Forsaith have been especially kind to us. Jeff is a useful first-grade club bowler on the fringe of state selection. Robyn is a radio personality; she is a gifted pianist and vocalist and we were always welcomed with musical honours

The DAILY HERALD
From Charles Bray. Perth. Monday.

Tyson Made Them Think

It's almost too good to be true. We shall leave here tomorrow night with the staggering record of two first-class matches played and won, the second against a stronger Combined Eleven by an innings and 62 runs

The performance against the State team was good. This was even better. Today there was no wind to help the bowlers and the pitch had lost much of its pace, so there had to be guile as well as speed and the bowlers had to be well supported in the field. And they were.

Without Alec.

Vic Wilson's one-handed catch which got rid of Carmody was one of the best I have seen for many a day. It was at leg-slip, and I think that nobody but the tall Yorkshireman would have reached the ball which went fast and low, Vic dived to his right and one great hand hung on to it.

Godfrey Evans who is rapidly becoming Neil Harvey's bogy-man, took the left-hander again by an acrobatic leap. Bob Appleyard also had a full-length catch.

There is cause for satisfaction in the bowling. So far, Alec Bedser whom we must still regard as our best bowler, has not performed. He will practice at Adelaide, but he won't be playing in the match.

Yet without him two matches have been won with remarkable ease.

Frank Tyson has made the Australian critics have second thoughts. They were inclined to write him off as just another fast bowling myth at Bunbury, but having seen him start off today with five extremely hostile and accurate overs without a run being scored and with one wicket obtained, they are now prepared to reserve judgement

Brian Statham is still the most accurate and dangerous of England's pace attack but in this match Trevor Bailey also bowled with intelligence, accuracy and controlled swerve.

Late this afternoon when the breeze sprang up and Appleyard bowled into it, he showed unmistakably how useful he is going to be on this tour. His change of pace and swerve had the tail-enders in knots and kept young Pavy quiet.

Good Prospect.

This 18-year-old has the makings of a fine player. He had the satisfaction of being unbeaten in the second innings.

The two Australian batsmen - Neil Harvey and Graeme Hole - who made the long journey from the eastern states to play in this game will return with mixed thoughts.

Harvey failed in both innings. Graeme Hole got a few today but he was morally bowled several times before he got out.

at the Forsaith home. Together they have produced girl triplets - each ash blond just like their mum and dad!

We shall miss this friendly state, its beautiful capital and its friendly people. And our quickies will certainly miss the fast wickets of the W.A.C.A. ground. But we must move on, and tonight we leave by air for South Australia and the eastern states. Air travel is still uncommon in Aussie and some of the side are openly nervous about the eight hour flight which lies ahead. When Freddie Brown's M.C.C. side toured in 1950/51, its airborne journeys were often complicated by the reluctance of its nervous leg-spinner, Warwickshire's Eric Hollies, to get on the plane. The only way they could coax him on board was to ply him with drink and get him totally 'legless'. Ansett airlines often took publicity photographs of the English side climbing the stairs to get on the plane. Eric Hollies is there in almost every shot, leaning against the side of the aircraft with a stupid grin on his face - completely inebriated! I'll bet that psychological tactic is not in the coaching manual!

The sting in the tail of our three-week stay in Western Australia came in the shape of a letter to Bill Edrich from his wife. One evening during our stay in Perth we were invited to a musical revue at the local theatre. It was a first-class West End show which we all enjoyed, and when we were invited to meet the English cast backstage we jumped at the chance. To show their gratitude for the evening's entertainment, several of the side agreed to pose for publicity photographs with the girls

of the chorus-line. Little did we know it, but some of the English press were in the audience, and when they saw photographs being taken of the players linking arms and doing a high-kick with a chorus-line of scantily-clad showgirls, they could not resist the temptation. They bribed the photographers and sent the shots off to their papers. The next day, the photos appeared in the London tabloids - with Bill in the centre of a bevy of beauties and one leg high in the air! 'Result? An angry 'please explain' letter from Mrs. Edrich. Moral? Never pose for suggestive photos with the press in the vicinity.

Later in the tour we heard on the jungle drums that Bill was not the only one to have lady trouble in Perth. It was rumoured that one of the English journalists decided to desert the tour in Western Australia. When we moved on to Adelaide it appeared that he chose to stay behind and holiday with a lady friend on Rottness Island. It says a great deal for the *esprit de corps* of the press that his journalistic colleagues filed his copy and covered for him for a couple of weeks after he absconded and until he came to his senses!

Chapter Four

Adelaide and Melbourne

OUR DAKOTA TOOK OFF FROM Perth Airport and headed east into the still pitch-black night, with everyone on board keeping everything crossed. But we quickly discovered that far from being exciting, flying was just plain boring. We droned on for hour after hour over the Australian continent, crossing what we were told was the featureless monotony of the Nullarbor desert - an aboriginal name apparently, meaning 'the plain with no trees'. Above the Nullarbor, we moved ever eastwards to meet the approaching dawn and the golden streaks of the sun's rays: the harbingers of Wednesday morning. At last the first officer informed us that we had begun our descent and we would shortly be landing in Adelaide. At first light, the captain eased the DC3 into the city's airport close by the shores of St. Vincent's Gulf. We gave a collective, audible sigh of relief as the aircraft's wheels touched terra firma, scattering the hordes of rabbits which have made the Adelaide Airport their home. Like cricket, the rabbits are an English export to Australia! The terminal buildings were little more than a collection of corrugated-iron huts; but the welcome which awaited us inside was worthy of a palace: a right royal greeting. Sir Donald Bradman had risen early to meet us. 'The Don' was, as ever, the polite Australian host and the absolutely correct member of the Board of Control. When the England side were in Adelaide, he regularly invited many of the members of the touring party into his home - especially the amateurs, the management and his pre-WW2 playing contemporaries in the media contingent. It was one of my great disappointments of the 1954/55 tour that I never won an invite to his house in Holden Street.

Adelaide, 'the Athens of the South' - and modelled on that Greek ideal - is paradoxically the most English of the State capitals. To its east, the Mount Lofty ranges dominate the city, rising to the height of several hundred metres and separating it from the Murray Valley and Lake Alexandrina. The River Murray, Australia's equivalent of the Thames, provides much of Adelaide's heavily chlorinated drinking water and, when it is flowing, empties into the sea via the lake. During the hot season - and Adelaide can be very hot - some of its citizens seek sleep by migrating to the cooler nights of Mount Lofty and commute daily to their city jobs. Adelaide occupies a wide coastal plain, sandwiched between the hills and the

Gulf of St.Vincent to its west. Its airport adjoins Henley Beach, its western boundary being only 100 yards from the sea.

We set up our Adelaide headquarters in the Pier Hotel, Glenelg: a seaside suburb on Holdfast Bay, where South Australia's first settlers landed from Tasmania. It is the proud boast of South Australians that the state was colonised by free-men - not a single convict amongst them. Glenelg is only a few miles along the beach road from the airport and, within an hour of landing, we were comfortably settled in the Pier. It is one of our favourites: a friendly country pub, just three storeys high, with the rooms on two sides of the first and second floors opening on to a wide verandah, overlooking the beach and cooled by a constant sea-breeze. A broad strip of lawn beneath this verandah separates the Pier from the Glenelg promenade, on the other side of which is the sea wall. During the Adelaide Test in January, the lawn becomes the camping ground for summer holiday-makers, most of whom seem to hail from the inland mining city of Broken Hill. They are a friendly lot - and some of the young ladies amongst them are quite attractive. We passed quite a few pleasant twilight hours chatting with them, as we sipped a cool ale and they cooked their dinners over their camp stoves.

On the verandah of our room at the Pier Hotel, Glenelg.

The lawns outside the Pier Hotel.

The Pier keeps a good table and its spacious colonnaded public rooms are floored in cool marble, have high ceilings and are ventilated by rotating fans. Our hotel rooms, however, are not air-conditioned and on nights of stifling heat sleep is only made possible by opening wide the windows of our large and airy rooms and admitting the sea-breeze. Unfortunately this also means letting in some of the local fauna: large and numerous mosquitos, which the fly-wire screens on the windows are apparently powerless to keep out. The result is that, on hot airless nights, my 'roomie', K.V., and I spend many sleepless hours chasing the b****y insects around our room, swatting them with rolled-up newspapers or spraying them with insecticide from the flit guns

- which the hotel kindly provides! Another inconvenience of the Pier is that Glenelg is a few miles from the city centre and therefore most forms of evening entertainment. We can, of course, summon our Holdens to whisk us along the Anzac Highway; or we can catch the brown Glenelg trams which take the short-cuts, rattle through the parklands and cover the distance into the city in a remarkably short time. But after a day on the cricket field, few of us were up to this extra trip. Our consolation lies in the assurances of our hosts that if we had chosen to stay in the middle of Adelaide, our hotel rooms would have been sweat boxes - 10 degrees warmer than those of our Glenelg pub. Not infrequently Adelaide experiences week-long temperatures of

The River Torrens, South Australia.

100 degrees Fahrenheit or more. The Mount Gambier stone buildings of city absorb and retain this heat so that, even at night, there is no cool relief.

Adelaide was founded in 1837, the last year of the reign of William IV, after whom the main avenue of the city is named. Adelaide itself took the name of William's consort, Queen Adelaide. Its planning was the brainchild of the government surveyor, Colonel Light, who laid out a city of spacious streets on a square grid system - enclosed on four sides by North, South, East and West Terraces and surrounded by open parklands. The River Torrens - a narrow creek dammed to widen it into a waterway 30 yards across - separates the thriving southern business district from the quieter northern residential areas. On a low hill overlooking the northern boundary of the Adelaide Oval, a statue of Colonel Light looks down on his work with satisfied approval.

Adelaide is a countrified city. Its eastern suburbs step into the foothills of the Lofty ranges and are blanketed by extensive vineyards. Wine and Adelaide are synonymous; the Barossa Valley and MacLaren Vale 'vignobles' are only forty minutes travel from the city centre; German 'vignerons' have established their own ethnic enclaves in the hills at Hahndorf and Mount Barker. One winemaking family, the Hill-Smiths, has cricket connections. One of its sons, 'Windy' Hill-Smith, played for South Australia. Alec Bedser tells me that a visit to the Hill-Smith Yalumba vineyard and its attached Lindsay Park horse stud is compulsory visiting on the Sunday of the Adelaide Test. We shall see.

Thursday October 28th.

With the state match only a day away, a full scale practice has been ordered for this afternoon. As was the norm throughout the tour, our cricket gear preceded the team and was sent directly to the Oval. South Australia is one of 'The Big Four' of the Australian mainland sides and a founder-member of the Sheffield Shield competition. Our game with it will be a better test of our steel than the previous encounters in Perth. But first this morning we have to attend the mandatory Civic Reception at the Town Hall. It is doubtful whether the net session which followed the function served much purpose. The wickets were green and we were weary after our overnight flight.

Denis Compton flew out to join us here after his knee op and his delayed departure from England. He must be feeling really air-lagged! At least our net work-out has given him the chance to get rid of some of the cricks in his neck and the stiffness in his muscles. After practice we paid a courtesy visit to Government House, just across King William Street and a few hundred metres closer to town than the Oval.

The Adelaide Oval is one of the most beautiful cricket grounds in the world. It lies in the foreground of a Mount Lofty landscape, just across King William Street from Adelaide University. It is protected from evil by the ecclesiastical presence of St Peter's Gothic Cathedral which stands behind the scoreboard on the gentle slope of King William Street, which climbs into the genteel suburb of North Adelaide. England first played on the Central Oval in March 1874, when W.G. Grace's touring side defeated Twenty-two of South Australia by seven wickets. In those days, of course, the Oval was not fringed on its western boundary, as it is today, by the red-roofed Victorian elegance of the Sir Edwin Smith, the Cresswell, the George Giffen and the Father and Son Stands. What a quaint custom - giving members the privilege of taking their sons to watch the cricket from a private enclosure! The number two oval lies behind the stands, catering for club matches which take place on it every summer Saturday. That ground is just a fraction of the adjoining acres which house practice nets, dozens of lawn courts for the tennis section of the club, and hospitality lawns which blossom with marquees on big match days. The ground's convenience lies in its proximity to the city, which is on the opposite bank of the River Torrens, immediately across Memorial Drive. Few transport problems there! The Oval is bordered on its three other sides of non-river frontage by a golf course and parkland which serves as a car park on game days. On its eastern boundary, access to the Oval is gained through the Victor Richardson gates, named after one of South Australia's most famous and versatile sporting sons. Alongside those gates and on a knoll just inside the ground, immediately in front of the

Anglican Cathedral, stands the score-board which provides a complete synopsis of the match in progress: the batsmen in, batsmen out, bowlers bowling or having bowled, runs scored, wickets taken, extras, umpires, bats-men's totals, bowler's analyses, fielders stopping the ball, taking catches, etc. etc. Everything, it seems, except one's most intimate and personal details!

Friday October 29th.

Right on cue and as ordered, the powers on high have delivered another glorious day. A brief jog on the beach followed by breakfast and then we 'holdened' once more up to town on the Anzac Highway, passing en route the handsome Morphetteville Racecourse. We got out in the Oval car park, next to the Adelaide Tennis Courts - the venue of many Australian Open and the Davis Cup challenge matches. Adelaide civic planners had a genius for a sensible grouping of sports facilities.

Having inspected the pitch for today's match, we came to the conclusion that it will be full of runs. The Adelaide Oval surface has the reputation of being a beautiful batting surface - with the qualification that the ball tends to keep a little low on the final day of a match. Our batting for this game will be strengthened by the inclusion of Compo, in spite of his recent arrival after what the press dubbed 'a tiring and adventurous flight from London'.

Batting first, we made a poor showing on a wicket that was yards slower than those we had encountered

in the West. Len persevered with Bill Edrich in the opening spot and W.J. failed yet again, being caught and bowled by Hornsell for a duck; Bill now has the grand total of two runs from three knocks. Len himself only scored a modest 37, Reg Simpson notched 26 and Graveney and Cowdrey could do no better than a score of runs. Compo alone showed any enterprise and, whilst his 113 was not out of the top drawer, it did enable us to scramble to a first innings total of 246. Jack 'Chucker' Wilson, a jovial and rotund orthodox slow-left arm spinner with no great powers of turn took five wickets.

Saturday, October 30th.

There was rain during the night, but the whole square was comprehensively swathed in tarpaulins and the wicket remains unaffected. The press corps is apparently unimpressed with our efforts with the ball today, dubbing Peter Loader and I as mere 'up-and-downers'. We certainly made heavy weather of getting rid of South Australia's opening pair of young David Harris and Les Favell. The latter, a salesman in a local sports store and a possible selection for the Tests, has an entrepreneurial approach to his batting task. He regards the bouncer as a calculated insult intended to cast doubts on his ability to hook. As a state baseball player, he is addicted to the cross-bat stroke and never hesitated to unleash it whenever we dropped the ball short. He lived a profitable but adventurous life, particularly outside the off-stump, where he constantly flirted with danger. He and Harris put on 119 before, right on the stroke of lunch, I got one through Harris's defences.

After the interval came the collapse! And what a collapse there was, my brothers! Graeme Hole, Col Pinch, Phil Ridings and Neil Dansie represent a considerable body of batting experience, but all failed to reach 20, and it was left to the tail-enders, Gil Langley and Bob Roxby, to add 60 for the seventh wicket. Then, with the scores dead level, the umpires upheld an appeal against the light and we called it a day. After the Saturday Night Club Meeting, the team were invited to, and attended, a party thrown by some air-hostesses, where I unwisely took off my shoes and lost them! They turned up mysteriously next day in Denis Compton's hotel room!

The MANCHESTER EVENING NEWS
From John Kay. Adelaide. Saturday.

Tyson, But M.C.C. toil

South Australia's batsmen gave Len Hutton and his M.C.C. bowlers plenty to think about here today by reaching 246 for the loss of seven wickets, before bad light ended play, ten minutes early.

The men mainly responsible were Les Favell, a salesman in a local sports store and David Harris, a young newcomer to big cricket, who put on 119 in an attractive opening partnership.

Harris fell for 43 just on lunch, but Favell went on to hit five fours and a couple of sixes in an aggressive 84.

Peter Loader and Frank Tyson then regained the advantage and six men were out for 186 before Test keeper Gil Langley and spin bowler Bob Roxby came together to put on 60 in an hour for the seventh wicket.

Loader had come in for some criticism for overdoing the bumpers but he worked hard for his 2/73, a return bettered by Tyson (3/60).

Over by over

There had been some rain throughout the night and early morning, but it did not affect the protected pitch and certainly could not be advanced as the reason for the M.C.C.'s poor showing in the opening stages.

Tyson and Loader were mere 'up and downers' and Edrich - used surprisingly as first change - offered few problems to Les Favell and David Harris.

Not only did they master the bowling, including that of Appleyard and McConnon, but they scored runs freely and when Favell reached 50 out of 79 in an hour and a half, he had hit Edrich for six and also picked up three fours.

The opening pair had three figures up in 110 minutes, neither batsman having made a mistake, although they had each survived an lbw appeal.

Rain proved something of a handicap when Tyson returned just before luncheon but Harris off-drove McConnon and ran so well that it brought him five.

Tyson shines

South Australia went in for the break with 119 on the board after Harris had been bowled by Tyson in the final over for a promising 43.

Favell was unbeaten with 74 in a little over two hours and it was a serious-looking Hutton who led his side in after a black morning.

Despite the rain, which held up play for 15 minutes after lunch and then enforced another stoppage after three runs had been added, the crowd was well above that of the first day when 10,200 paid for admission. They saw Loader quickly account for Hole who offered Simpson a simple catch at short-leg when 12. Then Favell soon foll-owed, giving Hutton at short-leg an easy catch with the South Australian total at 146 and his share an 84 that included two sixes and five fours.

It was a grand effort from this former Sydney grade batsman who now works in the sports department of an Adelaide store. He had certainly delivered the goods today. The wicket went to Tyson who then had two for 32 and looked far and away the best touring bowler.

Hutton then decided that the spin of Appleyard and McConnon would best follow up the pace success when Ridings and Pinch came together for the fourth wicket - and he was right. There was an element of luck about the dismissal of Pinch at 167, for the batsman chopped the ball from McConnon on to his stumps.

Tea came without further trouble to the home men, but the afternoon had been a pleasing one for Hutton.

Two quick wickets on the resumption completely changed the course of the game. Loader hit first by having Ridings caught behind the wicket for 19 and, four runs later, picked up another neat catch off Tyson to send back Dansie.

All square

Rather than risk a curtailment of play, Hutton brought back McConnon after Tyson bowled a six-over spell, but the Glamorgan bowler presented few difficulties and the seventh wicket pair added 50 in less than an hour. Roxby levelled the scores by cover-driving McConnon to the fence, but was palpably lbw to the next ball and at this stage the umpires finally called it a day with 10 minutes outstanding.

Sunday October 31st.

The day of rest! After a leisurely breakfast and a stroll along the beach, I joined the Bedsers at a barbecue at the family home of the Warrens in the Adelaide Hills. The Warrens are a wonderful family and own a large mansion high in the cool Lofty Ranges. Alec, I understand, used to take refuge from the city heat, after a hard day in the field, by staying overnight with them. I soon got to know the Warrens. Their children Rick and Debbie call me 'Mr. Snowman'!

Monday November 1st.

The South Australian innings continued today; but not for long. I quickly knocked over fast bowlers Drennan and Hornsell for the addition of another eight runs: the extent of the home side's first-innings lead. I finished with figures of 6/62 off 19: not a bad return on such a docile pitch.

Then it was the turn of our batsmen to continue their search for that elusive form; and once again they lost their way. What we would have done without Hutton, I shudder to think. He is not in his best touch, but at least he did stick around for a peerless 98 before falling to a great slip catch by Graeme Hole. The rest of us could

---

THE DAILY HERALD
From Charles Bray. Adelaide. Sunday.

M.C.C. find it tougher

Of course it had to happen sooner or later and will do so again. We knew the M.C.C. bowlers could not count on dismissing their opponents as if they were a lot of school kids. And my opinion that we had not scored anything like enough runs on the notoriously docile Adelaide wicket was well founded.

The inexperienced Frank Tyson, Peter Loader, Jim McConnon and Bob Appleyard faced for the first time by an Australian side in run-getting-mood on a most placid pitch stuck to their task remarkably well.

They were also sadly handicapped by the wet ball throughout most of the day. Conditions could not have been worse for them. Yet they came back in great style.

Never was the attack ragged or disjointed, while Tyson was given a lot of work to do and did it remarkably well. Hutton is still experimenting. That was obvious when he took Tyson off after two overs to bowl Edrich.

I'm handing out a bouquet also for the manner in which the tourists are throwing in. It's up to Australian standards and that's saying something.

What catches were going were held. So altogether the M.C.C.'s work in the field was satisfactory.

Apart from Les Favell, the batting was nothing to write home about. Graeme Hole failed again. Langley and Roxby had a good late stand against tired bowlers.

The DAILY EXPRESS
From Frank Rostron. Adelaide. Monday.

Only Tyson can save M.C.C. now

It's red for tour danger… Len Hutton at the wicket for four hours 18 minutes for 98 runs, while the rest of the M.C.C. team mustered only 81 between them.

This is the old story of the 1950-51 tour and here it is being repeated, so early in this tour, against a moderate (by Test standards) attack, and on a wicket which cannot be classed as unusually difficult by batsmen reared on English pitches.

South Australia's fast-bowling discovery, John Drennan, a 22-year old civil servant, destroyed the M.C.C. innings in the first three-quarters of an hour by dismissing Denis Compton, Bill Edrich and Reg Simpson. Three wickets were down for 31 when Compton played on.

After that only Hutton and Tom Graveney did not allow themselves to be mesmerised by the accurate but slight spin of Jack Wilson.

'English batsmen seem to be suckers for any slow left-hander who bowls over the wicket' was the verdict of the derisive crowd.

They slow handclapped and jeered as Hutton, in one moribund period, struggled unsuccessfully to penetrate the field and keep the strike from Jim McConnon.

In truth, our men, excepting one glorious 45 minutes of classic stroke play by Graveney and Hutton, in which they scored 50 runs, looked desperately uninspired.

Great Catch

Hutton and McConnon took 74 minutes to score 50. McConnon was an hour and three-quarters over 12, including one boundary.

Hutton sadly went at 98 - on the threshold of his second century of the tour - to a magnificent slip catch by Graeme Hole.

The umpires, spinner Wilson and South Australian skipper Phil Ridings, all said that the ball was turning only slightly, but admitted that the softish wicket was causing it to come through at varying heights. Ridings, a former Test selector, said, 'I think the M.C.C. is a much better side than last time, despite the result that is coming tomorrow. We're going to win.' Hutton disagreed: 'The pitch is just helpful enough to be tricky and they'll have to fight for every run. I still think we can win.'

I hope Hutton is right but doubt it - unless Tyson can blitz out opening batsmen Les Favell and David Harris. It will be a bad blow to lose a match so early. Even our last ill-starred team did not do that.

only cobble together an additional 83 runs and we were all out for 181, leaving South Australia a mere 174 for what looked like being our first defeat of the tour. My mate Keith Andrew collected a 'golden' duck, while for some strange reason, in what can only be called 'very gloomy conditions', Bob Appleyard, when he batted, refused point-blank to appeal against the light. Must have thought he was back in sunny Bradford!

I did not mind Drennan taking three wickets; he bowled well. But I was astonished that 'Chucker' Wilson boosted his first innings tally of five, with another four wickets - without really turning a ball!

I told myself that the South Aussies were not going to get these runs - and set out to make that thought a reality.

Tuesday November 2nd.

Before play began, 'Pancho' Ridings, the South Australian skipper, told the press that his side were going to win. Are they? We'll see. Len was confident but more circumspect, confining his judgement to the statement that the South Australians deserved to win if they got the runs.

David Harris soon departed, the victim of a fine Loader caught and bowled; but the odds were all on South Australia when Ridings and Favell - 'That Man Again' - advanced the local cause to 95 with only two wickets down. Favell really is a bonny fighter and loves carrying the fight to his opponent. *Le moment psychologique* came just after lunch, at which stage the locals needed only a further 70 runs for

victory. I summoned up the sinews and bowled Favell for 47. Then Bob Appleyard took over, with a four-over spell of 4/6 to finish with figures of 5/46 from 11. He really is an extraordinary bowler! He is all arm and little body, but he is tall and delivers right over the top, making the ball bounce even when it pitches close to the batsman. He swings the new ball both ways and unexpectedly late; and when he changes to cut, his movement off the wicket is pronounced and the ball keeps rising into the batsman, making it difficult to keep it down. Gil Langley put up a brave front for a while, but when Peter Loader came back, it was all over. He bowled Wilson with South Australia 21 runs short of our total. We were home, to the howls of a noisy and disappointed crowd.

Their howling and caterwauling are not to be wondered at, for today is Melbourne Cup Day: 'The Horse Race which Stops a Nation'. Several of the M.C.C. team who are not playing in the South Australian game went on ahead to Melbourne yesterday, so that they could enjoy all the fun of the Flemington races. Back at the Adelaide Oval, all afternoon nothing could be heard except the race-caller's Americanised screaming commentary emanating from thousands of portable radios turned up to full volume to relay the results of every race. Thank God umpires McInnes and Butler did not have any thin edges to adjudicate on! Just before 'the off' of the Cup, umpires, batsmen and fieldsmen all gave up the unequal struggle and sat down on the grass until the race finished. Rising

Fast! Rising Fast! A popular victory and the match resumed in front of a delighted crowd.

Wednesday November 3rd.

The skipper is angry and there is a compulsory parade today for our batsmen - morning and afternoon. Naturally the bowlers have to supply the opposition, so there is no respite for us. Bob Appleyard alone was 'excused boots'. He stepped on the ball during the last few moments of the South Australian game and slightly sprained his ankle. After two hard practices we are on the move again. We packed, said 'au revoir' to the Pier Hotel and this evening at 7p.m. we caught the Overlander train from the elegant North Terrace station - across the street from the South Australia Hotel, which for

The NEWS CHRONICLE
From Crawford White. Adelaide. Tuesday.

Len orders batsmen on parade

Appleyard Feat.

Len Hutton's first directive when he came off the field after the M.C.C.'s 21 runs victory over South Australia was to cancel tomorrow's day off and order special practice for all his batsmen.

'I have got to get them in form,' he told me, 'and hard work is the only way. We shall be down to it again, as soon as we get to Melbourne on Thursday too.' Hutton is right of, course.

The worrying factor is that so many of his men who look immaculate in the nets seem so awkward in the middle. His problem is how to achieve the carry-over from one to the other. If he could find a way to inject his batsmen with the skill, fight and confidence of his bowlers he would have a splendid team.

The way Bob Appleyard, Frank Tyson, Peter Loader and Jim McConnon pulled this match right out of the fire was magnificent. They never let up for a second and their effort today was as stimulating as Monday's batting failure was depressing.

Tyson Pleases.

Hutton is particularly pleased with the sustained steadily improving efforts of Tyson. The Northants lad is moving up to peak speed now and is gaining accuracy at the same time. I have yet to meet any Australian batsmen who like to face him for he is now making them play every ball and is two yards faster than anybody here.

Tyson did not repeat his five-wicket performance of the first innings today but his sheer speed knocked over the castle that really mattered.

That was Les Favell's, who had made another bold 47 and looked the man who could win this game for South Australia.

many years was the headquarters of most visiting touring teams.

The men who built the Adelaide-Melbourne railway must have been tough, persevering characters. Firstly they had to thread it through the Adelaide hills in a series of loops and graded climbs, which so increases the distance to be covered that this short phase of the journey takes more than two hours. Murray Bridge - and we were in the valley of the Murray on the river flats, before skirting the coastal wetlands of the Coorong and heading for Bordertown. Then it was on across the fertile Wimmera wheat lands to Stawell, Horsham, Ararat, Ballarat to Bacchus Marsh and the western suburbs of Melbourne. It was a jolting uncomfortable journey of stops and starts, and even though we had a comfortable sleeper we got very little 'shut eye'. I spent some time wandering up and down the train looking to borrow a good book. I shall make sure that I have something worthwhile reading next time I travel by train. The weather was cool in hospitable Adelaide and we looked forward to warmer treatment in Melbourne, where we arrived at Spencer Street Station at 9.30a.m. on Thursday morning.

Thursday November 4th.

Today is Ladies' Day at Flemington Racecourse. It is the day of fillies and fashion. The girls don their most elegant finery and flaunt it at the Spring Carnival. But we didn't play the gee-gees. In the morning we had a welcoming reception at our Melbourne headquarters, the Windsor Hotel: a stately Victorian edifice directly across Spring Street from the State Parliament. This porticoed building stands on the eastern side of Spring Street, looking down Bourke Street's hill towards the Central Business District.

In the style of most Australian cities, Melbourne is laid out on a rectangular grid plan. Running parallel to Bourke Street are the main avenues of Flinders, Latrobe and Collins Streets intersected at intervals by the main thoroughfares of Spring, Russell, Elizabeth, Swanston, Queen, William and Spencer Streets. Bourke, Elizabeth and Swanston Streets are the shopping malls, while eastern Collins Street is lined by cafes and up-market boutiques. This is the 'Paris' end of Melbourne. Elizabeth and Swanston Streets lie at the bottom of a hill on the other side of which is the city's business centre: the main banks, insurance offices, the stock exchange and clubland.

Two railway stations service the needs of Melbournians: Spencer Street which caters for inter-state travellers and is the station at which we arrived; and Flinders Street, which is linked to Spencer Street but is more of a terminus for suburban trains. On the southern extremity of the city block flows the River Yarra, a broad, brown water course, so muddy that the locals jokingly say that it is the only river in the world which flows upside down! At Williamstown, the Yarra disgorges into Port Phillip Bay, an almost land-locked and shallow bay, more than 50 miles from the narrow heads through which ships have to pass to reach Bass Strait and the open sea. In more general geographical terms, Melbourne is located at the northern end of Port Phillip Bay and a little way up the river which Governor Phillip navigated before landing to declare: 'Here is a good place for a village.'

There is a genteel and civilised nineteenth-century atmosphere about Melbourne. Green single-decker trams rumble up and down its broad avenues. Three live theatres lie within walking distance of our hotel. In the same quarter there are two or three good Italian restaurants, one of them, the Society, with a long family pedigree. Mario's restaurant opposite Her Majesty's Theatre has the added refinement of a staff of singing waiters, who each evening occasionally suspend their normal duties to give the customers a chorus or two. Yet in spite of these delightful *divertissements* there are some surprising less attractive paradoxes in Victorian and Melbourne life.

I was taken to one in the public bar of the Young and Jackson's pub at the corner of Flinders and Swanston Streets - during the 'Six o'clock Swill'. During the war, while the men were away, the women of Melbourne seized the opportunity of passing a referendum legislating for the closure of pubs at six in the evening. Thus, when their men finish work at five o'clock, they have only an hour in which to swill down gallons of beer. And how they drink! They drink before, up-to and for a quarter of an hour after six! They drink - often in large 'schools' - and as the 'Time Gentlemen Please' deadline

approaches, they each buy a round, until each man has as many as 10 beers in front of him; beers which they then have to dispatch in fifteen minutes! No doubt Chloe, the famous nude painting of a Junoesque young lady hung in the Young and Jackson public bar, could tell many tales of the 'Six o'clock Swill'!

It is ironic that such iron-fisted Puritanism - which Aussies dub 'wowserism' - directed at curbing drunkenness, has, in some instances, produced quite the opposite effect, and transformed former comfortable bars into Hogarthian beer shops!

The doyen of state governors, Sir Dallas Brooks, attended our reception at the Windsor, which was quite informal. We were delighted at the opportunity of meeting former Aussie cricketers like the fast bowler of the thirties, Ernie McCormick, now a jeweller. His great friend is the recently retired Australian skipper, Lindsay Hassett, now a partner in a city sports store. Ernie told us the story of his infamous fifteen-ball over which opened the Aussie tour of England at Worcester in 1938. After about his sixth no-ball, the Australian skipper, Bradman, came up to Ernie and asked him solicitously if he was alright. 'I'm fine,' replied Ernie, 'but I think the umpire's getting a bit hoarse!' The puckish Lindsay is a real card. Take him to a party and he never wants to go home.

In the afternoon it was down to the world-famous Melbourne Cricket Ground for net practice. What a ground! It was the scene of the inaugural Anglo-Australian Test in

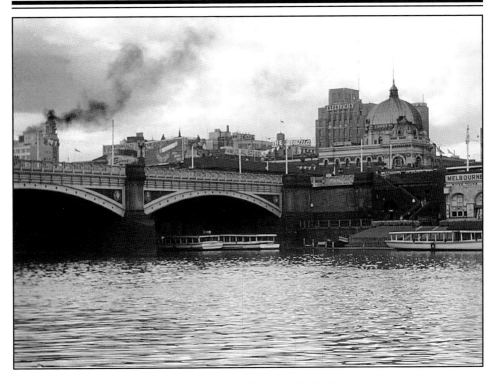

Two views of the City of Melbourne.

The "Paris" end of Collins Street.

1877, the setting for so many cricketing tragedies and triumphs, and, as far as we are concerned, it is the ground on which the Third Test will be decided. At the moment, the new Northern Stand is in the process of reconstruction in preparation for the 1956 Olympic Games. When it is completed, that stand alone will hold more spectators than Lord's! When it is completed the ground will finally seat well over 100,000 spectators - mind boggling!

The nets were good but soft - not suitable practice for the match tomorrow, on what will be a firm wicket - the square having been well protected against the rain. The heat which we longed for in Adelaide has not materialised and the skies remain overcast. I am being rested for the game against an Australian Eleven; if the weather holds, this will give me the opportunity of some quality practice at the Melbourne Grammar School nets.

The home selectors obviously intend to put us to the acid test in this game. They have chosen what looks like an Australian Second Eleven: a team which includes the Harvey brothers Ray and Neil, Briggs, the prolific New South Wales opener, Colin McDonald, Jimmy de Courcy, Richie Benaud, Ron Archer, Len Maddocks, Big Bill Johnston, Ian Johnson and John Drennan, the successful South Australian bowler of our previous match.

Getting into the Melbourne Cricket Ground is about as easy as penetrating the security defences of Fort Knox. Every player is issued with a ticket, plus a couple extra for guests. The ground itself is walled by stands and guarded by turnstiles. The gatemen manning these entrances seem to be brainwashed by a sense of their own importance. They demand to see a ticket each time one goes into the ground. Their dictum is: 'If you ain't got a ticket, you carn't get in.' The notorious stormy petrel of Aussie cricket, Sidney Barnes, once created a furore by vaulting an M.C.G. turnstile. During this Australian Eleven game, a party of us went out to practice at Melbourne Grammar, dressed in whites and M.C.C. blazers and carrying our gear - but we committed the cardinal sin of forgetting our tickets! When we returned a few hours later, we were refused re-admission to the ground because we hadn't got our tickets! It needed a referral to the gateman's supervisor to get us through the turnstile!

On the first day of the game, Compo stretched the sense of humour of the gateman on the players' entrance to its limit. In full view of the official, he stood 30 yards back from the gate, as though sizing it up before jumping it - a la Barnes. He began to run towards the entrance; the gateman, visualizing another incident, leapt in front of the turnstile and began waving his arms to stop him. Suddenly Denis stopped a few yards from the entrance, whipped a ticket out of the breast pocket of his blazer, showed it to the gateman and calmly walked into the ground!

Melbourne is the first major industrial city we have encountered on our tour of Australia. The business opportunities which it offers have brought to light some of the extra-mural activities of the team. Trevor Bailey, for instance, is acting as an agent for electrical switchgear, and on a couple of mornings before and after practice, went out on sales missions. I wondered why some of the lads were calling him 'Switchgear'! Players who have been to Aussie before are aware of the financial opportunities a tour can offer. They seek to supplement their cricket income with some business transactions on the side. For me the tour fee of £800 is reward enough for playing in Australia - but I am innocent in these matters and do not have expensive tastes.

Godders, on the other hand, does; he is a partner in a manufacturing jeweller's in Birmingham and has brought out a display case of marcasite broaches and rings. He never loses an opportunity of 'flogging' them - and he is a magnificent salesman! Alec and his brother Eric go about their business in a less flamboyant fashion; but they, too, seize every opportunity to promote their office equipment, stationery and typewriter business. Good luck to them!

K.V., my 'roomie', is missing Joyce, his wife of five months. Having a match off here has given him the chance to do a bit of shopping for her. Melbourne's Flinders Lane is the centre of the Australian fashion industry and he picked up quite a few attractive items for her at one of the fashion houses, to which he was introduced by Trevor Bailey.

In the Eye of the Typhoon

Friday November 5th.

Guy Fawke's Day! But no batting fireworks on the first day of our Australian Eleven match! Taking first knock on a good wicket, we were well served in the early part of our innings by Reg Simpson, who turned in an excellent 74, before being caught and bowled by Benaud. Reg stubbornly refuses to acknowledge that spinners present any threat to the batsmen. He does not think they can bowl! As soon as a slow bowler appears at the bowling crease, he goes for them bald-headed and often virtually throws away his wicket. Today, at 2/135, everything in the garden was lovely - but then came a cataclysmic collapse which saw us losing our last eight wickets for only 70 runs, to be all out for 205. Our leaden-footed batsmen failed against the spin of Benaud and Johnson, neither of them big turners of the ball. The non-spinning off-spinner Johnson took six wickets for 66, mostly with his arm ball. This performance was a real body blow for Len, who was looking to his senior batsmen to run themselves into form before the First Test. Edrich let him down again with a paltry 11; Compo could only manage 16, Vic Wilson a mere half-dozen and Trevor Bailey an insignificant four. P.B.H. did better, but ought to have translated his 45 into a major score - a lack of maturity. Tom Graveney promised much, but was left marooned on 22 not out.

Saturday November 6th.

It rained for most of last night and consequently the Australian batting reply was a dampish, dull affair which never broke the shackles of some accurate bowling. This was Alec Bedser's first game on a tour which is now more than a month old. Returning from his attack of shingles, he tuned himself up like a Stradivarius: sixteen accurate overs bringing him the reward of Benaud's wicket for 39 runs. Briggs top scored for the Eleven, reaching 48 before the meticulous Bailey bowled him. The Boil returned the best figures of our bowlers, finishing with 4/53. Trevor is a bowler of pernickety exactitude. He measures his run-up to the nearest tenth of an inch. He bowls so close to the stumps that his rear foot frequently clips the wicket; his bowling arm is always precisely over middle stump, exacting maximum benefit of cut and swing - in and out - from every ball. A veritable Isaac Newton of pace bowlers. 'George' Statham was his usual immaculate bowling conception, conceding only 29 runs in 14 overs and taking the key wickets of McDonald and Harvey. The pace of the innings, however, was pedestrian: 68 overs yielding a mere 167 runs at a cost of seven wickets. Jupiter Pluvius was master for the rest of our stay in Melbourne. It began to rain on Saturday evening and did not stop until Wednesday morning.

A most enjoyable Saturday Night Club cost me dear in fines.

Adelaide and Melbourne

Sunday November 7th.

A wet weekend was a good excuse to go to lunch at Ted Rippon's Auburn Hotel. The Victorian licensing laws forbid the opening of pubs on the Sabbath, but Ted holds open house and provides a meal for his theatrical, broadcasting and sporting friends and guests - one closest being Keith Miller. Ted's hotel is in the suburb of Auburn, close to the Hawthorn Footy Club and has a large beer garden, at one end of which is an elevated stage. Performers volunteer performances; the jokes fly thick and fast and are totally unrepeatable; sportsmen are interviewed for Ted's guests. Ted and his great friend Jack Dyer, a.k.a. Captain Blood, are recently retired Australian Rules Footballers who played for the Hawthorn and Richmond clubs. Great characters and rather physical sportsmen, they had recently returned from a trip to America and the U.K. In the U.S.A. State troopers had arrested them for driving too SLOWLY in the fast lane! Quite a switch on the usual story!

I had a look around the pub. In the Sportsman's Bar there was a wonderful photograph of Nugget Miller, sweat pouring off him, obviously after a vigorous bowling spell, and Keith, just in the process of licking his lips before downing his well-earned beer! Nugget was at the lunch. He came with a friend whom I escorted home. Quite a victory!

Monday November 8th.

This evening, after a blank and rain-spoilt day, the hopelessly optimistic Victorian Cricket Association announced through its secretary, Vern Ransford, that an extra day will be tagged on to the game in the forlorn hope - not that it might enable the match to reach a result - but rather that it might afford the players the opportunity of extra practice before the Brisbane Test. Alas, for their expectations on both scores! Melbourne did not live up to its fickle reputation of being able to turn on three different climates in the space of twenty-four hours - but it certainly turned on the rain: a deluge which did not abate until Wednesday morning. This was great for the Bedsers, The Boil, and Godders, who took the opportunity to do the rounds of potential customers, but it was not so good for those of us who did not know anyone in the city. To make matters worse, the hotel was jam-packed full of the racing crowd, in town for the Spring Racing Carnival at Flemington. Alec knew many of them and wheedled us an invite to a party in the hotel on Saturday evening. Most of those who were present were horsey and over fifty. Not much fun! George Tribe's father-in-law came in from Yarraville to meet Keith Andrew and me, and a pal of Reg Simpson's stopped off to spend some time with us.

One person who dropped in and whom I was delighted to see was Alan Jenkins, who played against me for the Medics in inter-college cricket at Durham University. Alan and his wife are G.P.s in the Victorian country town of Maffra, some 100 miles upcountry from Melbourne. Almost a year earlier, they emigrated to Australia with their three children and are enjoying their new home. They run the local general practice and the country hospital. Alan, Keith Andrew and I had a meal at Claridge's restaurant; we parted, promising to meet again at the Sydney Test and then, later in the tour, to spend a weekend in Maffra when the M.C.C. play against the Victorian country eleven in Yallourn.

The 'Windsor' is a wonderful hotel with a great reputation for client loyalty. Its Spring Street façade is dominated by twin towers, rented by sometimes eccentric tenants. The Prime Minister of Australia, Sir Robert Menzies, keeps a permanent flat on its second floor; its lounge, comfortably equipped with leather easy chairs and writing tables, smacks of a London men's club and is the meeting place of celebrities and nonentities alike. It has a magnificent dining-room in which the M.C.C. party has been allocated a central position. Here I made the acquaintance of oysters mornay - succulent Sydney rock oysters topped with melted cheese - and oysters Kilpatrick - oysters garnished with bacon and Worcester sauce. Manna from heaven!

The Windsor's public bar on the Bourke Street wing of the reception area has an oak-panelled air of solidity. It is airy and spacious, with civilised seating, even at the hour of the 'Six O 'Clock Swill'! On the other wing of the entrance hall is the underground luncheon 'Dive': a grill room with a mouth-watering menu. It serves fish which melts in the mouth. Everywhere in the building, one is surrounded by the elegance of curving staircases and wrought iron: a veritable throwback to the Golden Age of Edward VII and the times when the pink of the British Empire coloured much of the map of the world. Across Spring Street from the Windsor, the statue of General Gordon of Khartoum ponders on his plinth. He looks south towards the Melbourne Cricket Ground, over the hollow expanse of the Fitzroy Gardens, quarried to provide the bluestone for Melbourne's buildings. During our stay in Melbourne it was only a short walk from the Windsor, across the Fitzroy Gardens, through Jolimont, to the ground; and each morning we used to enjoy the stroll. It was a bit different to the days of the mid-nineteenth century, when, apparently, it was not wise for Melbournites to venture into the gardens alone - for fear of being held up by bushrangers!

Wednesday November 10th.

This morning it was luggage outside the rooms at 7a.m. We are off on our travels once more. The Australian Eleven match was abandoned to its watery fate, but we could not leave early for Sydney as we were booked on tonight's train for the Harbour City. After our soggy experiences in Victoria, we were not sorry to leave the Queen City of the South and head north towards warmer climes. So, seven o'clock found us at Spencer Street Station, seated in the comfortable sleeping compartments of the overnight inter-city train. Godfrey Evans whiled away the early part of the journey, teaching me how to play his card-racing game. It was quickly apparent to me that this was too rich an education. I retired to my book as the express rattled north-east through the towns of Kilmore, Benalla, Beechworth, Wangaratta, Wodonga, finally pulling into Albury on the Victoria-N.S.W. border just after ten. George Duckworth appeared in the compartment doorway.

'Come on,' he said, 'Everybody out!'

'At ten o'clock at night! Why?'

'We're changing trains!'

We tumbled out on to Albury's long platform and, taking advantage of our unexpected stop-over, headed for the refreshment room, a cup of tea and the Great Australian Snack - a meat pie! Our Victorian Railways train pulled out of the station and headed back towards Melbourne and its New South Wales replacement chugged into the platform opposite. Yawning our heads off, we headed for the train in which we were to complete our journey. Because Albury is on the River Murray and the Victorian border, our journey was to be completed in New South Wales and on a New South Wales train. It would have been physically impossible not to do so! The gauge of the N.S.W. railways is different to the Victorian gauge and our Melbourne train could not have gone further! Extraordinary! Perhaps not so strange, when one realises that before federation in 1901, the Australian colonies were separate entities, each with its own customs and immigration controls.

When we changed trains, we made a bad swop. The N.S.W. train was more ancient and grubbier than the Victorian rolling stock it replaced. Eventually, after chatting far into the early morning with my compartment mate, K.V., I fell into an uneasy sleep, broken only by our arrival in Sydney's Central Station.

Chapter Five

Sydney & the road to Brisbane

Thursday November 11th.

REMEMBRANCE DAY. A DAY NOT celebrated in Australia to the same extent as in Europe. Australia's principal Day of Remembrance is Anzac Day, April 25th: the day that the Australian and New Zealand Army Corps made its gallant but ill-fated landing on the Gallipoli Peninsula in 1915.

This morning our train pulled into Sydney's Central Station at about nine o'clock and we were greeted by what seemed to be all of the city's cricket enthusiasts. We were ushered into a fleet of Holden cars supplied by Stack's motors, the largest General Motors dealer in Australia. The two Stack daughters had returned from a European holiday on the Orsova with us. From the station we were driven to our hotel, overlooking one of eastern Sydney's beautiful ocean beaches. Our base during our initial stay in Australia's first city is to be the Coogee Bay Hotel: a large rambling pub perched on a hill overlooking the bay after which it was named. The view from the verandah of our room is spectacular: a crescent of white sand tipped by rocky headlands, and beyond the beach, the sapphire blue of the Pacific Ocean stretching to a horizon of lighter azure where sky meets sea. Rolling surf crashes ceaselessly on

to the shore and provides a soothing, background symphony. The white of the breakers and the occasional scudding cloud relieve an otherwise blue scene. Bathers and surfers either lay on the beach or skipped over the breakers on their boards, like ballet dancers.

It was warm when we checked in before going for a morning stroll along the beach. Appetite sharpened, we returned to the pub, ready for a good lunch. The Coogee Bay Hotel is a basic bush hotel with few refinements. It is, moreover, a good eight miles from the city and any form of entertainment. In the evening, piped music blares from the public bars, drowning the sound of the surf. I would guess that this might be our last stay in Coogee.

Sydney is 'The Big Smoke' of Australia: the country's largest city, boasting a population of about three million. It has a lot in common with London. Its population is cosmopolitan, and - unlike the other cities we have visited in this country, and like London - it is not laid out on a grid system. Sydney Cove is its focal point.

Here, in the almost landlocked harbour of Port Jackson, the First Fleet landed in 1788 to establish a convict settlement, intended to fill the prison vacuum created by the rebellion of the American colonies. Modern times have seen Sydney Cove develop into Circular Quay, sandwiched between Bennelong Point and the Rocks settlement. Green-painted ferry boats constantly ply constantly between Circular Quay and the many suburbs perched on the shores of the harbour. On the landward side of Circular Quay, the main thoroughfares of the city - Pitt, George, Macquarie, Castlereagh and Phillip Streets - funnel traffic towards the sea. Access to the quay is by streets which twist, turn, narrow and converge on the cove, indicating that Sydney had a far more organic growth than its more geometric cousins of other states. Further inland, the restful green expanse of Hyde Park faces the Mitchell Library. Government House is perched on Bennelong Point next to

Lady Macquarie's Seat, not far from St. Mary's Catholic Cathedral and State Parliament. The naval base of Garden Island lies seaward and beyond this anchorage rises the suburb of Woolloo-mooloo which ascends to the hill-top Australian Soho - King's Cross. From the night-clubs, restaurants and strip joints of 'King's-Bloody-Cross' - as the locals have it - and moving eastwards along the southern shores of the harbour, one encounters the posh inner suburb of Point Piper, then a string of bays, the shores of which are dotted with the mansions of the more affluent Sydneysiders. Vaucluse, Rushcutter's, Double, Elizabeth, Rose and Watson's Bays are desirable addresses. The march towards the Pacific Ocean ends at the South Head of Sydney Harbour.

The Gap, Sydney Heads.

The cliffs of this promontory rise 200 feet out of the sea and are known as the 'Gap'. Scarcely a month passes without some unfortunate throwing him or herself over its edge.

Beyond the Gap, to the south and facing the rollers of the Tasman Sea, lie Sydney's world famous surfing beaches. Bondi is perhaps the best known of them and it is certainly the most popular in the surfing world. But of equal beauty and repute with the 'Hang-Ten' club are Tamarama, Bronte, Maroubra and Coogee beaches. During our first stay in The Old Steak and Kidney, George Duckworth took us down to Maroubra beach, where he introduced us to a Surf Life-Saving Supervisor; apparently he is a famous rugby League player whom Duckie knows from previous football seasons spent following and broadcasting the games of his beloved Warrington.

Just over the Bridge and on the northern shore of Sydney Harbour is the modern business centre and some of the more popular residential areas of the city. Kirribilli House, the Sydney residence of the Australian Prime Minister, is perched on the headland which supports the northern pillars of the Harbour Bridge. To its east lie the suburbs of Mosman, Middle Harbour and the Taronga Zoo; North Head lies in the municipality of Manly which boasts both a Harbour and ocean frontage - the latter lined by a single rank of Norfolk Pines. To the north of Manly the never-ending succession of surf beaches continues: Manly, Whale, Newport and Narrabeen. But the real attraction of Sydney can be described in the two words: 'Sydney Harbour!' This unique body of water is the soul of Sydney; it swirls through its history; its fascination makes the city on its shores one of the most beautiful in the world.

Bondi Beach.

Sydney's southern surf beaches seen from the Bulli pass.

After lunch I phoned Margaret, my shipboard girlfriend, and arranged to have dinner at her home in Manly. Then it was off to the cricket ground for afternoon practice. I never cease to be amazed by the amenities of Australian cricket grounds. In Perth, Adelaide and now Sydney, there are practice grounds next to the main oval. These Number Two Grounds each have centre wickets, on which weekend club matches take place - plus a dozen or more practice nets. This means that the members of teams not actively engaged in the game on the number one ground can practise while a match is in progress. Wonderful!

The Moore Park cricket ground dates back to the 1870s and is but a small part of the greater complex which encompasses the New South Wales Agricultural Showground - the scene each year of the Easter Show - a trotting track, a golf course, and a barracks! The cream buildings of the Showgrounds and its tall clock tower abut the S.C.G. The scoreboard stands alongside them on top of the famous Hill, the former home of that Prince of Barrackers - 'Yabba': the 'rabbit-oh' with the aristocratic surname of Gascoigne! The Noble Stand is the sentinel of the western extremity of the playing area, standing next to the green-roofed pavilion, which in turn neighbours the Ladies' Stand. The north-western boundary is the home of the Paddington Hill, a miniature of its senior counter-part at the other end of the ground. Behind the Noble Stand lies the Number Two Practice Ground.

In the Eye of the Typhoon

In Melbourne we had been overwhelmed by the hospitality extended to us by the various clubs, who had made all of the team honorary members: The Public Schools' Club, the Victorian Club, the Commercial Travellers' Club and the South Melbourne Cricket Club. Now it was the turn of Sydney to see if it could roll out more welcome mats than Melbourne. Honorary membership cards flooded in from the City Tattersalls, the N.S.W. Leagues, and the Cricketers' Clubs. It is hard for the team to keep up with its social commitments! They seem never ending. Tonight, on the same day of our arrival in Sydney, and immediately after a hard afternoon's practice, we are committed to a cocktail party given to us by the New South Wales Cricket Association in the Cricketers' Club in George Street. K.V. was thrilled to meet Bert 'Smoothy' Oldfield, the fabled Aussie keeper of between-the-wars. Keith swears by the wicket-keeping gloves which Bert designed, endorsed and now sells. He keeps a sports shop close by the club. Stan McCabe, the fearless century-maker of the 'Bodyline' series, was also amongst the crowd. He too has a sports business, almost next door to the club.

No Harold Larwood though; George Duckworth has promised to introduce me to 'Lol', who is working for the Coca-Cola company in the eastern suburbs and living in Kingsford. Jack Fingleton, the former Aussie Test opening batsman and now a journalist, took French-leave from reporting a tour, to seek out Harold, who, just after the war, was keeping a sweet shop in Blackpool. 'Fingo' persuaded Harold to emigrate with his family to Australia in 1950. He is reputed to be very happy in his adopted country. Strange, to think that he has settled in Australia, where he was 'Public Enemy Number One' in 1932/33! 'Fergie', the celebrated baggage master and scorer, was also at the party; the little Taswegian has carted the baggage and kept the score-books of every touring side, no matter its nationality, to visit England or Australia since the turn of the century. It was hard to hear the many pearls of wisdom which passed the lips of the many celebrities present. The hubbub in a fairly small room was deafening!

A few lemonades and snacks and then it was time to head off to Manly and the Gregory's for dinner. This entailed catching a cab and crossing the Harbour Bridge for the first time. Sydneysiders call the Harbour Bridge the 'Coat Hanger'! Together with Tower Bridge and the Golden Gate, it is perhaps one of the most famous bridges in the world. The three customary questions which any Sydneysider asks visitors are: 'Whad'yer think of our beer?', 'Whad'yer think of our 'Arbour?' and 'Whad'yer think of our Bridge?' And one has to admit that it is immense and its construction is a wonderful feat of engineering, carried out by the north-eastern English firm of Dorman Long. The authorities still levy a toll for every vehicle which crosses it - but in spite of this impost it still remains mortgaged. Freddie Trueman likes to tell Aussies that they still owe its Yorkshire builders thousands!

**Harold Larwood, his cricketing days over,
kept himself busy selling "lollies".**

Our taxi driver told us that, at the opening of the bridge in the early thirties, the Premier of New South Wales, Jack Lang, was about to cut the ceremonial ribbon when an eccentric and disgruntled former cavalry officer, Captain de Groot, rode up on his horse and beat the politician to it, slashing the tape with his cutlass!

A quiet dinner with Margaret and her family and then it was back for an early night in Coogee. I am playing tomorrow against New South Wales; this will be a test of our true mettle. Keith Miller leads the strongest State team in the Sheffield Shield competition: a side which includes Morris, Briggs, Burke, Benaud, Davidson, the

The Sydney headlands.

eighteen-year-old Bobby Simpson and the new fast bowling phenomenon, Pat Crawford. This line-up - and a wicket that looks green - add up to trouble.

Friday November 12th.

Today Len was 'hoist on his own petard'. Our favourite tactic of inserting the opposition miscarried. We were beaten to the punch and we found ourselves 'the inserted' rather than 'the insertors'. Moreover, our habitual pattern of early batting insecurity surfaced once more. Very soon we soon found ourselves 4/38. Like Horatio, Len held the bridge to score a masterly 102 - but the news at the other end was all bad. Bill departed early, followed by Reg Simpson first ball. P.B.H and Vic Wilson fell to some smart slip-catching and the hostile pace bowling of Miller and Crawford,

supported by the nagging leg-spin of Treanor. Miller is a smart skipper. On today's showing he deserves to be captain of Australia. He rotated his bowlers very astutely.

Crawford was very impressive; a tall man, he bowls right over the top, moves the ball away and makes it rear from a good length. His explosive delivery is assisted by the fact that he is 'a dragger' - and a very long dragger at that! In the State game against South Australia, the home press accused me of taking unfair advantage by 'dragging' and releasing the ball with my front foot half a metre beyond the batting crease. In Sydney, an enterprising press photographer snapped Crawford delivering with his front foot more than a metre in front of the popping crease. The photo caption read 'Oh Tyson. You are an Angel compared to Pat!' A sweet irony! Another Sydney tabloid persuaded

Harold Larwood to put his name to an article: 'Replay Tests - Tyson Not Fair!' I was not expecting criticism from my childhood hero!

Showing great determination and concentration, Colin Cowdrey dropped anchor and helped Len add 163 for the fifth wicket. Kipper's was an outstanding knock; he is a natural timer of the ball and seems barely to touch the ball for it to speed to the boundary. The responsibilities which are being piled on Len Hutton are most unfair. The continual strain on the skipper is psychologically and physically draining and he is getting little on-field support from the expected senior sources. In our first innings against New South Wales, apart from the century contributions of Hutton and Cowdrey, only Godders got more than ten. The remaining eight batsmen scored precisely 40 and we were dismissed for a totally inadequate 252! This was a disgraceful effort when one considers that Alan Davidson, the Sydney paceman, was handicapped by an injured shoulder. 'Davo' always seems to have something wrong with him!

Saturday November 13th.

How inadequate our score of 252 is, became blatantly obvious today when New South Wales passed our total with only three wickets down! The batting revelation of this game is the 23-year-old Billy Watson, a Sydney grade opener, who, playing in his second first-class innings, hit his maiden hundred in any type of cricket! Watson is a short man and like many of his size, he loves to hook. I admire the aggressive intent which brought him a century and a half in only six hours, but his sense of adventure verges on the reckless. He is definitely a believer in 'a short life but a gay one!' He rode his luck, flinging his bat at everything, with the result that when he was sixth out l.b.w. to me on Monday he had 155 runs against his name in the scorebook. In the interim I had him caught behind off his gloves hooking - but not given - in addition to which he was twice dropped, once off a skyer and once in the slips.

The quality New South Wales innings came from the bat of Keith Miller: an imperious 86 which ended when Vic Wilson caught him off a much-below par Alec Bedser. Another Test veteran also turned in a disappointing performance; Arthur Morris played a very unconvincing innings of 26, before he too became a Bedser victim. There was one incomprehensible incident just before close of play when New South Wales were 4/294. Forty-five minutes before stumps, with the home side already in the lead, only four of its wickets down, our bowling tiring and the stage set for some quick scoring, 'Words' de Courcy suggested to Len that the light was too bad to continue and we left the field. We came back after half an hour - sent out again at the urging of a feisty Nugget Miller, who wanted to press home his advantage - but the light was worse than before and we soon returned to the pavilion. What a let-off!

The team meeting this evening was particularly enjoyable. I felt deliciously tired after having bowled hard all day. I was barman at the meeting, where a great deal of banter took place. After wards, the team went to a party given by John Human. A Northumberland-born Cambridge Blue, a Middlesex batsman and leg-spinner, Human toured India, Ceylon and Australia with the M.C.C. in the thirties, finally settling into a business career in Sydney. A varsity friend of Freddie Brown and some of the pressmen, he was a charming host, with many stories to tell about the largely amateur side which toured Australia and New Zealand in 1935/36, the trip which was intended to pacify Australian cricket officials in the stormy aftermath of 'Bodyline' - but he failed to capture the attention of K.V. who fell asleep in a comfortable armchair!

Sunday November 14th.

The invitation read: 'The President and Members of the Committee of the Cricketers' Club of New South Wales request the pleasure of Mr. F. Tyson at a Harbour Excursion on Sunday, November 14th 1954. The M.V. Provide will leave Fort Macquarie Steps at 11a.m. and return at approximately 5.30p.m.'

The excursion was what the Aussies would call 'A beaut day out'. The Provide turned out to be a miniature Orsova. Our hosts fell over themselves to do everything to make our day enjoyable: the lunch was delicious, and we were shown just about every bay, headland and island of wonderful Sydney Harbour. What strange names some of the islands have! How did Pinchgut Island get its name, I wonder? The mansions of the rich and famous were pointed out and the weather could not have been kinder - brilliant sunshine and a temperature which was moderated by a cool sea breeze. There was one disappointment. We had been told that the Harbour swarmed with sharks - but ne'er a one did we sight.

Monday November 15th.

This morning the home side continued its innings, finally being bowled out for 382 - a lead of 130. The situation could have been much worse. Bob Appleyard bowled with wonderful economy, conceding only 58 runs from 21 eight-ball overs and taking one wicket. I was not displeased with my final analysis of 4/98 from 25 overs, a performance almost mirrored by Alec Bedser whose 24 overs and four wickets cost him 117. All is not well with Big Al. I doubt that he is fully fit. He has a rash on his back and he certainly did not bowl with his usual economy.

In an effort to find a solution to the continued failure of our openers and take some of the pressure off the Skipper, Vic Wilson was promoted to open the innings with Kipper. Len dropped down to number 6. The experiment met with mixed success: Vic was 'castled' for nought by Crawford, but Colin, going in at number one for the first time in a first-class game, compensated for the additional failures of Reg Simpson, Peter May and Bill Edrich. His unbeaten 71 took the M.C.C. to a more comfortable position - eight runs in credit at 3/138 with seven wickets in reserve.

Tuesday November 16th.

A month short of his 22nd birthday, the 'Baby' of our side, Colin Cowdrey, today scored his second hundred of the N.S.W. game, against an attack which was the equal of anything Australia can throw at him: it was a superb response to the team's need and a wonderful display of a temperament, well in advance of his tender years. Kipper's double success in this match is all the more remarkable, since before this tour he has not even reached three figures in a county game!

Having wiped out our overdraft, we hung on tenaciously. Len was Colin's co-saviour of the day, falling to a Simpson slip catch off the bowling of top-spinner Jack Treanor when he was an unlucky 13 runs short of his second century of the game. The alarming statistic of this match is that between them, Cowdrey and Hutton scored 402 - or 70% of the M.C.C.'s aggregate of 579 runs. The other nine batsmen could only manage 117 runs in 16 innings. Not a good augury with the First Test coming up! Another lesson which we take away from the New South Wales game is that we have a long way to go before we can match the fielding standards set by Simpson, Watson and Davidson.

We held out until just after tea when we were finally dismissed for a creditable 327. This left New South Wales just 75 minutes to score 198 for victory: an improbable task as Miller acknowledged when he sent the junior members of the N.S.W. side in to bat out time. Scrubs Loader, learning from the experience of the first innings, picked up the wickets of Watson and Simpson cheaply; at the other end Alan Davidson helped himself to 27 gift runs off what Colin Cowdrey later assured us would have been leg-spinners had they bounced! I bowled two overs for one run; Colin sent down 24 balls for 38! One of Davidson's hits off Cowdrey from the Paddington end cleared the top of the Ladies Stand! It was one of the biggest hits I have ever seen! Kipper, an accomplished mimic, then concluded the inconclusive with a series of imitations of the bowling actions of Miller, Lindwall, Benaud, et alia!

Wednesday November 17th.

Last night I enjoyed a pleasant meal with Godfrey and Margaret at Kinneir's Restaurant. Today the team flew out of Mascot airport at noon - destination Brisbane and a game against Queensland before the big one: The First Test. The enjoyable first Sydney phase of the tour is over. In spite of the wonderful times we spent there, I still felt miserable when it ended with Margaret's tears.

Chapter Six

Brisbane and the First Test

The DC3 to Brisbane - a bumpy ride.

THE FLIGHT NORTH WAS THROUGH thunder clouds and extremely bumpy. When we disembarked in Brisbane the heat and humidity met us like a brick wall! Queensland has the appearance of a last outpost of civilisation: the type of city one meets on an excursion up the Amazon! The houses are weather-board square boxes with pointed roofs, raised on stilts to allow the cooling passage of air beneath the living quarters. Roofs are of painted corrugated iron and give off noises like an orchestra's timpani when it rains, which, at this time of year, is quite often. Thank God for Lennon's Hotel, our headquarters in the centre of Brisbane. It seems to be one of the very few air-conditioned refuges from the heat and humidity in the city! The nearby Bellevue Hotel, which is where George Duckworth tells us that previous M.C.C. teams stayed, seems to have few of such modern comforts. The boredom is crushing. There seems to be nothing to do, other than practise and play cricket. Even that veteran networker, Alec Bedser, knows no-one here.

The Governor of the State, His Excellency Lord Lavarack, is a military man and was present at the formal dinner which the Queensland Cricket Association put on to welcome us to the northern state. The dining room was not air-conditioned, was stuffy, and ill-suited to the team's thick English dinner jackets. Never have I been so hot at a supposedly enjoyable function. The sweat rolled off me. My starched shirt crumpled in two minutes flat - and the speeches droned on and on! The relief at regaining the coolness of our hotel room was indescribable.

The city of Brisbane is situated on the banks of the broad river of the same name, a few miles upstream from where it winds through mangrove swamps and into the waters of Moreton Bay. Like most Australian towns its streets follow a rectangular, gridded plan, which the river divides into the northern CBD area and the suburb of South Brisbane. The Queensland Club, the Parliament House, the Treasury Buildings and Government Buildings have a Victorian elegance. They perch on the northern bank of the river and look across to South Brisbane from the heart of the city. The railway from New South Wales and the southern states goes no further than South Brisbane and travellers hoping to reach Cairns and the far north of Australia have to change trains and stations to cross the river and continue their trip. I seem to remember having to make similar changes at Peter-borough in England, when going from Durham to Northampton.

Brisbane has an attractive location, set on hills which rise steeply from deeply cut valley floors, prone to flood. On the heights perch the city's 'Nob Hills' - residential areas such as Hamilton and Paddington. High on Mount Cootha one finds the renowned Botanical Gardens, inside which is the Brisbane Observatory. On the crest of one hill, we discovered 'Cloudland' - a well-patronised and popular dance hall - whose flashing lights illuminate the tropical evening: a magnet for the young at heart . On one side Cloudland overlooks the 'Valley': Brisbane's Soho and China Town. Further down the road the Breakfast Creek flows into the Brisbane River. On the banks of the creek is the famed Brekkie Creek Hotel, renowned for the size of its T-bone steaks, Australia-wide. Brisbane's two most famous landmarks are the Storey Bridge and Kangaroo Point - the first linking the latter to the city centre by road. Storey Bridge is Queensland's 'Coathanger', although it is but half the size of its Sydney counterpart. Kanga-roo Point houses the flat dwellers of the city who commute each morning on quaint little ferry boats servicing equally quaint pontoon jetties. Close by the river estuary is the airport, which is, in turn, cheek by jowl with the Doomben and Eagle Farm racetracks. Moving along the river banks in the opposite direction, one is surrounded by expanses of sugar cane, the main cash crop of Queensland. The tennis centre of Milton - sometimes the venue for Davis Cup matches - is also in Brisbane.

Thursday November 18th.

Off to the ground early for practice in the cool of the morning. The Queensland Oval is known as the 'Gabba' - short for 'Woolloongabba' - which we are told means 'the place of the flowering gum-trees' in the aboriginal language. Others claim that it means 'a place of whirling waters', while others maintain that it means 'meeting or fighting place'. Any name would struggle to do justice to the ground. The playing surface is blameless: a bounceless batsman's paradise, positioned in the centre of an excellent outfield and incongruously surrounded by a greyhound track which batsmen have to cross to access the playing area. Brisbane's humidity certainly assists swing, but once the ball loses its shine, it also loses its movement through the air. After the ball pitches, it seldom deviates any further.

The spectator and player amenities are a different and uncomfortable story. Like the Sydney Cricket Ground, the Gabba has its barrackers' grass-covered Hill, crowned with the usual comprehensive Aussie scoreboard - in this case, however, somewhat difficult to read because of the smallness of its figures. The pavilion - or what substitutes for a pavilion - is on the Vulture Street side of the ground facing south, away from the city. At the opposite Stanley Street end is a single-storeyed, whitewashed stand which extends to the eastern side of the ground where it merges with the 'Gordon Chalk' pavilion. On the eastern boundary, the Gabba is flanked by a primary school, whose grounds, on big match days are used as a parking lot. The Queensland Cricketers' Club stands to one side of the pavilion and provides its members with tasty barbecue lunches; on the right flank of the pavilion is the main members' stand, a wooden structure which rises to a height of some forty feet and provides bum-numbing partan seating. The pavilion is an antique: two wooden dressing rooms cobbled together with bathrooms at the rear, a dining room to one side and a players' viewing facility on a verandah in front. Access and egress to and from the changing rooms is along the passageway between the members' stand and the pavilion; player protection comes from barbed wire strung along the top of a fence which separates the teams from their public. The dressing rooms do not even have a fridge; just a large galvanised iron bathtub filled with drinks and kept cool by ice blocks placed on top of them. On the first floor, above the players' heads, but only in the physical sense, is the press box, while on the roof of the building, the Australian Broadcasting Commission have erected a small temporary broadcasting box. It is in a wonderful position behind the bowler's arm, but I doubt that it is comfortable.

Once, when an England-Australia Test match was held up by one of the thunder, rain and hail-storms which are frequent summer visitors to this neck of the woods, Sid Barnes, the Australian opener and 'Artful Dodger' of the side, tested the gullibility of the English visitors with the tall tale of a previous

The antiquated pavilion at Brisbane.

game, interrupted by hailstones the size of half-bricks falling on the Gabba. Hail the size of golf balls the Poms could already see falling on the turf before their very eyes - but the size of half-bricks!!! Sid slipped quietly away from the front verandah and, as he passed the galvanised bathtub-cum-fridge, extracted a large block of ice. Going to the back of the pavilion he lobbed the ice over the roof of the pavilion on to the oval! The Pommie players goggled as this giant ersatz hail stone bounced on the grass in front of their dressing room!

The Gabba only came on to the Test match circuit in 1931, before which time first-class games were played on the Exhibition Grounds on the other side of the river. Since that time the Gabba has developed into a pretty, but basic, picket-fenced ground. But its practice amenities are totally inadequate for a Test arena. There are only a couple of cramped, usually under-prepared, nets alongside the pavilion. Today we held practice at the nearby 'Churchie' school: a leading Brisbane private school, which did us proud, providing us with wonderful facilities.

I am not in the side to play Queensland tomorrow, but I am looking forward to seeing Ray Lindwall - formerly a New South Welshman - bowl for his adopted state. The 'Banana Benders' will be led by Ken Archer, who travelled with us on the Orsova, after a season as a pro in the Lancashire League.

Friday November 19th.

Ken Archer is an accomplished opening batsman and a wonderfully athletic cover fieldsman. His brother Ron is in no way inferior to him; a fine attacking number five batsman and a decidedly brisk opening bowler with pronounced outwards and inwards movement in the air. He is firm favourite for one of the all-rounders' places in the Aussie side for the First Test. Indeed five of the Queensland side might justifiably lay claim to a slot in the Aussie side: Lindwall, Grout, Archer, the promising Peter Burge and 'Slasher' Mackay - an ungainly left-handed bat with a formidable Sheffield Shield record.

When Ken Archer and P.B.H. went out to the middle and spun the coin, the humidity was stifling. It was like breathing in the vapour from the spout of a boiling kettle. Ken won the toss and asked us to bat. What is it about this tour that makes sides reluctant to bat first? Len asked Peter to continue the experiment of opening with Colin Cowdrey, but this time it failed. Kipper was caught behind off Lindwall in the first knock and played on to Ron Archer in the second; Len never fiddled again with the batting order or interfered with Kipper's batting future.

The familiar batting pattern asserted itself yet again and Cowdrey, Bailey and May were out with only 18 on the board - the last two for ducks to Lindwall and Archer. They made way for a wonderful stand of 234 from Simpson and Compton. Reg Simpson - The Native - is a real enigma. There is not a better player of pace in our side; he dominates and dictates terms against the fastest of bowlers. But he has a fixation: he does not believe that slow bowlers can bowl at all - an underestimation of the spinner's skills, which, more often than not, eventuates in the most ludicrous of unforced errors and dismissals. Today his concentration never wavered and he reeled off 136 wonderful runs, before my colleague from the Central Lancashire League, the veteran leg-spinner Wally Walmsley, had him caught behind.

Reg Simpson - a real enigma.

Compo contributed 110 inventive runs, but only two more batsmen exceeded ten and we were all out 20 minutes before stumps for 304. Denis and Reg scored all but 58 of our total! Again, this alarming batting dependence on just a couple of players! Let me say in mitigation of this imbalanced performance that this first-day pitch was moist, green and helpful to all of the quicker bowlers for most of the humid day. If the curator prepares a similar pitch for the Test we are in for some fun and games!

'Lindy' finished with the fine figures of 4/66 off 15 overs, but was not looking too well as he left the playing arena. At the close, Queensland had scored 15 without loss - but, more importantly, had reduced our playing strength by one. Off-spinner Jim McConnon, fielding close in at forward short-leg, collected a hard drive from opener Mick Harvey, right in the groin, and was carted off to hospital where he spent a week worrying about the continuance of the McConnon line. Poor Jim! The injury was just the beginning of a series of misfortunes which were to lead to his early repatriation.

Saturday November 20th.

Today was even muggier than yesterday. Intermittent rain allowed only two and a half hours on the field. Keith Andrew was brilliant behind the stumps. Standing up to Alec, he caught Ken Archer - the only wicket to fall today - for 23, and at close Queensland were 1/97 with Harvey unbeaten on 47.

Jim McConnon - a series of misfortunes starting in Brisbane led to his early repatriation.

It was a disgruntled bunch of English cricketers who piled once more into our Holdens to make our way back along the road to the city, over the Storey Bridge and into the cooling comfort of Lennon's, where dinner was preceded by a lively Saturday Night Club meeting. Fortunately our hotel is excellent: modern, comfortable and with a good dining room. There doesn't seem to be many decent restaurants in

Brisbane, although Godfrey says that you can get a good steak and plateful of pasta at 'Mamma Luigis', an Italian eatery miles away down in the Valley. It is not the sort of place one feels like seeking out after a hard day's cricket.

Sunday November 21st.

According to the Meteorological Office, the humidity in Brisbane last night reached 92%, which meant it must almost have been raining. We spent this morning with Jim McConnon in hospital, to see if we could cheer him up. It was an almost impossible task; Jim felt as if the whole trip had been wasted. He certainly was not looking forward to a week in hospital. In the afternoon a doctor friend of Len, Godders and Bill Edrich took us under his wing and we headed south-east on the two hour drive to the beaches of Southport and Surfers' Paradise. Lunching at the Southport Hotel, we crossed the Broadwater and the River Nerang and, a couple of miles down the road, found ourselves in the town centre of Surfers: a crossroads distinguished only by a hotel on one corner, a bank on another and a petrol station on the third. All around were sand-dunes, which sheltered holiday shacks, and beyond the dunes, the beach. And what a beach! Fifteen miles of white sand stretching as far as - and beyond - the New South Wales border. The surf provided the background music to a scene of sun and heat. The only tall - or tallish - building visible seemed to be a large modern hotel a couple of miles down the highway at a place called Broadbeach. We paused for a drink at the Surfers' Paradise Hotel and there met the local 'character': an enormous cockatoo, whose spacious cage hung in the shady courtyard of the pub. Unwary visitors were manoeuvred so that their backs were against the bird's cage, at which stage the cocky was prompted into startling them with a selection of profane language, the like of which has never been heard this side of the black stump!

We found the beach and the Surf Life-Saving club and spent a couple of pleasant but safe hours kicking a ball on the beach and being pummelled by the Pacific Ocean. The sea was wonderfully warm and we learned that its temperature even in winter seldom falls below 19 degrees centigrade. We also learned that £500 can buy a beachfront block of land. I do not have a spare £500 - but I wonder if this is an opportunity missed? Before we knew it, it was time for home. It being Sunday, the pubs were shut. With a few of the boys wanting a drink, we took a detour on the return journey, stopping at a hinterland hotel in Advancetown, which the Doc assured us would still be open. So it was! But it is the only pub which I have ever seen serve beer through a spigot out of a keg lodged on a sawing horse, and kept cool by a large block of ice on top!

Monday November 22nd.

Rose early, breakfasted and were at the ground by 10 am. The overnight threat of rain had disappeared and the day was fine and dry. No nets were provided and so we had to content ourselves with a light fielding workout. Before lunch we watched the Queensland innings, which eventually dawdled along for seven and a half languid hours. Alec Bedser bowled splendidly to claim 2/56 off 31 overs - a tremendous workout and a wonderful preparation for the Test. Bailey and Statham were equally economical and effective, each claiming 3 wickets for 74. My mate Keith Andrew was in tremendous form behind the stumps, adding the scalps of Harvey, Ron Archer and Bratchford to that of Ken Archer. Queensland dawdled to a total of 288, in the equivalent of 129 six-ball overs - but I was not there to see the funereal innings, in which every batsman who went to the wicket reached double figures. Those of us who were not playing in the game took off after lunch for the Milton tennis courts where the Australian/American professional tennis troupe were playing. We saw Pancho Gonzales defeat Frank Sedgman and, in the doubles, Sedgman and McGregor lose to Gonzales and Segura. The tall, athletic Gonzales was unbelievably good - strong, incisive and absolutely precise in his placement. Ray Lindwall took the afternoon off because of his stomach upset and joined us at the tennis.

**Pancho Gonzales defeats Frank Sedgman
at the Milton Courts in Brisbane.**

When we returned to the Gabba we got the full story: at the end of the third day the M.C.C. were 20 or so runs ahead for the loss of opener Cowdrey's wicket. Other news was that Vic Wilson had claimed his first wicket in the first-class game, clean bowling Peter Burge. Peter will never live that down! Another promotion story was that of my 'roomie' K.V.'s elevation to number three in the second innings - P.B.H sent him in as night watchman after the fall of Cowdrey's wicket. The following day he was bowled by Bratchford for a duck!

Tuesday November 23rd.

Today, with only one day of the Queensland game left, we are a score of runs ahead and, with two more innings remaining to be completed, nothing but a bowling miracle can rescue the match from a draw. The poor quality of the two Gabba nets, the lack of net bowlers and the previous day's rain, made practice a rather unattractive prospect. The boys batted for most of the day and equalled Queensland's first innings score of 288 precisely: good batting practice. Trevor, Peter May and Denis each scored half centuries, and Reg Simpson, though unable to regain the touch which yielded him a century in the first knock, once more amazed - this time with the ball, taking the wickets of Mick Harvey and Ken Archer in Queensland's second innings for five runs!

Wednesday November 24th.

Two days to 'D-Day' and the First Test. I can't say that I am happy about our preparation for the important match. True, we had nets today and more of the same are scheduled for tomorrow. But the practice facilities at the Gabba are very sub-standard - the two nets are cramped and usually green enough to make batting a lottery. They are not a very good introduction to what looks as if it is going to be a perfect wicket on the day after tomorrow. Indeed, as I have commented before, the practice pitches at the local grammar school nets are infinitely better.

I wonder if our bowling on the green Gabba practice pitches - and on the lively wicket served up for the Queensland match - have pre-disposed the tour selectors to choose a Test attack entirely slanted towards pace. After practice today, Len, Peter May, Bill Edrich, Godders and the 'Ger put their heads together and named Bedser, Statham, Bailey and myself as the bowlers for the First Test. Not a spinner in sight! The die seems to have been cast as to what our tactics will be on Friday; it looks as if we want to bowl first - as we have so often on this tour - hoping to exploit what early life there may be in the pitch. Quite a gamble when you consider that the weather forecast is set fine and hot for the next few days. So why have the selectors plumped for this course of action?

I believe that they have made their decision, first and foremost, because the fast men have been the form bowlers of the tour to date. Of the slower bowlers, only Bob Appleyard has troubled the batsmen in the earlier games. Secondly, they are hoping that the last Saturday's rain and the humidity of the subsequent days hold out some slight promise of early assistance to the new-ball bowlers. Mostly, I suspect, it is because Len, as an opening batsman, respects quick bowlers more than the slower men. It is a puzzle as to why the committee has not opted for Appleyard; he can use both the new and old ball and his inclusion would in no way have weakened the side. Another alternative would have been to bolster our batting with the inclusion of Tom Graveney or Vic Wilson in the side. Bill Edrich has hardly scored a run on tour. But Vic has lost form in the last few games and Tom was compelled to withdraw from the Queensland game with flu and, in consequence, has scarcely touched a bat for three weeks. Let us hope that Reg Simpson maintains his Queensland form.

The press corps were warming up their typewriters before they had even left the conference at which the England side was announced. They are witnessing the greatest gamble of Hutton's career as England's first professional captain.

Thursday November 25th.

The final practice before the Test and it seems that the two teams could not be more disparate in character. Australia will enter this game replete with all-rounders: Ron Archer, Richie Benaud, Keith Miller - and we may even include Ray Lindwall in that category. England

on the other hand has opted for a side of five specialist batsmen, one all-rounder and three pace-men. Ray Lindwall has now fully recovered from the gastric upset which caused his retirement from the Queensland game and is confident that he will be 100% for tomorrow's encounter.

In the England camp, Alec still has a nasty reddish-brown rash on his back and Godfrey came off the field after practice today feeling sweaty and a little woozy. No wonder! It has been hot, and Godders, as usual, was flat out throughout the session.

The bookies have the odds on both teams at evens. It seems that the '53 tour has shaken the Australian public's confidence in the invincibility of its side's batsmen. We had our final team meeting before the match tonight. We will give it our best try.

Friday November 26th.

From its outset this was not destined to be our day. I awoke with a smile of optimistic anticipation on my lips, breakfasted, and jumped into one of the Holdens for the short trip to the ground. There my happiness quickly dissipated. A quick trip to the Test wicket, now stripped of its covers and exposed to the hot Queensland sun, was enough to confirm my suspicion that the grounds-man, who is reputed to have forecast that the wicket will be similar to that of the Queensland game, was wide of the mark and there will not be a green beginning to the game. It was a beauty - full of runs. A downcast Len Hutton entered the dressing room bearing the

**K.V., a pioneer of the wicket-keeping science,
was selected for his first Test cap in Brisbane.**

bad news that wicket-keeper, Godfrey Evans, was out of the side with an undiagnosed ailment which could be either flu or heat stroke!

My Northampton colleague K.V. was about to win his first England cap! It was not the way in which he would have liked to earn it; but he is worthy of it. I have known Keith since he and I faced one another in the Central Lancashire League; he playing for Werneth and me for Middleton. We both joined Northamptonshire in 1952 after completing our National Service - he in the R.A.F. and me in the Royal Signals. While we were qualifying for the midland county, we shared digs. Over time we have come to know each other's strengths and weaknesses, likes and dislikes.

By profession Keith is a qualified electrical engineer; by inclination he is a cerebral person. Once, when travelling by coach to an away game, I caught him counting the telegraph posts as they flashed by the bus's windows, occasionally looking down at his wrist watch. When challenged about what he was doing, he told me he was calculating the bus's speed by counting the number of posts we passed in a minute and multiplying that number by the known distance between them, times 60! That is Keith, ever precise and ever calculating. His keeping is equally exact. His work pattern standing up to the stumps is based on predetermined angles and glove work. He is a pioneer of the wicket-keeping science. His gloves are always positioned above the top edge of the batsman's bat - or outside its outside edge. What is the use, he says, of positioning the gloves behind the ball when it looks like hitting the bat, plumb in the middle? Over the top edge and outside the outside edge, the gloves are already in position to take a top or outside feather. Keith is acknowledged, almost without dissent, as having the best pair of hands in the county game - the best accolade a keeper can ever receive. What goes into his gloves stays in them.

His reading of the spinners is impeccable. Rarely has there been a keeper who can detect the turn of wrist spinners like Keith. Each Northamptonshire match is a competition between George Tribe's ability to hide or invent a new delivery and Keith's Hercule Poirot-like sniffing out of the mystery. But Keith had to keep in an age of pace bowlers: an era when mobility, agility and speed over the ground, allied to useful batting skills, were deemed essential for a keeper worthy of Test selection. And Keith was no Godfrey Evans - just as Godfrey's hands were not the equal of Keith's.

In Brisbane's First Test, there would be no opportunity for Keith to keep to spin bowlers. The die was cast. Having chosen a team for seaming conditions, and having won the toss, we were committed to inserting the opposition. From there it was all downhill. In the opening overs both Favell and Morris flashed repeatedly at Bedser and Statham outside the off stump, to the accompaniment of the 'oohs' and 'aahs' of the 10,000 crowd; but they failed to make the necessary contact. Then K.V. fumbled an impossible leg-side, inside-edge chance off Arthur Morris in Alec's second over and the press opened its file on 'chances missed'. Miraculously 'Artie' and Favell survived, although Morris took 20 minutes to open his account. At the end of the first hour, our misfortunes were compounded by the disaster of Compton chasing a Morris slash past cover and stabbing his left hand into the picket fence at point. Compton gritted his teeth and stuck it out. Ten minutes before lunch we enjoyed our first success. Favell mis-hooked Statham to Cowdrey at square leg and we went in at the first interval with the scoreboard showing 1/56. Slow going at 40 runs an hour.

Lunch turned to ashes in our mouths when we learned that Compo, who had gone to the hospital for an x-ray, had broken a metacarpal bone in his hand and would take no further part in the match. After the interval the batsmen continued to enjoy charmed lives, playing and missing repeatedly. The new batsman, Miller, hooked me high to Vic Wilson at deep fine leg, but it was ruled a no-ball, much to the delight of a crowd who love seeing Australia on top - rather more, in fact, than it does watching cricket. Miller interspersed his flashy existence with some superb back-foot driving, and then, when he was one run short of his half century, he chopped a Bailey long-hop on to his stumps.

His departure changed nothing; for it was now the turn of Harvey to flick and miss outside the off-stump. The little Victorian left-hander needed 20 minutes to get off the mark. The snicks continued, but we could not lay a hand on them. At the end of the game, the *Wisden* correspondent calculated that 12 chances went begging in the Australian innings. I would have guesstimated the figure as being closer to 14; but who am I to quibble!

The normally reliable Boil gave Morris yet another life when he dropped him at deep fine-leg just after tea, when the opener was 55 and the total 145. There was nothing to do but to keep on keeping on. Still the edges did not carry or go to hand, and with the batsmen failing to seize the initiative and creeping along at 20 an hour, the crowd greeted each bouncer with cries of 'don't wake them up'. At close of play, Australia was 2/208, with Morris still there on 82 and Harvey 41. Statham left the field of play with just one wicket to his credit, but having conceded only 29 runs in 16 stingy overs.

Saturday November 27th.

With a good night's sleep under our heads - thanks to Lennon's air conditioning - we arrived at the Gabba early, optimistic that we could still dismiss Australia for under 400. It was a horrible Brisbane day, stuffy and humid, with never a breath of wind. Exertion brought a breathlessness which in itself was an effort not unlike sucking in damp cotton wool.

The morning's papers concerned themselves largely with what they dubbed Hutton's monumental blunder in sending Australia in to bat yesterday. Not everyone, however, towed the popular line. The groundsman, Jock

Morris hits a no-ball from me for four.

McAndrew, reported that he never discussed the pitch with Hutton before the game. The England skipper had asked him on Wednesday when the wicket was last watered and was told that it was that morning. McAndrew also expressed his opinion to the press that he, personally, expected the Test wicket to play as fast on the first morning as the next-door pitch had played in the first session of the Queensland match. That was enough for Alex Bannister of the *Daily Mail* to write that he did not blame Hutton for his gamble, adding that most of the people who saw the Queensland match and the way the turf behaved at the start, would have a great deal of sympathy for England's captain.

Morris and Harvey resumed the home side's innings with the obvious intention of speeding up the scoring rate. They succeeded to the extent that their association realised 202 runs in 232 minutes before Morris departed for 153, caught by Cowdrey off Bailey. Harvey and Hole then added 131 in two hours when the left-hander was taken off a full-blooded pull by Bailey at square-leg. I inveigled Hole into attempting one run too many and ran him out with a hard low return from fine-leg. The local lad, Ron Archer, was caught by Bedser in the gully without scoring. Four wickets fell in an exhausting day at the end of which Australia were 6/503. We laboured to save runs; oh how we laboured and

—THAT TEST WICKET—

Groundsman Says 'I Never Discussed The Pitch With Hutton'

Yes . . . no . . . yes . . . NO ! Peter May just misses when Morris drives past him off Bedser's bowling during the second day of the Brisbane Test.

By ALEX BANNISTER

ENGLAND face a desperate situation in the first Test match at Brisbane. Assuming that Ian Johnson declares tomorrow morning, he will have 20 hours in which to bowl out England twice.

sweated - bowling off short run-ups, just short of a length and to defensive fields. It went very much against the grain to be so negative, but what could one do?

Our fielding let us down again, and the skipper's statement to the press at the end of the day said it all. His main contention was that no matter what tactics are used or how good a team's bowlers are, it is useless if the fielders don't hold their catches. At this stage of the game, the press were probably running a lottery on how many catches we would drop - and they were already up to seven! I thought it was far more!

High above Stanley Street's buildings on the southern side of the Gabba, there is an elevated neon sign advertising a petrol company. As the day grew more torrid and bowling became harder work, the sign seemed to absorb the sun's rays, growing and glowing as red-hot as my anger. Frustration increased as our luck held - and it was all bad. Batsman after batsman either flashed and missed or edged and saw the ball fly wide of the fieldsman.

The Saturday Night Club meeting tonight was far from a jolly affair. But we all wore the blue club tie, with its boomerang and kangaroo motif, woven for us in Melbourne; and we recommitted ourselves to its motto, thought up by one of Kipper Cowdrey's ecclesiastical friends - a bishop no less.

Perduravimus - 'we shall endure'.

And our day will come!

Sunday November 28th.

A welcome day of rest and recuperation after the tour's most gruelling day in the field. But my experience of the two previous days shows me quite clearly that when we take our catches - and when we have just a modicum of luck - we can beat this Aussie side. This will be my dream come true: the vision which I used to conjure up when, in the late 1930s, I read of the Test exploits of England and Hammond, Australia and Bradman, in the used newspapers which people brought in to my aunty Beatty and Uncle Joe's shop in Wallasey - to wrap their fish and chips in. To them it was just paper to wrap their meal in; to me it described sporting romance. And how I longed to get back at that Don Bradman, for all the mammoth scores he piled up against my English bowling heroes!

Monday November 29th.

The Australian innings came to a merciful end today with a lunch-time declaration by Johnson at 8/601. Lindwall, Benaud and Langley contributed an additional 98 runs in the morning session for the loss of Benaud's and Langley's wickets. I claimed my sole success of the innings when I had Benaud caught at deep extra cover by Peter May. It was not exactly a typical fast bowler's wicket; but I am convinced that I deserved better figures than 1/160, off what was the equivalent of 40 six-ball overs.

Ray Lindwall showed his all-round competence by compiling an excellent and unbeaten 64 - and in so doing provoked what looks like developing into a fast-bowling feud between him and me. His chase after quick runs towards the end of the Australian innings led him to play what I can only describe as several cheeky and disrespectful strokes off a fellow fast bowler. And - I am shame-faced to admit it - I broke the quick-bowler's code of honour and let him have a bouncer! Lindy ducked under the bumper, but the look he gave me left me in no doubt that he had stored that delivery in the memory bank and I would hear more of it later on!

What ensued when we batted was more the aftermath of seven exhausting and dispiriting sessions in the field than the result of devastating Australian bowling. Lindwall, seemingly unaffected by his ninety minutes at the batting crease, ran in like a two-year-old and within an hour England lost four wickets with only 25 runs on the board. Before this afternoon I had never seen Lindy doing his stuff in the flesh. I had watched him on film sending England to an all-out total of

IT LEAVES 'EM SPEECHLESS!

PICTURE OF ENGLAND'S SPIN BOWLERS
(Not considered worth a Test place)
REFUSING TO COMMENT ON THE
PERFORMANCE OF OUR OPENING BATSMEN

52 in the Oval Test of 1948; but Brisbane was my first face-to-face encounter with him.

I must confess to being surprised by a couple of aspects of his bowling: I had not realised just how slowly he runs up to the wicket. He appears to be just jogging his fifteen yards up to the stumps - until the last couple of strides of his approach, when he suddenly explodes into his delivery stride. The result of those last two energised paces is impressively fast; but what is even more impressive is the amount of swing he obtains. He often moves the new ball as much as a foot in the air. The other surprising facet of his bowling is that his action is far from being classically high, as I always imagined it. Indeed when he releases the ball, his bowling arm is so low that it borders on the round-arm.

Round-arm or over the top, Lindwall produced the breakthrough. He induced Hutton into edging to keeper Langley, then rattled P.B.H's stumps. With Miller and Archer dismissing Simpson and Edrich, we were in deep trouble. Cowdrey hung on desperately and The Boil dropped anchor as only he can do. Together they added 82 in the remaining three hours of the third day, Cowdrey being caught off 'Big Bill' Johnston on the stroke of time when the scoreboard read 5/107.

Tuesday November 30th.

Having fought the good fight for 160 minutes and only 38 runs, Bailey - *Cunctator* - continued his 260-minute resistance today. He was the last man out, for 88 of the paltry 190 runs which we managed to scrape together in our first innings. Neither K.V., Alec, 'George' Statham or I were much help

'The Boil' - The Prince of Stonewallers.

On the verandah at Brisbane during the first Test. Bradman is in the hat.

to the obdurate Essex man; we were all bowled 'neck and crop', on a wicket on which 'Blind Freddie' should have scored runs. What infuriated me was the fact that I was bowled by an Ian Johnson 'straight break', which drifted with the off-spinner's arm to hit the off-stump - as I played down the line of middle! 'George' and Alec fell for the same Johnson 'three-card trick'. Our dereliction of resistance duty meant that Compo tried a foolish 'King Canute' act - attempting to stem the bowling tide by batting with a broken hand. It was useless of course, and seeing Denis' agony each time he hit the ball, Bailey stepped out of character, laid into the Aussie bowlers with a will and tried to score as many runs as he could before the inevitable happened.

Compton's quixotic gesture in batting one-handed produced at least one totally unexpected bonus. Before the match a local businessman put up a £100 prize for the batsman who hit the first six of the game. Never in his wildest dreams could he have imagined that Trevor Bailey, the 'Barnacle', a.k.a the 'Prince of Stonewallers', would be the first man 'to score the ton'. Yet this is precisely what happened; on the stroke of lunch Trevor slogged Ian Johnson high into the crowd on the Hill, pocketed the money, and earmarked it for the post-match champagne party to mark our determination to win the series!

The Brisbane heat went a long way to convincing me that I should shorten my lengthy run-up. It has also changed my dietary habits. 'Woozer' Dalton - our physiotherapist - thinks that it is a bad idea in a hot climate to eat a heavy lunch and then run around after the interval with undigested food bouncing around my stomach. He has introduced me to a 'liquid lunch': two raw eggs, beaten up in milk or orange juice, sometimes spiked with a measure of sherry! It is not exactly appetising, but it is sustaining. It served me so well in Australia that I stuck to it when I returned to England and county cricket.

After the interval, Ian Johnson asked us to follow on, 411 runs in arrears. Opener Reg Simpson thereupon committed batting *felo de se*. He was run out by a mile when he called for a single off a Favell misfield: the sequel of the South Australian dropping Hutton at slip. What is it that we always tell schoolboy cricketers? 'Never run on a misfield!' Then the Skipper fell l.b.w. to his *bête noire*, Keith Miller, who was now really bending his back and putting everything into his bowling - as only he can. It took the overdue Bill Edrich and Peter May to put some backbone into the innings with a stand of 107. This took us to 130 at close of play - plus the hundred quid, of course!

Wednesday, December 1st.

Seventeen runs into the day, Peter May became the second l.b.w. victim of the innings. He played back and missed a Lindwall delivery which did not bounce on the fifth day pitch. No complaints about the umpiring, however! Col Hoy and Mel McInnes are good blokes and conscientious. Off the field, Col has been especially kind. He is a public relations officer at Ansett Airlines and has bent over backwards to be of assistance. Mel is a South Australian and a good umpire; but his failing eyesight is a worrying factor.

The lack of bounce and pace in the wicket also accounted for Bill Edrich, when Bill Johnston took his middle stump with a delivery which found 'W.J.' completing his favourite hook stroke miles too early, and far too high. Edrich's return to form saw him batting for 190 minutes for his 88; but we needed him to translate that score into a big hundred if we were to survive. There was also the possibility of being saved by rain - a brief flurry arrived forty-five minutes before lunch - but it proved a mirage of hope. Cowdrey could not repeat his first-innings form, and was bowled by an undetected Benaud 'wrong-un' for 10. I determined to sell my wicket dearly and lent what support I could to Bailey. We hung on and hung on. It was not all that difficult and if I were to be born again and play cricket in Australia, I would probably come back as a quick bowler - because I love bowling fast - but I would also pay more attention to my batting. Down Under the odds are all in favour of the man with the bat in his hand.

Surprisingly it was The Boil who succumbed before me. Lindwall took the second new ball and produced an outswinger, which Trevor edged to be caught behind by Langley. He is a remarkable 'keeper - this bloke Gil Langley. Never has there been a more ungainly mover behind the stumps. He is tubby and unathletic. He is not really quick on his feet and often dives to get to the line of the ball - a basic fault in the wicket-keeping coaching manuals. But once the ball is in his hands, it seldom escapes. It is almost as if his gloves are magnetised and the ball is metal.

The end came half an hour after tea. I watched helpless, as Benaud and Johnson bought our last four wickets at a negligible cost. I had played in my first England side to lose to Australia. I did not enjoy the experience. Indeed, I hated it, and I swore that it would never occur again if I had any means of preventing it. That night we put Trevor Bailey's £100 prize to good use. The champagne corks popped on our floor at Lennon's hotel, as players and their friends wandered from room to room - surprisingly happy and optimistic about the future. But we kept our socialising and our optimism to ourselves, away from the public eye and the press. We still feel that we had the measure of the Aussies. We have lost, it is true. But under what circumstances? A mistaken selection policy, an unbalanced team, a minimum of twelve missed changes, two crucial injuries, a wrong insertion and the worst of dismal luck. It lies within our power to correct many of these mistakes. We are not deficient in the talent department. We have the ability and youth to win the series. Len called half a dozen of us into his room and told us that he is completely confident that we will win the series. Even after a crushing defeat by an innings and 154 runs, he knows in his heart of hearts that he has a side with the talent and commitment to beat the Aussies. Last night I slept the sleep of the confident.

Thursday December 2nd.

Critical, but not condemnatory is perhaps the best way to describe the media reaction to our loss of the Brisbane Test. Without exception, the scribes lambasted Hutton's decision to send Australia in to bat. Personally I feel that Len had little choice in the matter, once the selectors had landed him with a top-heavy pace attack which would be at its most effective on the first morning. Still, it is gratifying to learn that some of the press corps have discovered a few golden nuggets of promise amongst the dross of defeat. They singled out the performances of Bailey, Cowdrey and myself for praise. John Arlott, the doyen of commentators, came closest to an accurate diagnosis of our faults when he wrote that Australia won because England missed too much in the field and because neither Hutton nor Bedser produced his usual larger-than-life-size performance. He is closer to the truth than he realizes. Alec still has that ugly rash on his back and 'Woozer' Dalton's treatment doesn't seem to be doing any good. For Alec, the Test ending one day early is another bonus rest day.

Friday December 3rd.

The walking wounded have been given a game off after the First Test. Compo, Godders and Jim McConnon have been invalided back to Sydney, accompanied

by those of the side in need of rest and recuperation: 'George' Statham, The Boil and myself. This morning, the main body of the M.C.C. party headed north towards Rockhampton - 'Mighty Rocky' - where they are scheduled to play a Queensland Country XI to-morrow. Manager Geoff Howard left Denis Compton in charge of the splinter group, who are booked to head south by train to Sydney. Making Denis 'Officer Commanding' is like handing over the keys of the asylum to the inmates. Taking the slow train south will take, we are told, about 24 hours. With the bright lights of Sydney beckoning, there is no way that Denis will tolerate such a waste of time! No sooner had the Rockhampton contingent left the hotel for the airport, than Denis was on the phone to umpire Col Hoy, who today swopped his white hat for that of an Ansett marketing man. The deal was finalised; train tickets were exchanged for airline reservations and within a few hours we were on a plane heading for Sydney. This time we are staying at Usher's Carlton Hotel, in the very hub of Sydney happenings: Martin Place and restaurants such as Prince's and Romano's are just around the corner.

K.V. the cameraman.

Saturday December 4th.

Today the working group of the touring party find themselves in the heat and humidity of sub-tropical central Queensland, playing on Rocky's grassless and dusty rodeo ground. Later K.V. told me that the dust was everywhere. It blocked the eyes, and got into the nose and mouth. It coated shirts and trousers so that when, in Melbourne, the boys unpacked the clothes they had worn in Rockhampton to send them to the laundry, they pulled out of their bags shirts that were stiff, brown and impregnated with a brown mud made up of sweat and rodeo dust! They could have propped their 'strides' up against the wall!

Had there been any grass growing on Rocky's Rodeo Oval, our batsmen in this game may have been described as 'having made hay while the sun shone'. Bill Edrich, Peter May and Vic Wilson all reached the half-century mark, while Len scored 40. For the selectors the problem remains to be solved as to what they are going to do about our long batting tail. Today in Rockhampton, our last five batsmen only contributed 21 runs to the 317 aggregate. There is also the anxiety of our top order not being able to translate good starts into three-figure scores.

In Sydney, Margaret and I went sightseeing. She has a little car to which she has given the name of a Kiwi princess, 'Hinemoa'; today we drove to the Bulli Pass and from its summit looked down the beautiful southern Sydney coastline laid out before us like a map. Later in the evening we visited another of our favourite spots and parked overlooking the southern Sydney Harbour Head and the Gap. The immensity and the power of the Pacific Ocean is mind-boggling!

Sunday December 5th.

Cameras whirled while my co-film director, Keith Andrew was in Rockhampton. Today the M.C.C.'s country hosts took a party from the side to visit an Aborigine settlement just outside the city. Keith expended a couple of reels of film on what they saw. Filmed from the top of a water tower, the Woorabindi reservation looks like a tropical version of 7 Training Regiment, Royal Signals, at Catterick Camp: rows of low wooden huts with corrugated roofs grouped around a central hall and facilities. It does not look very comfortable - and if it is anything like 7 Training Regiment, it isn't! The aborigines laid on entertainment for their visitors. The show consisted of a miniature informal rodeo, the highlight of which was one of the locals riding a buffalo - backwards! Literally - No Bull! The rider could only see the Bull's Dust! Keith tells me that Woorabindi means: 'Where the Kangaroo Sits Down.'

Margaret and I spent the day in the Blue Mountains, visiting Katoomba and the Three Sisters. It is amazing how the canyons of the Blue Mountains all seem to end in sheer, impassable rock walls. I am told that in the early days of settlement, the colonial explorers tried to cross the mountain range by following the valleys, but were frustrated by all of the valleys ending in box canyons. It was only when they travelled along the highland ridges that they conquered the Alps and reached the Western Plains beyond the mountains.

I have had several meals with Margaret and her family at their home in the Manly suburb of Fairlight; I cannot help but feel that I am being treated very circumspectly. Perhaps they regard me as a fortune hunter! It is better that Margaret and I keep our distance.

Monday December 6th.

The Rockhampton match has proved to be all the more-to-be-missed - because of the complaints it provoked. One of the things which I have already learned in Australia is that there is no such thing as a friendly cricket match! All games are played to be won - and losses are to be avoided at all costs! Today therefore, when Len persuaded the Queensland Country Eleven skipper to give him a short extension of play, so that his bowlers could finish bowling the local team out a second time, his bending of the rules came in for a lot of petty criticism. His critics conveniently forgot that, after the M.C.C. had batted all of the Saturday to score 317 and, in the process, had reduced the pitch of rolled earth to the status of a golf bunker, Hutton agreed that the wicket be remade on the rest day. Without this mid-match surgery to the playing surface, the spectators would not have had a game to watch today! As it was, the two Country Eleven innings were day-long processions, with the locals bowled out for successive totals of 95 and 210. Bob Appleyard underlined his indispensable value to the side with a nine-wicket haul; less convincing was Johnny Wardle, who, on a pitch very much to his liking, could only manage two wickets in thirty overs. He is a worry.

With so few of the side in Sydney, it is hard to arrange practice, especially since Denis still cannot hold a bat and Jim McConnon is still tender around the gooleys. Godfrey, though still not 100%, keeps himself fit by roping me in to play squash with him. I try to keep up, but the man is perpetual motion personified and far more skilled at the game than me. 'George' is George and keeps fit by bowling in matches. Our new accommodation, Usher's Hotel, is much superior to the Coogee Bay pub, but its main advantage lies in its central situation and not in its comforts, which are little better than our former headquarters. And even its city location has its drawbacks, for our rooms are four storeys up and overlook one of Sydney's main thoroughfares. The traffic passing outside our windows puts sleep well out of the question until well after midnight.

Tuesday December 7th.

Today we rejoined the team as it made its way south from Rockhampton to our next fixture: tomorrow against the Prime Minister's Eleven in Canberra. The Australian capital is only a half-hour's flight south-west from Sydney. And what a lovely spot it is! Set in a natural mountainous bowl in the Australian Alps, at a height of 1900 feet and overlooked by the Brindabella ranges, it is completely man-made. Apparently, subsequent to the federation of the Australian states in 1901, the two major contenders for the title of the Commonwealth's premier city, Sydney and Melbourne, could not settle which city was to house the Australian Parliament - such was the jealousy which existed between them. It was therefore decided to carve a completely independent Australian Capital Territory out of the bush on the N.S.W/Victoria border. There Australia built its capital. The planning of the city was put out for competition and tender amongst the international community of architects. The winner was the American Walter Burley Griffin. Canberra proved to be his masterpiece. It flouts the conventional grid plan of other Aussie cities and makes a wonderful use of that plentiful Aussie commodity: space! Every avenue seems to be either a crescent or circle, ringing the Houses of Parliament and Central Business District, perched on the banks of man-made Lake Burley Griffin.

It is so easy to lose oneself in its circular maze. Satellite suburbs ring its diplomatic heart, which groups together Parliament, the Prime Minister's Lodge, Yarralumla - the Governor-General's residence, foreign embassies, consulates and the greatest cluster of architectural

Parliament House, Canberra.

culture in Australia: the National Library, the Art Gallery, the Law Courts and the National Theatre. The Houses of Parliament are housed in a long, low, white colonial-style building which overlooks an immaculate and immensely broad lawn. This, in turn, gives way to a wide Australian *Champs Elysees* which bridges the lake, traverses the city, and leads up to the Australian War Memorial on the hill opposite.

Canberra was declared the official capital of Australia by the Duke of York in 1927, and, in my opinion, easily carries off the accolade for the most beautiful capital in the world. Yet in some respects it is a soulless city. Few of its inhabitants are native to it. Most are part of a shifting demographic pattern which alters with every change in government and each diplomatic transfer. I suppose it will take a few hundred years for a permanent bureaucracy to take root there.

We, too, are just transitory inhabitants; we paused for only one evening and a day - but it was a most enjoyable time. Our hotel is the Hotel Canberra: a low, rambling, white building of similar design to the Parliament, where tonight we were entertained at dinner by the cricket-loving Prime Minister of Australia, Bob Menzies. Tomorrow we are playing a one-day social match against a team which the P.M. himself has chosen; he is not a bad selector and usually manages to put his finger on one or two promising youngsters for inclusion in his eleven. The outlook for tomorrow's game, however, is not promising. The weather was unsettled even as we sat down to the meal. Canberra is notorious for its violent thunderstorms and our plane was tossed around even on the short flight from Sydney. Now, even as we take our places around the dinner table, thunder rolls and lightning flickers in the peaks of the Brindabellas. Let it flash and crash, we still enjoyed ourselves, dwelling on a feast of wit from one of the best speakers of the cricket world.

During the evening, the P.M. recalled his early days in politics and at the cricket. He told of being invited into the President's box at Lord's and there being bored to death by a member of the English nobility, who sprinkled his conversation with the expletive: What! Mr. Menzies had to endure a conversation which went along the following lines:-

'Splendid day, what!'

Menzies; 'Yes, your Grace!'

'Excellent pitch, what!'

Menzies: 'Yes your Grace!'

'Stout fella, this Bradman, what!'

Menzies: 'Yes your Grace!'

'The Australians look like winning, what!'

Menzies: 'Perhaps your Grace.'

After half an hour of this lively banter, the P.M. had reached the end of his tether and interjected :

'Not Watt, your Grace. Menzies! Menzies!'

On yet another occasion when Mr. Menzies was again rubbing shoulders with the English aristocracy, one of their number patronisingly commented to the future Australian P.M. that Bradman - then at the outset of his career - was 'A very agricultural batsman.'

'Maybe, Sir Humphrey,' replied Menzies, 'since he is certainly very fruitful!'

In my younger days, my father had the ambition that I should become a politician - perhaps even the Prime Minister of England! Well, I suppose that every English boy has that potential within him; just as every boy in Napoleon's day was said to have a field-marshal's baton in his knapsack. The closest I ever came to fulfilling the ambitions my father held for me was to be invited to the Australian Prime Minister's Lodge in Canberra. In 1954/55 Bob Menzies took the England side home after the dinner at the Hotel Canberra for a nightcap. It was a very hospitable gesture - and it taught me a thing or two about politics and politicians! A couple of the English team members were invited to a game of billiards, with a little wager on the side. Fancying their chances, they took up the invitation - but quite quickly discovered that they simply could not sink a ball! The cue ball refused to run straight and they could not hit a red in the middle. It was only then that they found out that each time they took their stroke the P.M. was substituting a biased cue ball for the white! Tricky - these politicians!

Wednesday December 8th.

The Prime Minister, Bob Menzies, rolled out his big guns for this game: Neil Harvey, Keith Miller, Richie Benaud, Ian Johnson, Lindsay Hassett and Sam Loxton. All agreed to play in what is to be, by common consent, a light-hearted match. The performance was stage-managed by the Test opener of the 1930s, Jack Fingleton, who is a member of both the Cricket Press box and the Parliamentary Press Gallery. The game was Jack's brainchild in 1951, when he persuaded John Goddard to bring his touring West Indian side to Canberra to play in the first of these charity games.

Our game was patronised by Sir William Slim, the Governor General, who joined in the spirit of the day by catching one of Benaud's six-hits which lobbed into his enclosure. The gate money of the game went to local charities - plus an extra £35.10s paid by local businessmen, who contributed 30/- for each six and 10/- for every four hit. It was a festival affair, overseen and umpired by Jack himself, who tried to manipulate the scores to as close to a tie as could be arranged. He failed to achieve equality - but only by 31 runs! The spectators were treated to some spectacular big hitting, with both Benaud and May making centuries. I sometimes question the wisdom of facilitating such scores from Test players - even in giggle games. It can

Hutton and Edrich open for the M.C.C. in Canberra.

only boost confidence - albeit subconsciously - when it comes to more serious contests.

The most keenly anticipated innings in this game was that promised by the former Australian skipper, Lindsay Hassett, at last night's dinner. As he rose to say a few words of welcome to the touring England side, he denounced the faint-heartedness of the Australian batsmen when confronted by our fast bowlers. He ended with a rather bold boast.

'They say that this bloke Tyson is fast!

'Faster than Larwood, so they say!'

'They also say that he takes a run-up of a hundred yards!'

'Fast - psshaw! I'm not scared of him and his long run.'

'Tomorrow when I bat, I'll hook him out of sight!'

As he was speaking, there was a terrific Canberra thunderstorm raging outside the hotel windows - flashes of lightning, explosions of thunder and downpours of sheeting rain. As Lindsay finished his boast, there was one extra-loud clap of thunder and a flash of lightning which lit up the room.

'Listen,' added Lindsay, 'he's just started his run-up!'

When Lindsay came in to bat today, I had already bowled my ration of overs. But seeing that 'Taskett' had to face up to the next delivery, Len immediately handed me the ball for another over. I measured out an exaggeratedly long run, paused for effect as Hassett took guard and looked around the field. Then I hared in and bowled - the slowest, highest donkey drop of all time! It was so slow and high that Lindsay had time to take a couple of swipes at it as it came down - and he still didn't hit it! Then I bowled a second ball: a fair dinkum fast bouncer! It hit him on the hand and he held up his hands in mock surrender! Thankful that no-one was hurt, I gave the ball back to Len - honour satisfied!

Thursday December 9th.

We are on the move again. This time we are off to Melbourne for the match against the State side. In State ratings, Victoria ranks number two. It is a pretty formidable combination and includes two of the Harvey brothers, Ray and Neil - one a Test man and the other close to being one, Test opener Colin McDonald, the Aussie skipper Ian Johnson, leg-spinner Jack Hill, who played three Tests against England in 1953, the left-hand Test paceman, Big Bill Johnston and the leading all-rounder in Bradman's 1948 touring team, Sam Loxton. It looks like being a tough tussle.

It is only a short flight of under an hour from Canberra to Essendon Airport and in no time at all, we were back in our comfortable stomping grounds at the Windsor. After the Prime Minister's match and its attendant hectic social round, afternoon practice was optional and relaxation was the most popular order of the day, or rather what was left of the day after travel time. I practised. I was keen to smooth out my remodelled run-up and I knew that, after our top-heavy pace selection in Brisbane, one fast bowling position in the side for the Sydney Test could be on the line. With 'Big Al' still not fully operational, I had a chance of clinching that place in the Victorian match.

Friday December 10th.

Melbourne's weather was distinctly ominous when Len won the toss from Sam Loxton and took first strike. The Victorian pace trio of 'Strawberry' Power, Loxton and Big Bill Johnston is enough to shake the strongest of batting line-ups. It was therefore with a great sense of satisfaction that the rest of the side looked on as the Skipper and The Boil put on 97 for the first wicket - one of our best starts of the tour. Tom Graveney chipped in with a beautifully struck 48 and Colin Cowdrey was well on his way to another century when he was run out just 21 short of his goal. At the end of a profitable batting day, we had accumulated 253 for the loss of eight wickets.

Saturday December 11th.

Yesterday's threat of rain became a reality and reduced today's scheduled six hours of play to just two. When the Victorian batsmen were finally forced off the field, the home side's score stood at 33 without loss in reply to our total of 312.

This evening, after a riotous Saturday Evening Club get-together, K.V. and I were invited to the home of Keith Burnham, a real estate agent and the president of the Footscray Cricket Club, one of Melbourne's District teams. We enjoyed a homely evening, Keith and his wife Vicki proving to be excellent hosts.

Sunday December 12th.

More than two inches of rain fell in Melbourne yesterday and today. We shall be lucky to start on time tomorrow. There is some bad news on the injury front. It looks as if Denis Compton will still not be fit enough to resume his place in the side for the Second Test in Sydney; his broken hand has not mended as quickly as was expected.

After having given some thought to the subject of my run-up, I think that I will revert to the approach which I used in my league, Army and University days. This is based on ten long final strides before delivery, prefaced by shorter steps leading to the acceleration point into those final strides. It is an approach which served me well for some years. It is not too long - about 20 yards including the shorter steps, and it should enable me to retain my forward impetus in the delivery stride and follow-through. Hopefully, I should retain my speed and increase my accuracy.

Monday December 13th.

It has finally stopped raining. But I fear that it will be too late to save the match from a watery grave. When the pitch was uncovered this morning, its straw colour was in stark contrast to the greenness of the saturated outfield. It promised fun and games for the Victorian opening batsmen, Jeff Hallebone and Col McDonald, when the home side resumed its innings at 0/33. Moreover, the heavy M.C.G. has transformed our score of 312 into a total far more formidable than that suggested by the scorebook. At the end of first innings, had our catching not been lamentable and the umpiring indifferent, Johnson's batsmen would never have come close to the flattering deficit of 35 runs with which they finished.

I began with a bang. In the second over of the day I bowled Hallebone off the inside edge, after he and McDonald had added four to the overnight total. In his first over, Scrubs Loader stuck McDonald on the pads plumb in front - but the umpire's mind was elsewhere. The same may be said of the umpire at the other end, when the new batsman, Neil Harvey's elder brother, Ray, enjoyed a similar escape off the first ball I bowled to him. McDonald is a determined defender, planting his body solidly in behind the line of every delivery. He is a chest-on player and scores his runs mostly by cuts and leg-side deflections. His patience is unlimited - but he showed me his weakness when he fanned the air several times outside the off-stump without making contact. Finally my luck turned and he edged a rising delivery into the safe gloves of Godfrey Evans behind the stumps. Five runs later, the fraternal Harvey partnership came to an abrupt end when I bowled Ray, for 11.

For his part, Neil was leading a charmed life, playing and missing at a couple of balls an over. A construction worker employed in the rebuilding of the Northern Stand in preparation for the 1956 Olympics summed up the situation pretty well when, after interrupting his lunch break to watch me bowl a couple of overs to 'Nina', he bawled out the advice: 'Typhoon! Bowl 'im down a piano! P'rhaps, 'e can play that!'

Lunch arrived with Victoria having collected 125 fortunate runs for the loss of three wickets. After the interval, Harvey and Chambers feasted off the spin of Wardle and McConnon; but they received scant fare from me. I bowled a bouncer at Chambers. The confident 'Cocky' lived up to his nickname and, never one to refuse a challenge, he tried to hook it. He missed - so I bowled him another. This time he made contact with the top edge - and lobbed a 'dolly' catch to square-leg, where Wardle stood under the catch and awaited its arrival - singing!! As the ball descended he was actually singing his tune of commiseration - 'Give me your shoulder to cry on!' I could have forgiven his ambition to become another Bing Crosby except HE DROPPED THE CATCH!!! Chambers did not add to his score of 42 - Wardle, rubbing salt into the wound he made in my bowling analysis by immediately running him out with a fine return to Jim McConnon! To add insult to injury, the next man in, Sam Loxton, feathered the next delivery to Godders and was given not out! What a day it was turning out to be!

NEWS CHRONICLE, TUESDAY, DECEMBER 14, 1954

TYSON TORNADO UPROOTS SIX

...But our spin bowlers disappoint

From CRAWFORD WHITE : MELBOURNE, Monday.

THE magnificent bowling of Frank Tyson against Victoria here today had the pavilion critics of Melbourne classing him with the great Ted McDonald, Harold Larwood, Ray Lindwall and Keith Miller.

In his first five overs he had three wickets at a cost of 15 runs. He finished with an analysis of six wickets for 68 for the innings, having taken five by hitting the stumps.

Using his shorter run—18 yards instead of 30—he achieved tremendous pace, and once again we had evidence that no batsman relishes really good fast bowling spiced with the occasional bumper.

Tyson had Neil Harvey hopping around in an agitated way before he bowled the ball which cut back from his leg stump to wreck the wicket.

None of the other batsmen was any more comfortable, and Tyson might easily have had much better figures than his six for 59 today.

It was an eve-of-Test performance which was welcome and stimulating.

Hutton's bad day

Tyson's triumph, however, should not blind us to the less palatable fact that Len Hutton had a bad day as captain, and the slow bowlers—Johnny Wardle and Jim McConnon—did not show up too well. In fact, I would say that both probably did more to bowl themselves out of rather than into the next Test.

That, of course, is a pity, for one of them, or Bob Appleyard, will have to come into the England side to take some of the strain from our pace men.

Which of them it will be remains as much a mystery now as it was at the beginning of this eventful day's play.

Hutton's handling of the situation on several occasions was mystifying. After Tyson had struck those first three lightning blows, Hutton brought left-hander Wardle into the attack to bowl to the two left-handed batsmen—Neil Harvey and Chambers. Wardle put down several very good overs which troubled Chambers but the situation cried aloud for an offspin bowler like McConnon, who could turn the ball away from the edgy bats of the Victoria pair.

100 partnership

McConnon did not bowl until after lunch, when Harvey and Chambers had scored 79 of their partnership of 100.

Hutton's next surprise was his removal of Tyson immediately after he had had Chambers dropped, had then clean bowled Harvey, and had had Loxton all but out first ball.

Hutton's hat-trick of mysteries came when he recalled the then tiring Tyson when the new ball was still 14 runs away.

I have no doubt that much of Hutton's strategy today was concerned with trying men out for the Test rather than achieving a result in this match, but it certainly did not look convincing.

CASUALTY REPORT. — Denis Compton will not be fit to play in the second Test at Sydney on Friday. Keith Miller says : "I should be OK."

SCOREBOARD

M.C.C.

First Innings.—312 (Cowdrey 79, Bailey 60).

Second Innings

L. Hutton not out	12
T. E. Bailey not out	2
Extras 2. Total (no wkt.)	16

VICTORIA

Saturday : 33 for no wicket.

C. McDonald c Evans b Tyson	24
J. Hallebone b Tyson	17
Ray Harvey b Tyson	11
R. N. Harvey b Tyson	53
J. Chambers run out	43
S. Loxton b Bailey	28
L. Maddocks c Cowdrey b Leader	35
I. W. Johnson b Tyson	5
J. Hill not out	34
J. Power b Tyson	5
W. A. Johnston c Leader b Wardle	4
Extras 18. Total	277

Bowling: Tyson 21-3-68-6, Bailey 10-0-48-1, Leader 15-2-00-1, Wardle 12.5-2-41-1, McConnon 11-2-45-0.

Frank Tyson's bowling for M.C.C. at Melbourne, yesterday, when he took six wickets that of the best fast bowlers of all time.

There was consolation for me in the shape of a delivery which seamed off this still sporty wicket to castle Nina Harvey for a courageous 59. But no further reward came my way; Len immediately removed me from the attack - presumably to await the arrival of the second new ball. This tactic resulted in wicket-keeper Maddocks and his captain, Johnson, making themselves at home and adding 65 for the sixth wicket. The new ball at 205 brought me back to the crease, but it was Loader and Bailey who made a double breakthrough at 225. I tidied up the innings, bowling Power and Johnston and, with Wardle chipping in with the wicket of Johnston, Victoria was all out for 277, leaving us just 15 minutes to bat before close: a period which Bailey and Hutton safely negotiated, scoring 16 runs in the process.

I am happy with my performance against Victoria. I bowled fast and reasonably straight and probably should have had two more wickets. My analysis of 6/68 is the best of my career in wicket-terms - but 8/68 would have been better. But I must not delude myself. The M.C.G. pitch was very green and extremely helpful. Taking wickets will be much more difficult on harder pitches.

Tuesday December 14th.

The equation is six hours batting time, divided by two teams on an almost equal footing - and it equals a declaration which will set an impossible run-chase, leading to a draw. The Skipper and

Tyson can be trump card in the Test

From ALEX BANNISTER

MELBOURNE, Monday.

NOW that Denis Compton is pronounced unfit for the second Test, which starts at Sydney on Friday, and Frank Tyson today hit his best form of the tour, the sole remaining doubt again concerns the unhappy position of the spinners.

Hutton is back to exactly the same predicament as he found himself in before the first Test when he gambled and lost by relying on an all-speed attack because his spinners had failed him.

If anything, he is worse off, for Compton could at least be classed as a useful change spinner, although Hutton seems to be the last to admit it.

We may be assured, however, that Compton will be available, barring further accidents, for the third Test.

5 CLEAN BOWLED

M.C.C. owed their 35 runs lead over Victoria almost solely to Frank Tyson, the fastest bowler since Harold Larwood.

Apart from one spell, Tyson concentrated on a full length, making the batsmen reach forward, instead of pounding away a yard short.

The happy result was that five of his six victims were clean bowled—a feat which should encourage him to pitch the ball up. At his speed he could deliver, like Lindwall, a devastating yorker.

Again Tyson used his shortened run, consisting of six walking paces developing into 10 running strides, which is five fewer than in his normal approach to the wicket. He should seriously consider adopting it permanently, particularly as his speed does not suffer.

I have never seen Tyson bowl with such venom and accuracy and but for one of Wardle's rare lapses in the field—he later atoned with a brilliant run-out—his tally would have been seven.

If he can maintain this speed and form and ability to keep the ball pitched well up to the batsman, he will be a trump card for England in Sydney.

Trevor added a mere 11 runs to their overnight total before The Boil was castled by Power. The Victorian bowlers did not hand out any gratuitous practice to our out-of-form batsmen. They made them fight for every run. Loxton had Len caught behind off a thin edge and 'Long Tom' Graveney followed his leader both in the manner of his dismissal and his journey back to the pavilion. His lack of form in serious games is worrying. He has not scored a fifty in one first-class game of this three-month-long tour so far.

Graveney's dismissal opened the door for our best partnership of the match; P.B.H. and Kipper came together to add 120 for the fourth wicket, May doing the lion's share of the scoring to finish with a masterful 105 not out. Cowdrey played the role of sleeping partner to perfection, contributing 54 to the joint venture. Hutton delayed his closure until May reached three figures, by which stage any hope of a result in the game had been extinguished. Understandably, Victoria refused the challenge of scoring 272 in two hours, and contented itself with occupying the crease against an attack which was merely going through the motions. When stumps were drawn the home side had reached 3/88.

There were, however, two outcomes of Test significance to emerge from this game. The Aussie skipper, Ian Johnson, pulled a muscle while fielding and is out of the Second Test in Sydney. It also looks as if 'C.C' McDonald is out of contention for selection after retiring hurt in Melbourne.

Chapter Seven

The Sydney Test

LAST NIGHT WE ONCE MORE LEFT Spencer Street Station on the Melbourne/Sydney overnight train. After a speedy trip through the Victorian countryside, we again suffered the inconvenience of having to disembark at Albury shortly after 10p.m. to catch our New South Wales connection. Like an idiot, I forgot my normal precaution of guarding against boredom by buying a decent paperback. It was all very well to study my English set texts for a couple of hours. But there was only so much Virginia Woolf, William Wordsworth and Geoffrey Chaucer I could take, and I liked to break up the heavy stuff with a bit of light reading. After dinner I wandered up and down the corridor outside the team's compartments asking if anyone had a good book they were not reading - but I didn't get a touch!

After Albury I spent half-an-hour gazing out of the carriage window at the darkened countryside of the southern New South Wales highlands. This was Bradman and O'Reilly country, the Land of a Legend: rich pastoral hills dotted with towns bearing strange-sounding names like Wagga Wagga; I remembered that as the place which the Aussie comedian Bill Kerr

came from. Then there were Junee, Gundegai - where 'The Dog sat on the Tucker Box' - and Cootamundra, Bradman's birthplace. Back to a few pages of Virginia, William and Geoffrey before bed in the berth underneath K.V.

New South Wales sleeping compartments must be amongst the most uncomfortable in the railway world. The trains which pull them usually jolt along at a stop-start thirty miles an hour, frequently coming to an unexplained halt for long periods of time: a clanking, bone-jolting journey not especially conducive to sleep. Geoffrey Howard, the 'Ger', told us at breakfast that the train had been creeping along in this manner at six this morning, when he was woken from his doze by the conversation of two gangers outside his compartment window. One of the Aussies, who had apparently been celebrating the night before, was quizzed by his mate:

"G'dy Blue. 'Owyer goin'?"

To which came the hung-over reply:

"Jeez! 'Ow crook can'yer be before yer die!"

Now we have just two days - two days in which to do the Christmas shopping we have so far neglected to do. There is only just over a week to go before Christmas Day! And there are only two days of net practice in which to prepare for our chance to square the series. Never great on the shopping front, I am however quite determined and enthusiastic about my cricket preparation. After my showing in Melbourne, I am raring to go. I am working hard to put the finishing touches to my New-Old-Fashioned League run-up. Team-wise there are plenty of worries about: the continued unavailability of Compo, the indifferent form of our spinners, an opening partner for the Skipper, our top-order batting, our catching and the fitness of Alec, who still has not rid of the mysterious rash on his back.

Thursday December 16th.

A solid morning practice for the whole squad - helped out by a few club bowlers recruited from Sydney grade cricket - at the nets on Number Two Ground.

This evening Ronnie Aird, the M.C.C. secretary, who is spending some time with the side as an observer, told us that a most unlikely supporter will be turning up to see the first day of the Test tomorrow. His name is Henry Sayen: a middle-aged American, a graduate of Princeton, a top-class player of his day in Yankee cricket and wealthy industrialist. Henry's uncanny habit of turning up in odd corners of the world at critical times to watch England play and either win or stave off certain defeat, has earned him the title of 'England's Mascot'.

He performed his magic at Lord's in 1953 when Willie Watson and Trevor Bailey held the Aussies at bay for almost the whole of the last day, enabling England to go on to win the Ashes in the deciding Oval test. The following winter, he was present in Kingston to see England come from behind, win the Test and square a West Indies series that looked lost beyond redemption. Now he is coming to Australia, defying the orders of his doctors who, a month earlier, had operated on him for a serious intestinal complaint. This gutsy Yank is coming once more to England's aid, bringing with him his own incentive scheme: that of financial rewards for performance. The senior members of the side tell me that the rate of pay will be:-

£3 for 30 runs
£4 for 40 runs.
£5 for 50 runs.
£6 for 100 runs.
£1 for catches or stumpings.
£1 for a wicket.
£? for spectacular play.

The B.B.C. commentator and author, John Arlott, is on the tour with us. It is his first visit to Australia and he is not too enamoured with the country. He does, however, like its red wines and the waiters in our hotel have quickly become aware of the fact. They seek to please his discerning palate at every opportunity. Tonight, however, one of them rather overstepped the mark by promoting himself to the rank of wine connoisseur and bringing John an uncorked Australian Burgundy: a pleasant drink but certainly not chambred. Indeed it was so cold that beads of condensation streaked its sides. The waiter plonked the bottle down in front of John - who also holds down the post of food and drink critic for one of the London evening tabloids - and declared triumphantly: "There you are Mr. Arlott. A nice full-bodied burgundy. If you want another bottle, we've got one in the freezer!"

The unsettled Sydney weather is also something of a worry. Tonight, the eve of the match, a celestial *Son et Lumiere* thunderstorm lit the Sydney streets and rattled its buildings. It appears that whoever wins the toss tomorrow might have to face the dilemma which confronted Hutton in Brisbane: to insert or not to insert. One thing is sure: the side batting first will have a green wicket to contend with. Personally I would not like to face Big Al on such a track.

Friday December 17th.

A rather dull and overcast day. But there's a match to win, and a series to square. So it's up and at 'em! Off early to the Moore Park ground, courtesy of Stack's Holden cars, which inch their way through the crowd in front of the members' gate, drive into the ground and deposit us immediately behind the green painted entrance to the Members' Bar and the players' dressing rooms. Then it's a trip to the middle to see what the groundsman has to offer for us to play on.

The pitch looks extremely 'juicy' and good to bowl on. We shall miss Denis Charles Scott, whose broken hand has still not mended - and our batting will be depleted accordingly. But Big Al must be licking his enormous fingers at the prospect of

bowling on a 'greentop'. I have a locker on the inner changing rooms and am quickly into my whites and off to the pre-game practice. I return half an hour before start of play. When I do, there's a white slip of paper pinned to the notice board: The batting order and I am number seven - followed by Godders, Wardle, Appleyard and Statham. But where's Alec's name? It is inconceivable that England could drop the man who, virtually alone, has carried its quick bowling since 1946! But that is precisely what has happened! And the tactless manner in which Bedser was cut - by a team sheet on a notice board - is more than ungrateful; it is insulting! Surely the Skipper must have taken Alec to one side and explained whatever reasons were behind his being dropped? It is an unpleasant duty - even when the player to be dropped is a close friend. But it has to be done. And Len, who is beginning to look careworn - apparently had no stomach for it!

What can explain the selectors' decision to 'put Alec over the side'? In mitigation of their seemingly callous action, even Alec must admit that his form on tour has not been good. He has only taken eight wickets in the four first-class games in which he has played in the two and a half months we have been in this country. Nor has his health been good. His shoulders are still not free of the shingles rash which has plagued him for weeks. I only salvaged my spot in the side by a reasonable performance in the Victorian game; the same may be said of Bob Appleyard, who has been bowling very impressively of late. Johnny Wardle's place in

Sydney Cricket Ground.

the line-up is more difficult to explain; he has not been bowling well, but his is a case of 'Hobson's Choice'. There is no other completely fit specialist spinner in the party; and if the wicket turns later in the game, we will need one.

Arthur Morris, Australia's acting skipper, although handicapped by injuries to both Johnson and Miller, was obviously unfazed by Hutton's disastrous example in Brisbane. He won the toss and, thinking quite rightly, that conditions would suit the swing, seam and pace of Johnston, Lindwall, Archer and Davidson, asked Hutton to bat. The subsequent events of the first day proved his judgement absolutely correct. Encouraged by the successful experiment of opening with Bailey against Victoria, Len tried the gamble again. This time the results were less encouraging, and although he survived for 35 minutes, Trevor was eventually bowled by Lindwall without scoring. May was then caught at short leg to make us 2/19. But it was the loss of Hutton which was the real body blow. After scoring 30, the skipper leg-glanced Big Bill Johnston, only to see Alan Davidson stick out his famous left 'Claw' and conjure up a catch off a stroke which Hutton thought was four! With Graveney caught at slip and Langley picking up Colin Cowdrey and Evans behind the stumps, our innings fell away until we were a disastrous 9/111. Then followed an amazing piece of North Country bloody-minded contrariness: Lancastrian 'George' Statham and Yorkshire's Johnny Wardle defied everything bowled at them to add 43 for the last wicket: a partnership which could prove a decisive factor in the match. It was the method in which the runs were scored which was as remarkable as their number. Statham blocked while Wardle strolled down the wicket to every Aussie paceman and swung or sliced them high and hard through the vacant spaces in front of the wicket or over the spreadeagled ranks behind square. They survived to take our total to what seemed, at one stage, an unlikely 154, and keep us in the game.

A freshet of rain delayed the Aussie innings and spiced the pitch. When Morris and Favell eventually took strike it was against the accuracy of Bailey and Statham: a good move which paid dividends when Morris edged Bailey to leg-slip off the last ball of the day - the score 1/18.

Saturday December 18th.

The press were pretty scathing this morning, asking why Alec has been dropped - and demanding, quite rightly, to know why he had been given so little opportunityto bowl himself into form in the early part of the tour. They particularly wanted to know why he had been rested in Melbourne and allowed to precede the team to Sydney. I have no answers. I just thought that selectors who had adopted such a policy and then dropped the key player in question, have a few embarrassing questions to reply to. But it has to be admitted that the press do not know the full fitness picture.

Today, the pitch had less to offer than yesterday. A lot hinged on the bowlers keeping the ball in the area which forced the batsmen to play and give them no scope to play shots. Trevor Bailey was just the man for the job. But he began from the wrong end, allowing Favell and Burke to score with ease in the opening overs of the day. As soon as Bailey changed ends, the scoring rate slowed and he picked up the wicket of the South Australian caught at second slip. At lunch Australia was 2/88. It was the turning point of the match.

Bailey bowled splendidly, time and time again drawing the batmen forward to beat the outside edge and evoke leaps of expectation from the slips. He was so impressive that the usually anti-Bailey Hill began to harass Jimmy Burke and barrack for the The Boil! "Burkey," shouted one wag, "You're so like a statue, I wish I were a pigeon!"

Then it was my turn. A little ragged to begin, I soon found my rhythm and my enthusiasm was sustained by Harvey's continual fanning outside the off-stump. Imitating Keith Miller, I bowled a round-arm delivery. It pitched on the seam in line with Nina's leg stump and moved towards the slips as he tried to turn it towards mid-wicket. The resultant edge curled lazily off the shoulder of his bat and into Colin Cowdrey's hands at gully. Graeme Hole had a dozen to his name when his high flourishing back-lift left him far too late for a full-length ball which he could only edge on to his stumps. Now it was George's turn; he trapped Benaud l.b.w. before knocking Davidson's middle stump out of the ground. In 110 minutes between lunch and tea the home side lost 4/70 and we were back in the game with

Hole drives. Benaud is the non-striker and I am at mid-on.

a vengeance. Ron Archer wafted and waved his bat outside the off stump - yet amazingly survived to score 49 and take Australia into the lead. The second new ball accounted for him, as his luck ran out and he edged a bootlace catch to Hutton at first slip.

Ray Lindwall marched to the wicket. There and then I determined that there was to be no repetition of his 60 in Brisbane. A bouncer soon followed, and, within minutes, he had edged a short delivery to Evans behind the wickets. Little did I know it at the time, but this bumper and the bouncer I had bowled at him in Brisbane were to be the triggers for a fast bowling feud between Lindy and me: a psychological combat in which anticipation far outweighed eventuality. So much so that, ironically, this Sydney bouncer proved to be the last I bowled at him in the series!

With stumps approaching, we slowed the tempo of the game, not wanting to bat again this evening. The crowd hooted, but we ignored its disapproval. Precisely ten minutes before close of play, Bailey removed Gil Langley's middle stump with an air of affected ease and we retired to the pavilion 74 runs in arrears, but still very much in the game.

Sunday December 19th.

Last night's Saturday Night Club's meeting was a bit of a flat flop. Afterwards Compo was supposed to have taken most of the side out to a barbecue on Middle Harbour. The Yorkshire contingent was reluctant to come. One of them - who shall remain nameless - voiced his reservations in a question which became his recognised call-sign:

"Do we 'ave to pay?"

It did not much matter. We discovered when we arrived that D.C.S. had got it wrong again! The Christmas

TYSON WAS LIKE A TIGER

By IAN PEEBLES,

former England and Middlesex cricketer

ENGLAND, yesterday the despair of their friends, today regained a lot of lost ground and self-respect. On a wicket which had dried up and played true, apart from a very occasional "lifter," they made Australia fight every inch of the way.

At one stage it looked as if they would finish the first innings on pretty even terms, but the seventh wicket stand between Archer and Davidson carried their side out of immediate danger.

The fast bowlers all had good spells at one time or another, but Bailey was consistently hostile through the whole day.

In the morning he alone was able to move the ball, and acted as path-finder in getting rid of Favell and Burke. Alec Bedser, in his true form, would have been a decisive factor in this match, but as it was, the only three seamers were pretty hard pressed to keep going the whole day.

Happy return

Burke made a happy return to the Australian side, and while he and Favell were going it looked as thought a big score was in the offing. Statham, bowling to this pair from the hill end, dispensed with third man and fine leg, and was expensive, but later in the day he switched and then worried all the batsmen.

Tyson, similarly, looked unimpressive in the morning, but bowled like a tiger in the afternoon. Neither Benaud nor Archer could cope with him and were lucky to survive their early struggles.

The fielding was keen and pretty good on the ground, but several possible chances went astray, although none had really disastrous consequences. At the same time such things should not happen in Test matches, and this may well be a match in which every run is going to count.

party had been on the night before!!! Margaret and I enjoyed our evening and today, as the temperature soared into the nineties, we accepted an invitation to the Christmas festivities at the Watson's Bay Naval Base. It's hard to imagine that Christmas is just around the corner. At home, no doubt it is freezing. It might even be snowing. Mother will be buying in the Christmas goodies and making plans to spend the festive season with her friends and family. Here in Sydney, hundreds of thousands pack the weekend beaches, bronzing their bodies, surfing and swimming. Margaret and I relaxed in the Officers' Mess and watched as Father Christmas, sweltering beneath his traditional scarlet costume, arrived by car to distribute presents to the servicemen's families. A few miles back along the bay, Sydneyites bustled along Pitt, George, Castlereagh and Elizabeth Streets, frantically window shopping for last minute presents for Auntie Dot and Uncle Bill. They gazed into shop-windows, full of sequinned models of Father Christmas and incongruous northern winter scenes of houses covered with spangled frost and snow - glittering in a hot Australian sun! For the English and Europeans, Christmas remains the same all over the world - talk about Mad Dogs and Englishmen going out in the midday sun!!

Monday December 20th.

A short shopping jaunt this morning as K.V. and I picked up a few gifts for the folks back home. We could not go back without a koala bear or two and the odd aboriginal boomerang. On the serious

gift side, I bought a couple of opals for mother: one green and another a beautiful black with real fire in its belly.

Back at the S.C.G, the Aussie bowlers were waiting for us. So effective was their initial assault on our batsmen on the third morning that Hutton, Bailey and Graveney were all back in the hutch before lunch with only 58 on the board. It took a fourth wicket of 116 and three and a half hours of resolute batting from May and Cowdrey to cancel out our first innings deficit and set our feet back on the steep path towards victory. What marvellous young batsmen these two men from the universities of Cambridge and Oxford are! As one watched their afternoon dominance of the Aussie bowlers, one sensed that here, before our very eyes, we were watching the arrival of a fresh, young generation of future England batsmen. All through the afternoon session the 22-year old dark blue and the 24-year old light blue stuck to their task like two veterans with a hundred Tests to their credit. Both of their birthdays fall immediately after this game and we are hoping that they really give us something to celebrate!

P.B.H. was at his most masterful, repeatedly drawing himself to his full height to despatch anything minimally short of a good length to the mid-wicket fence with a savagery which seemed out of place in such a cultured individual. No doubt he sent it on its way with his favourite utterance: "Do you mind?" Kipper's brooding con-centration sat heavily on his shoulders, but did not inhibit his natural penchant for playing strokes. He hid his intensity

Kipper edges Archer past Benaud in the gully.

behind a bland impassive expression. But when his concentration finally snapped and Benaud enticed him into giving a catch to Archer at long-off, four runs after passing his half-century, it opened the floodgates of pent-up emotion. Colin came back to the pavilion utterly despondent. The green door of the dressing room had barely closed behind him when he burst into an ocean of child-like tears! "I've just thrown the Test match away, Frank!" he sobbed. "It will all be my fault!" "Not if I can help it," I thought! He and I share the same depth of feeling about certain issues.

Kipper was dismissed half an hour before stumps, by which stage, Bill Edrich had helped Peter May to shepherd the England total to 5/204. P.B.H was two runs shy of his hundred, but such was his composure that he made no extravagant bids to get to three

figures. He waited for the next day and the second new ball, as if George Duckworth had already written his century in the scorebook.

Tuesday December 21st.

Brian Johnson, the B.B.C. commentator, enjoyed an eventful dinner yesterday evening. He is staying at Kinneir's: a private hotel and a splendid restaurant at the top of the King's Cross hill. Yesterday evening, he dined out with friends and returned to his lodgings just before eleven. Unfortunately the proprietors of Kinneir's had omitted to tell him that in order to get back into the hotel after a certain time, he had to be escorted through the gardens by a member of staff, since one of their security precautions was to loose a guard dog in the grounds at night. Consequently 'Johnno' made a very hurried entry into the hotel - with the seat ripped out of his beautiful tan suit and the dog snapping at his heels.

Brian is a very superstitious person and, ever since England's elusive and only post-war victory against Australia in Melbourne in 1950, he insists on going to Tests wearing the same two-toned brown and white shoes and the suit he wore on that occasion - just doing his bit to conjure up another win! That was all very well and good - and the dog incident at Kinneir's should have caused no immediate problems - except for the fact that the suit and shoes were both borrowed! Now he is faced with explaining away the seatless pants and the muddied shoes! Quite a night!

It rained heavily overnight and when it was time for Peter and Bill to resume the struggle - while the wicket was perfectly dry - the grass on the outfield was wet and heavy. It was obviously an inopportune moment to take the second new ball, which was now due. This gave P.B.H the opportunity to move to his hundred off the second ball of the morning. But the Aussies kept things tight and Peter was then only permitted a further three runs in the next fifty minutes - at which stage Morris took the new ball.

The result was dramatic. P.B.H. played all around a Lindwall inswinger and departed after five hours at the crease and a wonderful innings of 104. It was at this stage, just before lunch, that Ray Lindwall made what many of his side thought was Australia's major blunder of the game. The fast bowler decided to repay me for my two bouncers at him in Brisbane and Sydney and my violation of the fast bowler's unwritten code of behaviour. He let me have a very fast, short-pitched delivery. The lowness of his delivery arm meant that his point of delivery was outside the white background of the sightscreen. I completely lost sight of the ball. Instinctively I turned a defensive back on the ball which skidded through and hit me a sickening blow on the back of the head. I sank to the ground and as I slipped in and out of consciousness, I was dimly aware of the players gathering around my prostrate body. Indistinctly I heard my fellow batsman Bill Edrich saying: 'My God, Lindy, you've killed him!' I was hoisted to my feet, supported from the field and went to hospital for a precautionary X-ray. There the thickness of the Tyson skull was proved beyond doubt. Later in the afternoon, I returned to the batting crease, but failed to make any further substantial contribution to the England score and in no time at all we were 9/250. At this stage, had it not been for the initiative and the judicious hitting of Bob Appleyard and George Statham, the match would have been lost there and then. But the two bowlers added 46 in 50 minutes, interspersing cross-batted slogs with solid blocking. Their courageous defiance delayed matters, but it seemed doubtful that it could do more than postpone an Australian win. Australia still had more than four sessions in which to score 223 for victory: ostensibly non-too-difficult a task.

But crucially, from the point of view of England's victory aspirations, I was very, very angry with Ray Lindwall. And the whole of the Aussie team knew it - and were inclined to the opinion that I would return the complimentary bouncer with interest! Moreover, from this juncture in the series, Ray was always on the look-out for the bouncer when he batted. Knowing this, I kept the ball well up to him - and he never made another score!

When Australia batted a second time, just before tea, it was quickly obvious that a home victory was far from a foregone conclusion. Brian Statham had Favell dropped at slip in his first over, and then beat Morris four times in the over before the interval. He finally trapped him l.b.w. with the penultimate delivery of the session. Tea brought a breather for Brian and I, and with my sixth ball after the resumption, I had Les Favell caught chest-high at slip by Bill Edrich. Shakily, Neil Harvey and Jimmy Burke survived somehow, playing and missing frequently, but never paying the full price for their uncertainty. Burke did not score for almost an hour, giving his critics on the Hill much more to shout about! At close of play, Australia were still 151 runs behind with eight wickets in hand.

Wednesday December 22nd.

The outcome of the Second Test was decided in today's first hour. In my second over from the Randwick end, I produced a full-length delivery which moved back up the hill, found the gate in Burke's defence, and flattened his middle and off stumps. Graeme Hole once again flourished in the back-lift, and failed to get his bat down on a yorker. Len thereupon rested George and I, choking the scoring rate with the parsimonious accuracy of Bailey and Appleyard. But Benaud is not a patient man. Frustrated, he went for a big hit in Appleyard's second over, only to find the ball was too wide outside the off-stump to control. The resultant top edge steepled high into the air, wobbling as it went in the sullen day's stiff breeze. God! It was coming in my direction! I sat under the catch in what I thought was the right position. But the breeze caught it again and moved it another yard to my left. I made a despairing last minute lunge at the ball - and wonder of wonders - caught it at shoe-lace height! A relieved cold sweat dampened my forehead. But Benaud had gone and Australia was five down for 106! At lunch Harvey and Archer were still together and the score had advanced by another 12 runs.

The first fifty minutes of the afternoon session settled the issue beyond doubt. I rattled the furniture of Archer and Lindwall and Statham accounted for Davidson and Langley. Lindy's dismissal from a half-volley which he made into a yorker, was, in the outcome of his expectations, the perfect example of a fast bowler being hoist on his own petard! Australia's last hope, Big Bill Johnston, joined Nina Harvey with the score standing at 9/145, and the home side still 78 runs short of victory. Then followed one of the most agonising hours I ever spent on a cricketing field. Harvey played a masterly innings - the best of his career in my estimation - controlling the strike and shielding Johnston from the tiring attentions of Statham and me. I bowled a 90-minute spell downwind but George did the donkey work: 85 minutes from the Paddington end into a stiff sea breeze.

There would have been no victory without George. He was indefatigable. Many batsmen undersell Brian's ability to move the ball. It is true that he rarely moves the ball through the air; indeed when he does - as he told me he did once in Guyana in 1953 - he finds it difficult to control. But his ability to move the ball off the seam is second to none. He has one special delivery which he calls his 'nip-backer', which cuts back from the off like a fast off-spinner. He holds the ball with the first two fingers of his bowling hand to the left of the upright seam, his third and fourth digits to its right, and delivers with a closed action. It rarely fails to cut back, and George invariably pitches it on the right spot - on a length and just outside the off-stump. He also has a ball which pitches on the seam, behaves like a fast leg-spinner and leads to the downfall of many leg-side players who try to hit it through mid-wicket. His accuracy is phenomenal - to the extent that a batsman is lucky to get one ball in three overs to hit.

Bill Johnston did his bit for his team with true Aussie grit. His speciality stroke was a right-handed, one-handed, back-handed, glancing scoop off the line of his bum - cricket's equivalent of tennis' back-handed retrieve. It brought him a dozen runs - plus a considerable

amount of pain when he failed to make contact and the ball clipped his maximus gluteus! Bill's luck could not hold, however, and he finally laid a thin edge on a delivery which 'George' had advised me to bowl a little closer to his body. Godfrey Evans did the rest and

6 for 85

FRANK TYSON sends them down like this. It's frightening and effective. His six wickets for 85 runs broke the back of Australia's second innings.

THE TOAST IS:
TYPHOON TYSON!

From ROSS HALL

Sydney, Wednesday

THE toast here tonight—the toast of both Englishman and Australian—is Typhoon Tyson, who made this second Test his own by bowling England to a 38-run victory that squared the rubber at one-all.

But for Tyson we might so easily be facing next week's third Test with a disastrous 2—0 deficit and little hope of retaining the Ashes.

Instead, we shall go in at Melbourne with a tremendous moral advantage, for the Australian batsmen—Neil Harvey excepted—have become flinching shadows against the fiery, blinding pace of young Tyson.

Ten wickets in the match for 130 runs — six of them in Australia's second innings for $5! What a performance by Tyson—and what justification for the few of us who supported his tour selection!

Model Sportsman

This boy has greatness walking beside him. . . Ever eager to accept advice—as with shortening his run—and at all times a model sportsman. They can be proud today in the Northamptonshire that has nurtured his talents.

This was the tribute of the Australian captain. Arthur Morris;

● "Such fine bowling deserved to win what was a great game of cricket."

And England's Len Hutton, not forgetting Statham's three for 45, while bowling into the wind ALL the time, said:

● "The best fast bowlers I have ever played against were Lindwall and Miller in their prime, but I just could not visualise better bowling on that still-good wicket of today than we got from Tyson and Statham.

● "Frank Tyson is far exceeding any hope I had for him when we left England."

Yet Tyson's final domination of this thrilling struggle was but the peak of a match in which England players won a battle with themselves.

'WONDERFUL,' SAYS HIS MOTHER

"DAILY MIRROR" REPORTER

GREY-HAIRED Mrs. Violet Tyson, 62, mother of The Typhoon, has "hardly slept a wink" since the Test began last Friday.

Worried that the team might be beaten, she stopped getting up early to listen to the radio commentary, and waited for a summary of play later.

Neighbours Told Her

She had no need to wait yesterday. Neighbours called at her home in Valley-road, Middleton, Lancashire, clamouring to tell her the news of her son's match-winning effort.

"Wonderful," said Mrs. Tyson—and out she dashed to cable her congratulations.

"Now I can get a good night's sleep," she said. "This is the best Christmas present I could have had."

England was home by 38 runs. I had taken 10 wickets in the match and the magnificent Harvey remained unbeaten on 92!

As we sank a few drinks in the drinks in the dressing room after the game, Scrubs Loader threw an arm around my shoulders. "Today," he announced, "you bowled like a 'Dingbat"! The nickname 'Dingers' stuck. I flatter myself that it means someone who gives his all to a cause.

Importantly, we were one-all in the series, and we knew as a proven fact that we could beat Australia! What a Christmas present! To celebrate the festive season and our victory, we were invited to a Christmas party tonight. When we got there someone had drunk all the beer! But what the hell!

Chapter Eight

A Very Happy Christmas and a Wonderful New Year

Thursday December 23rd.

HENRY SAYEN, ENGLAND'S YAN-kee mascot, has done it again! Just as he was the presiding genius in Trevor Bailey and Willie Watson's rescue act against Lindsay Hassett's team at Lord's in 1953, he is now the talisman of our Sydney triumph. To mark the event, he joined the England team in a celebratory dinner at Prince's Restaurant in Martin Place last night. Everybody in the team went - no excuses were permitted and no curfew was imposed. It was a joyous, wonderful night! And no-one enjoyed it more than Henry himself. For him it was the culmination of a wonderful week in Sydney, in the course of which he has dined with Sir Donald Bradman, Jack Ryder and Bob Menzies and breakfasted with Ian Johnson. He has placed a wreath on Victor Trumper's grave and forked out what he reckoned to be a £4 incentive bonus for every run scored in the Test match. He has hugged and jigged with the M.C.C. secretary, Ronnie Aird, at the fall of each Aussie wicket in the Sydney Test and proved himself a one-man band of supporters.

Ronnie and his wife have journeyed to Sydney on holiday, more, I suspect, in hope than in expectation of an England win. But we have been able to make their trip a happy one. It is only right that Henry should celebrate our win with us. We recorded our appreciation of his support with the presentation of a silver salver engraved with all the autographs of the touring party. We even tried to persuade him to linger longer in Aussie - but he was not feeling too well in the aftermath of his earlier surgery in America and felt that if he was to die, he should do it in his own bed. He left with our best wishes - and admiration. It took a lot of guts and determination to make the journey that he undertook in his precarious state of health.

To the victors went the spoils and our reward for winning was two optional days of light training - which, none-theless, our out-of-form batsmen took advantage of. Today Margaret took me Christmas shopping in Sydney. It was an odd experience of unseasonable unfamiliarity. Every shop, in every street seems to have a loudspeaker, each providing a different contribution to the conflicting cacophony of carols which pound the eardrums and provide a non-stop background of noise which numbs the senses and defies the definition of Christmas as the season of peace - if not goodwill. It is all very Americanised. Continuous streams of Sydneyites shuffle down George, Oxford, Pitt,

BILL BOWES WRITES ABOUT

The bowler who has got Australia guessing

HATS off to Frank "Typhoon" Tyson, England's fastest bowler since the days of Larwood. His magnificent fast bowling in the Second Test at Sydney, when he took six wickets for 85 runs, enabled England—after the debacle at Brisbane, when they lost by an innings and 154 runs—to level the series at one game apiece.

His bowling in the second innings of the Third Test match at Melbourne last Thursday, when he returned the amazing analysis of seven wickets for 27 runs—six for 16 on the final morning of the game—has given England a one-up advantage, which it will now be difficult to shake.

In Tyson and Statham, Australia have found bowlers capable of putting them on the defensive. Just as we clamoured for batsmen, with Hutton, capable of withstanding an initial onslaught of speed, so are the Australian critics and selectors looking anxiously for replacements.

And the reason is nothing more than Frank Tyson, who has grown overnight. He is not the same bowler as a month ago. Who, watching Tyson bowl against Pakistan at the Oval last August could have prophesied success for him in Australia?

Shorter run-up

In the early matches in Australia there was no improvement, and then he adopted a suggestion that he bowl with a shortened run.

It was found that it did not affect his speed and it improved his accuracy out of all recognition.

Tyson himself then found that he could afford to pitch the ball up to the batsmen, give them a ball like Lindwall—a yorker or a half-volley—and by sheer pace through the air hurry the batsman into mistakes.

It is this amount of hurry given to batsman, rather than any measurement in actual speed, which decides the success of a speed bowler.

For instance, the big, tall bowler like Ken Farnes, who delivered the ball from nearly nine feet up and sent it to the ground in oblique angle, is much more difficult for batsmen to see than a short bowler whose trajectory is slightly above the eye level of the batsman opposing him.

The ball is another yard or so on its way before it is focused, and the feeling of hurry is more noticeable to batsmen.

Like Larwood

Australian batsmen, while admitting Statham is steadier and more accurate, say: "He does not hurry you so much as Tyson." Either in sheer pace, or because Tyson gathers himself to his full height before delivery, he's the more dangerous bowler.

When comparing Trueman with Tyson our England batsmen say the same thing, and as I watch batsmen of repute face up to Tyson I am forced to the opinion that he almost gives the same amount of hurry as Larwood.

Tyson, like Larwood and Lindwall, has a big starting advantage in that he has proved he can hurry batsmen into mistakes without the need for anything else.

It has still got to be seen if he holds such a reserve of energy like Larwood, Trueman and even Statham; that he can come back at six o'clock and bowl like he did at 11.30.

His shortened run-up has made him into a different bowler—a new bowler—and new opinions must be formed. So far he's done all, and more, that could be asked. He has reached greatness and I raise my hat to him.

Bill Bowes

Castlereagh and Elizabeth Streets, pausing to gawk at the incongruous northern hemisphere Christmas scenes in the shop-fronts of Myers, David Jones, Horderns and all the major stores. These illuminated snow scenes, peopled by mannequin Santas, reindeer, robin redbreasts and cotton wool snowmen are as close as many Aussies get to a European Christmas. The lady shoppers themselves wear only skimpy dresses - the men are in shorts, flip-flops and broad-brimmed hats. Each December they sweat beneath a Christmas sun which generates temperatures approaching the century mark. My heart went out to the many Father Christmases who threaded their way through the crammed stores, melting beneath their scarlet uniforms, yet still ringing their handbells defiantly as sweat poured down their faces, gradually darkening their red coats and pants. Down on Circular Quay, close by the cooling breezes of the harbour, the green ferry boats arrived from every point of the compass, from Manly to Mosman, bedecked with yuletide bunting and scarlet cut-outs of Father Christmases. Outside the First and Last pub stand the drinkers, pushed into pavement exile by the crowds inside.

Team plans for Christmas Day involve a team lunch in the Australia hotel, after which Keith Andrew and I have been invited to have an evening meal with Margaret and her parents at their home in the harbour suburb of Manly.

Friday December 24th.

It is hard to absorb all of this adulation which has suddenly descended on me. Pressmen want interviews. Their papers want to sign me up to write articles. Meanwhile the best idea is to get away from it all, relax and go sightseeing. One particular joy was a trip on a bone-shaking Sydney tram up Oxford Street, down Anzac Parade, past the cricket ground, skirting the Randwick Racetrack and finally descending in Kingsford, where my companion, 'The Admiral', George Duckworth, disappeared into a pub to re-emerge with a few bottles of beer in a brown paper bag. We were on our way to 7 Leonard Ave, Kensington, the home of one Harold 'Lol' Larwood, my schoolboy hero of the 1930s, and a team-mate of Ducky's in the 'Bodyline' series of 1932/33. We were met at the front gate of the trim, wooden, bungalow by Harold and his complete family: his wife and five daughters - most of whom are either teachers or training to become teachers. Then it was into the Larwood lounge to open the beer and examine the trophies of Lol's memorable triumphs: the photographs of Jardine and Chapman's teams of twenty years earlier, illuminated addresses from admirers and a heap of silverware. Pride of place was given to a small silver ashtray, inscribed 'To Lol, for the Ashes, the Skipper, Douglas Jardine'. Harold said he admired me - but I admired him more. I came away from that meeting with the Larwoods and their daughters with my head spinning, clutching a few treasured photographs, which he had given me together with the assurance that, 'When you hear 50,000 Aussies shouting at you, you know you've got 'em worried.' As George and I left, I invited Harold to visit me in the England dressing room during the coming Test match. He turned me down flat. The hurt of his treatment at the hands of the English cricket authorities in the years just before W.W.2 ran too deep.

As I write Christmas is only hours away. Tomorrow we shall plumb the depths of homesickness and the longing for our loved ones. Phone calls have been booked to our families and the traditional Christmas messages will be

With my hero at his Sydney home.

exchanged. But the media will be sniffing around and it will be hard to speak heart to heart without interference. How we would like to be around the yuletide table, sharing the turkey and the Christmas pud! It is hard to be 14,000 miles from home at times like this. Well, at least I shall have the bonus of an extra five days off. I have not been selected for our next game against the New South Wales Northern Districts. It will be a tough match. Newcastle, an industrial city like its namesake in England, is about 100 miles north of Sydney and it breeds some doughty opponents: men like 'Words' de Courcy. The boys head off for Newcastle on Boxing Day.

One man I feel sorry for is K.V. He wants to get a game in so much, but he has been passed over for the Newcastle match. He has not kept wicket since the Queensland Country Eleven clash on December 6th. The trouble is that Godders is so determined to regain match fitness that he is making every post a winning post. It seems that Keith will not get another opportunity behind the stumps until we go to Tasmania, immediately after the Melbourne Test. A month between matches is a long time - even for the most patient of reserve keepers!

Saturday December 25th
Christmas Day.

Kipper was off to church early. What a fine individual he is! A true Christian who practices and preaches! Lunch was a team occasion, full of high spirits and traditional fare; a little bit of England in distant Australia. Speaking to our families by phone was great - but it was no substitute for being with them.

Until today, I had no idea of the impact which our victory in Sydney had made back home in England. Thanks to the *People* newspaper, I spoke to Mother on the radio-telephone and she told me that the press and friends had been beating a path up to her door since early Thursday morning. In my home town of Middleton, the Mayor, Councillor Wellens, went to congratulate mum. My former second team mentor at Towncroft Avenue, Councillor Tom Heywood,

announced he will be calling a cricket club and council committee meeting to organise a welcome home function for me in March. An additional honour was the decision to open a public subscription for me. It was the same story across Manchester, where, in the Denton home of Brian and Audrey Statham, the great news was that Daddy's team had won the Test match and baby Terence had cut his first teeth.

A bitter-sweet day! We rested in the afternoon, then Margaret picked us up in 'Hinemoa' just after six and we spent the evening with her family in Fairlight. It was a very subdued affair, and I had the distinct impression that Keith and I were not the most welcome of guests. It was a very subdued affair. We opted to take our leave early and were back in bed at the hotel at 10pm.

Sunday December 26th
Boxing Day.

By tradition, Christmas in Aussie is holiday-time, given over to the beach and major sporting events. I don't know how he did it, but our wonderful 'Ger, Geoffrey Howard, got hold of a few tickets for the final Davis Cup Challenge Round which is to be contested in the next few days between America and Australia at the White City Stadium. To get tickets for even one day is like winning the lottery.

So it was that Len, Trevor, 'George' myself and K.V. found ourselves walking down towards Rushcutters' Bay and taking our seats in the boiling sun. The tennis Test match was to be contested by Harry Hopman's young gladiators, Lew Hoad, Ken Rosewall and Frank Sedgman, and the Americans. There is no denying the natural talents of the Aussie squad. They are youthful, athletic and gifted ball players. But today Vic Seixas and the Yankee squad proved themselves mentally tougher and more focussed. These were the qualities which carried the day - and eventually won the trophy in the days that followed.

Monday December 27th.

Light practice this morning at the S.C.G. Spent some time with Len. We had lunch with some of the Cricket Association 'Big Nobs' at Tattersall's Club. It is a magnificent establishment complete with an indoor pool and gym. Len was in his best form - very dry in his observations and very amusing. In the bar before lunch he spent half an hour watching a couple of young men playing the 'pokies' or slot machines. At the end of this unproductive period with the aptly named 'One-Armed Bandits', Len, with a twinkle in his eye, turned to one of our hosts and enquired, "Why don't they play at something useful - like cricket?"

The evening's news from Newcastle is mixed. The match is not billed as first-class, although three days were allotted to it and the standard of the opposition is far superior to some of the so-called first-class teams we later met in Tasmania. The early bulletins were bad and at one stage the N.S.W. Northern Districts, batting first, reached 4/171, and looked like accumulating a handsome total. Then it was that

Above: A huge crowd gathers for the Boxing Day Davis Cup match between Australia and the U.S.A. at the White City Stadium in Sydney.

Below: Lew Hoad loses to Trabert.

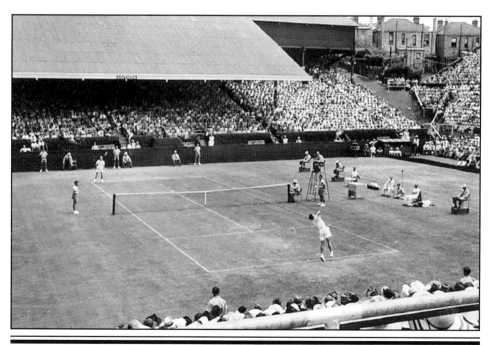

Johnny Wardle broke through with his wrist spin, took the last six wickets for 11 runs and restricted the home side to a disappointing first-innings score of 211. Wardle's performance and, later in the game, Appleyard's 5/59 return, added a lustre to our spin attack which so far on the tour has been notably lacking in penetration.

Tuesday December 28th.

More light training in the morning, but now, with the Melbourne Test only three days away, we are working up to maximum effort. The news from Newcastle continues to be good. On the second day of the game, 465 runs were notched in only 320 minutes. The M.C.C. total of 438 included a classically savage 157 from Peter May, his fourth century in as many matches. Denny proved that he was over his hand injury with a splendid 60, before, in typical cavalier fashion, he dashed down the wicket to be stumped off O'Sullivan. Two hundred and twenty-seven runs in arrears, the locals batted with far more assurance in their second knock, taking their score to 161 at the fall of their fourth wicket. Then their resistance crumbled in the face of a fine spell from Bob Appleyard. Jim McConnon opened the batting in this game and helped Godfrey Evans, yet another unfamiliar opener, to knock off the 20 runs needed for victory. Finishing the game just after lunch on the third day, the boys joined us in Sydney. They were glad to be back in the big smoke, not being too impressed with ind-

ustrial Newcastle, which apparently was a queer mix of heavy industry and beautiful surfing beaches. Personally I was sad not to have played in the game in the Hunter Valley. As a Royal Marine, my brother David had been stationed at Newcastle during the war in the Far East and had made some very good friends - Mr. and Mrs Nesbitt - during his stay. I would have liked to have met them. Reunited once more, the M.C.C. party headed off to Melbourne and the Third Test in high spirits and fine form.

Wednesday December 29th.

Travelling once more by overnight train, we disembarked this morning at Spencer Street station, just as Melbourne's office workers were making their way to work, rubbing the sleep from their eyes. Then it was into the waiting Holdens and up Lonsdale Street to the Windsor at the eastern extremity of the Central Business District. Keith and I were once more sharing a room and, having checked in, we unpacked and rested an hour or two before having an early lunch in the Windsor's elegant dining room - a throwback to gracious Victorian times. A long table in the centre of the spacious eatery had been reserved for the team and meals around it were, by and large, convivial affairs, digested to the accompaniment of lively and humorous banter. We ate a light meal and, as it was only a short walk across Fitzroy Gardens to the cricket ground, decided to dispense with the services of our cars. Stepping out into the bright

Aussie sunshine, we crossed Spring Street and nodded to the statue of poet Adam Lindsay Gordon before we traversed the top of Collins Street and passed in front of the State Government Offices in the Treasury Buildings. On the southern boundary of Fitzroy Gardens, Melbournites with a sense of history raised, in the late nineteenth century, the cottage of Australia's discoverer, Captain Cook. They dismantled it brick by brick, and beam by beam in its Great Ayton home in north-eastern England, and transported it to this corner of a foreign field.

We skirted Captain Cook's cottage and crossed into the suburb of Jolimont and Yarra Park, the home of the Melbourne Cricket Ground. On our right we passed the Jolimont railway yards, built on the site of what was formerly the East Melbourne Cricket Ground, one of the oldest cricket clubs in Victoria. Turning left we approached the red-brick members' entrance of the M.C.G. On the high ground to our left was the Yarra Park School, which, we are reliably informed, was the site of the police troopers' headquarters which gave the M.C.G. its original name: the Richmond Police Paddock.

After the building congestion which surrounds most of England's major cricket grounds, the vastness of Australian sporting venues is an eye-opener. Not only are the playing arenas larger, but the parking areas for cars are far more extensive. Everything is on a bigger scale.

The Houses of Parliament in Melbourne, Victoria's legislative assembly.

Keith and I passed through the members' gate, turned right and made our way to the Grey Smith stand at the base of which the dressing rooms of both teams are to be found. The stand is a tall, elegant, colonnaded piece of Victorian architecture brocaded with red, white and blue cast-iron railings decorated with the Melbourne Cricket Club's insignia. During important sporting events on the ground, it seats the press corps, V.I.P.s and feminine elegance - leaving the Members' Pavilion to cater for the committee members, their friends and those men whose fathers had had the foresight to enrol their sons at birth in a members' waiting list twenty years long. Access to the dressing rooms is barred by an official who never seems to leave his post and allows only players to enter the most holy of holies. The changing rooms are situated on each side of the single entrance door and each has an elevated wooden viewing platform and panoramic window set in the wall facing the playing arena. This is where the players sit in directors' chairs to keep track with the goings-on in the middle, looking over the heads of the spectators, who in their turn gawk back at their heroes in white. The Southern Stand - built for the Bodyline Tour of 1932/33 - houses the hotbed of Melbourne barrackers in its Bays 13 and 14. Together with the terraces beneath the black multi-storeyed and encyclopaedic score-board on the western side of the ground, it is one of the favourite vantage points of the M.C.G. groundlings.

As per usual, our cricket bags had been forwarded directly from the train to the ground, and we were quickly into practice gear. The nets were on the periphery of the ground just in front of the Southern Stand, into which several hundred people had already crowded to get a glimpse of the "Poms'" afternoon practice. Brian and I did not stretch ourselves but bowled fast enough to elicit several 'oohs' and 'aahs' from the watching Aussies. We had a solid work-out on fairly good practice surfaces. But our main interest was not with the turf in the practice nets, but with the 22 yards of Merri Creek soil in the middle of the arena. We had heard that, in an attempt to quicken up the Test pitch, this season the curator had not followed his usual practice of planting couch in the square. This policy had certainly removed the cushioning effect of the coarse grass and its root system; but in so doing it had also robbed the wicket of its main binding agent. In the course of the State game which preceded the Test, the pitch had broken up and had to be repaired. Now the same thing looked like occurring in the Test. Panic! The Melbourne Club called in Jack House, by reputation the best groundsman in the land. But when we strolled across from the practice nets to have a look at the Test pitch, the cracks in it were already visible to the naked eye! The batsmen, it seemed, were in for a torrid time.

This evening we were entertained at the South Melbourne Cricket Club: the cradle of five Australian skippers. And what an evening we had! Horace Lindrum, the master of the billiard cue, gave us an exhibition of his skills, which had to be seen to be believed! He must be a magician to make the ivory balls behave the way he did! What a spinner he would have been! The other star of the evening was South Melbourne Cricket Club's resident parrot, whose command of Australian blasphemy had to be heard to be believed. The trick was to position his cage behind the eminent visitor who was to be shocked. Then, when someone threatened to pour a glass of beer over the bird, the invective began - !!##**^^%!! We were told that the parrot's performance had produced a startled reaction from the Governor of Victoria quite recently!

Thursday December 30th.

The eve of the Third Test was crunch-decision time for the selectors of both teams. After our win in Sydney, there seemed to be no reason to alter the composition of our side, except to bring in the freshly fit Denis Compton for Tom Graveney. Later, it transpired that Reg Simpson was none too happy about the selectors' continued perseverance with Bill Edrich in the opening spot, in view of W.J.'s continued lack of success. Reg, after all, is a specialist in that position and he can point to a previous outstanding success against Australia in Melbourne in 1950/51. And, to be truthful, Bill has not really outperformed the Nottingham batsman. I later learned that another more critical selection drama was taking place behind the scenes. Len was not a well man, crippled as he was with fibrositis

in his back. He did not want to play. But if our captain abandoned the ship, it would be a devastating psychological blow to our chances of victory.

The Australian selectors stood by the men who had won the Brisbane Test - with one exception. Len Maddocks, the diminutive Victorian 'keeper, who performed very well against us in the State game, replaced Gil Langley, who had been hit in the eye by a flying bail during a Shield match. This was a well merited promotion for the likable Lennie - but it later led to a remarkable exhibition of South Australian parochialism when he was preferred to the local lad, Langley, and retained for the Adelaide Test. He was actually BOOED by the local crowd as he made his way into the Australian dressing room on the first morning of the Fourth Test! Keith Miller was back in the Australian side for the Melbourne game, but right up to the first ball of the game, he was a doubtful starter because of 'a crook knee'.

The preparation for tomorrow's match was hard and demanding. The game was not going to be a rehearsal. On my way back to the Windsor, I took the time to examine the tunnel which runs behind and around the M.C.G stands. During the Second World War the tunnel was weatherproofed and used to accommodate the thousands of American G.I.s who passed through Melbourne en route to the War in the Pacific - a fact recorded on brass plaques on the back wall of the pavilion. The breezes which even now whistle through the long cavern explain why the Americans dubbed it

M.C.C. in Melbourne.

'Pneumonia Alley'. I could not explore the tunnel beyond the Members' Pavilion. It was blocked by the bull-dozers of the builders who are building the new Northern Stand for the 1956 Olympic Games.

This evening was spent at the cinema with a girl friend. After the show we went back to the hotel for a nightcap, and at about 10 o'clock there was a faint tap on the door of the room and the Skipper entered. 'Just to remind you,' he said, 'you have a hard day in front of you tomorrow.' Superb psychology! Ten minutes later the girlfriend had departed and I was safely tucked up in bed!

Friday December 31st.

Real drama unfolded in the early hours of this morning - not at the Melbourne Cricket Ground but in Len Hutton's room at the Windsor Hotel. I learned later that The 'Ger, Duckie and a couple of the senior members of the team were summoned to the Skipper's bedside before breakfast. Len's fibrositis was killing him and he had a heavy cold, He did not want to play in the Test! Len was obviously below par and in pain; but his uncharacteristic reluctance to tough it out in true Yorkshire fashion could not have come at a worse time. After our Sydney win, we were on top psychologically. Now was the time to rub the Aussies' noses in the dirt! And to do that, we needed Len's experience and presence on the field. As an eight-year-old kid, I remembered how he dominated the Aussies in 1938 at The Oval with his world record innings of 364. And how many times since has he stood firm when others around him failed! We needed him to show us the way to a series victory.

Fortunately the persuasive powers of George Duckworth and northern common sense won the day. Len agreed to play and went out to toss with Ian Johnson. This time he called correctly and decided to bat. Within the hour, Len's 'bogey', Keith Miller, gave him cause to regret that decision. Nugget made a nonsense of his 'bung' knee and the doctor's advice not to bowl. He turned on a dazzling display of pace and late swing which reinforced my opinion of him as the greatest match-winning all-rounder who has ever drawn breath. He really turned it on for his native Melbourne. In an inspired, pre-lunch, ninety-minute spell, his accuracy, speed and late swing netted him the prime wickets of Edrich, Hutton and Compton in nine overs at a cost of only five runs. Never has a player undersold himself before a game as much as Miller did before this match. There were only two positive shots played off his bowling - one by Compo and the other by Kipper. With P.B.H. bowled by Lindwall, four wickets were down half-way through the session.

Cowdrey and Bailey then steadied the boat with a 74-run fifth wicket stand before Evans and Cowdrey contributed another 54 runs to our total. Runs did not flow; they were grafted from a pitch which kept the batsmen hopping around as delivery after delivery tickled their ribs.

Colin was icily superb. For four hours his concentration never wavered. He unhesitatingly got behind the line of the short, rising deliveries and, as soon as the bowler overpitched, he stroked the ball through the cover and mid-wicket gaps in the field. Shooters became more frequent; but Colin dug them out. When I joined him at the wicket he was a run short of his maiden Test century: a goal which he reached with a scampered single. If he ever scores a better hundred, I hope that I am there to see it. He is a superb striker of the ball and is completely unflappable. He exudes a total dedication to cricket and his side.

Two runs later, off-spinner Ian Johnson bowled him with a remarkable delivery which was an indication of what was to follow. Never a great spinner of the ball, the Aussie skipper bowled a length ball a foot wide of the off stump. Kipper disdained the delivery and padded up to it, moving so far to the off that the middle and leg stumps were visible behind his legs. The ball hit the edge of one of the cracks in the wicket, which was now assuming the appearance of a tessellated pavement. It jagged back to pass behind Kipper's pads and hit his leg-stump! Small wonder, therefore, that when our last wicket fell on 191 shortly afterwards, our bowlers looked towards the second day in an expectant frame of mind!

Saturday January 1st.

New Year's Day. Our New Year's Resolution is to win this Test and start 1955 in a winning vein, which we shall strive to extend to the remaining two Tests. Today the B.B.C. broadcast our previously recorded New Year's messages to our families. To a northern hemisphere person, this is a strange New Year's Day! When we reached the M.C.G. at nine o'clock, the temperature was already into the nineties. Breathing was like inhaling lukewarm water. Bowling is going to be hard, enervating work.

Our main task is not just to bowl Australia out; the flawed pitch will ensure that we do that - in good time. Importantly we have to stop them getting too far ahead of our total and playing us out of the game. In this respect, George Statham and Bob Appleyard bowled magnificently today - penetrative and economical by turns. 'Stat' took 5/60 and, with Appleyard disposing of the dangerous Harvey and the explosive Benaud at a cost of 38 runs, we have every right to be pleased with restricting the home side to 8/188 at stumps. We might have been even better placed. Favell and Artie Morris both fell cheaply, l.b.w. to Statham and me. Keith Miller preceded the South Australian opener to the pavilion, caught behind for seven. Then Harvey and Hole were 'hobbed' by George and me. Benaud followed, pouched at short-leg by Vic Wilson - substituting for Compton, who was nursing a bruised thumb. At this stage Johnson's men were 6/115 and staring down the barrel at a sub-150 total. Fortunately for them, Ron Archer tore off a quick-fire 23 and Lindwall chipped in with 13, before Maddocks and Johnson steered their side to within three runs of our total at close of play.

It was far from exhilarating cricket. The over-rate was painfully slow, with Hutton deliberately using his fast bowlers in short but effective bursts in the torrid conditions, tactics with which the vocal crowd obviously disagreed. But who could blame him? For his part, Maddocks did not do much to quicken the pace of events. His 36 runs occupied 135 minutes. Sleep tonight is going to be a sweaty affair.

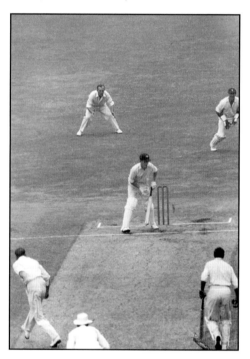

Maddocks in scintillating form, playing a defensive stroke against my bowling.

Sunday January 2nd.

The Boil has more connections than one of his switchboards! Today he arranged for us to spend the rest day with a party from W.R.Hughes', a leading Melbourne couturier. They took us on a surfing excursion to Point Leo, a beach on Westernport Bay some 30 miles from Melbourne. We had an enjoyable day cavorting in the 'briny' - which was the only civilised place to be. It was stinking hot and by mid-afternoon the mercury had reached 105 degrees. Even bathing could not bring physical comfort. The north wind whipped up the sand which stung the legs like wasps. God knows what effect the heat will have on the already badly cracked Test pitch! The sun and wind made life so uncomfortable that we abandoned the beach and made our way back to town, edging past ranks of overheated cars abandoned by the roadside. By five o'clock we were home, ready for a quiet evening meal and then bed.

It really is remarkable how hospitable Australians have been towards us. They have made us one of their families. One of the Holden car drivers and his wife, Stan and Rosemary Bentley, keep open house for the M.C.C. players. Scarcely an evening passes without one or other of the team having a meal with them in their pleasant St. Kilda Road home. Alan and Rita Jenkins have taken a few days off from their Maffra practice and driven the 100 miles from Gippsland to support England. It is great to have some 'Pommies' barracking for us - especially someone from the old 'alma mater'.

Monday January 3rd.

We arrived at the ground expecting the worst: we fully anticipated that yesterday's 'scorcher' would have reduced the wicket to a state of total fragility. The cracks in the pitch must have widened. Batting will be like threading one's way through a minefield! Before play, I went up into the Members' stand to speak to a 'Pommie' radio commentator. Imagine my surprise when, looking down from the broadcasting position on the third balcony of the stand, I saw that the colour of the Merri Creek soil on the square was not the dried, baked grey I had expected - but black, as though it were damp!

It fell to George Statham to bowl the first ball of the day. On Saturday he had slipped several times in his run-up on the glass-like approaches - his spikes unable to provide the necessary purchase. Today he moved back to his bowling mark and glided into his smooth run-up, accelerating ready to leap into his delivery stride. As was his habit, he grounded the side of his right boot and stepped forward to deliver the ball. The spikes on his rear boot sank into soft turf and skidded slightly. The ground was wet! How could this be? The pitch had been exposed to the tropical sun and hot northerly wind for the whole of Sunday. It should have been bone-hard and crumbly. Close inspection revealed that Saturday's mosaic of a wicket was now whole once again. The cracks had mysteriously closed and the holes where pieces of the surface had crumbled had been filled. Rumours abounded. One incredible explanation was that there was a subterranean spring under the M.C.G. wicket. The verdict of the official M.C.C. committee appointed to investigate the 'mystery' was that the wicket had sweated under its tarpaulin covers.

The most credible and probable reason given, however, was that of Percy Beames, the Melbourne Age's chief cricket writer who stated quite bluntly that the pitch had been watered during the wee hours. He had seen it with his own eyes when walking past the ground. Apparently, after the pitch broke up during the M.C.C. versus Victoria game, the Melbourne club recruited the services of the best curator in Victoria, Jack House, to prevent a recurrence of the problem in the Test. Faced with the dual disaster of a disintegrating pitch and an air temperature of 105 degrees on the rest day, House chose to turn on the sprinklers rather than risk not having a wicket at all on the third day.

The result of House's initiative was obvious from the first delivery bowled on Monday morning. The bounce was even and slow. Maddocks, Johnson and Johnston helped themselves to 43 additional runs, hoisting the Australian total to 231 and establishing a useful 43-run lead. When the *Melbourne Age* published Beames' story on Tuesday morning, the Victorian Cricket Association and the Melbourne Cricket Club issued a joint communiqué:

After a searching enquiry it is emphatically denied that the pitch or any part of the cricket ground has been watered since the commencement of the Third Test on Friday, December 31st.

I thought that the gentlemen do protest too much. The men in the middle knew the truth.

By an ironic twist of fate, the actions of an Australian groundsman spelt defeat for his own team. The much improved pitch enabled our batsmen to give a far better account of themselves in our second innings. We had all but wiped off our arrears before a Johnston delivery turned sharply from leg to clip the top of Bill Edrich's off-stump. Our vice-captain and captain then dug in, playing some scintillating drives to add 56 runs for the second wicket. Then the gremlins in the pitch began to re-appear as it dried out, and the cracks in its surface widened. After a dogged 42, Len got an Archer off-cutter which crept, hitting him on the ankle in front of middle stump. He slouched back into the dressing-room, slumped in his corner, buried his head in his hands and did not even bother to take off his pads for another hour. He was not a well man. In the interim, Kipper was dismissed in a most unfortunate manner. Playing defensively at a Benaud leggie, he dropped the ball at his feet where it behaved as if it had a life of its own, curling like a spinning top around his pads. P.B.H.'s warning shout came too late. The ball clipped his stumps, toppling a bail. With steely determination, May played the role of

Tyson to Ian Johnson. Note the wicket - wet black.

Horatio, helping Compton to hold the bridge against all attacks. Stumps found them still together with England's score at 3/159: 119 runs to the good and with seven wickets in reserve. When we joined the press for a beer in the Snake Pit bar at the Western end of the Grey Smith Stand, the consensus of opinion was that England had had the better of the day. The wicket was bound to deteriorate and if we could put together a half-decent total, we were in with a chance of winning the Third Test.

The Aussie press seem a decent bunch and treated the story quite impartially. John Priestley of the *Melbourne Herald* and Rex Pullen of the *Sun* respected our requests for confidentiality on our opinions of the watered pitch.

With the Test having run three-fifths of its course, this was not the time for high jinks. We ate a quiet meal in the Windsor dining room. I had a beer with Alan and Rita Jenkins in the mahogany surrounds of the hotel lounge - and then to bed, tired but ready for the last supreme effort.

Tuesday January 4th.

Another fine hot day and another test of pitch durability. Its life span was shortening - rapidly! After adding a few runs to his overnight score of 83, May was disappointingly bowled by a

YOUNG MAN, I CONSIDER YOUR REMARK "DO I WANT A SPOT OF WATER WITH IT?" TO BE IN INFERNALLY BAD TASTE

TEST WICKET WATERED

16 runs in one over and collecting 38 in just 40 minutes. Even so Australia's ultimate task of scoring 240 in its last innings did not appear daunting to the happily sanguine home crowd of 60,000. Its optimism refused to be dampened - even by Kipper catching Morris off me at short-leg and Appleyard yorking Favell as he tried to drive him over the Southern Stand. In the final wash-up of the day's play, Johnson's batsmen have been left to score a further 165 for victory tomorrow: a task well within the capabilities of the remaining nine batsmen.

Wednesday January 5th.

The cryptic entry in my handwritten diary says every-thing about today's events: 'This Wednesday morning has been remarkable and today is perhaps the luckiest and happiest day of my life. We finished the Test before lunch, Australia adding only 32 to its overnight score.

Johnston delivery which turned across him; he fell nine runs short of the coveted and well-deserved hundred. Twelve runs later Compo was caught behind on the leg-side by the mobile Maddocks off Archer. It looked as if it was all over. We would not be able to set Australia any challenging victory task. But Bailey blocked, as only he knows how, for nearly three hours and Evans hit gaily. The wicket-keeper's 22 set the mood for Johnny Wardle, who took the long handle to Bill Johnston, scything

They were all out for 111 and we won by 128 runs. I took 7/27 in the innings and 6/16 in the 6.3 overs I bowled today from the Richmond end!'

Early this morning 50,000 spectators pushed and jostled their way into the M.C.G., chattering and laughing in happy anticipation. They were in a jovial frame of mind as they swarmed into the vast amphitheatre, convinced that an Australian victory was in the bag. Many had set off early in the day to journey in from country centres around Melbourne, carrying their packed lunches and thermoses. Little did they realise that they were destined to eat their mid-day meal outside the ground in the nearby Fitzroy Gardens. The M.C.C. caterers were also in for a nasty shock - the game finished before they could sell their stocks of meat pies and they were left with thousands on their hands!

There was no hint of the drama which was to follow as I took the comparatively new ball, gave it a vigorous rub and began proceedings from the southern end. It was the first time I had bowled from the end at which Keith Miller had bowled so destructively on the first morning of the match. The approach is slightly uphill and the breeze was slightly in my face. No matter! It was the psychological moment for a flat-out effort. The penultimate ball of the first over was slanted into the pads of the overnight batsman, Neil Harvey. When the left-hander glanced it off the full face of the bat, he must have thought that it was a certain four. But he had reckoned without wicket-keeper Godfrey Evans, who danced a few steps to his right and flung himself at the ball like a circus acrobat. He gathered in the most extraordinary wicket-keeper's catch I have ever seen, directly in front of Colin Cowdrey, who was fielding very wide of the pitch at leg slip! It was the catch which turned the game - perhaps the series - not merely because it dismissed one of Australia's best batsmen, but largely because of the dispiriting effect it must have had on the batsmen waiting in the dressing room. It had quite the opposite influence on Brian and me. After that, I never doubted that we would win.

George and I turned the screw and runs became as scarce as hens' teeth. Nugget, the new batsman, was all at sea against Stat and Benaud champed at the bit as he failed to get the scoreboard ticking over. Rashly, he attempted to hook a short delivery - the first bad ball I had sent down all morning. But it was far too wide of the off-stump and he bottom edged it on to his stumps! The Gods were certainly with me!

Miller's batting torment ended when, after keeping out a couple of shooters, he got a lightning delivery which lifted, clipped the shoulder of his bat and appeared to be going high over Hutton's head at first slip. The Skipper thrust a despairing hand skywards and tipped it high 'over the bar'. Miraculously, Bill Edrich, at second slip, anticipated the deflection. He retreated a few yards to take the catch and complete the dismissal. Five for 87 became 6/97 when Hole edged Statham to Evans. Wicket-keeper Len Maddocks could not repeat his first innings heroics - but he was desper-ately unlucky. He departed much in the same manner as Cowdrey did in our innings. The first ball I bowled him was a yorker. He dug it out, but did not stun it completely. Like a billiard ball with side on it, it spun in an arc around the batsman's pads, passing behind his legs to clip the leg-stump - just hard enough to dislodge one bail! Two balls later, Ray Lindwall, still waiting for the bouncer which never came, played back to a full-length outswinger and was l.b.w. I was bowling in a euphoric daze. At times like this sportsmen seem to operate on instinct. To recollect such moments is like passing from one's corporeal being to observe the unfolding drama from the outside. I am sure that years after the event one will be able to recreate the bio-feedback of such pinnacles of success to produce the same elevated levels of arousal.

Ron Archer enjoyed a charmed life outside the off-stump, but finally Brian Statham torpedoed his innings with a devastating yorker. Nine for 110 was translated into 111 all out when Bill Johnston hung his bat out to dry wide of the off-stump and was pouched by Godders. We were home and dry by 128 runs! The clock on the Members' Pavilion showed the time to be just 1.25p.m.! We had only been out in the middle for 80 minutes. The crowd, now muted, trudged off to munch their sandwiches in the surrounding park-lands.

My elation was unimaginable! But I could never have done it without Brian. What a partner! Wise and reliable - just the man to have alongside you in the trenches when you are up against it. As the crowd swarmed over the fence, I strode up the walk leading to the dressing-room with my arm around 'George's' shoulder. Len Hutton was delirious with happiness. He, England's first professional captain, was leading a triumphant team - in Australia! A side which, after a dismal start to the Ashes series, had been written off by the pundits. A side which had risen like the Phoenix from those Ashes, turned the tables on Australia, and were now a game to the good in the series! I feel that

if we can clinch the rubber, Hutton will die a happy man!

Yet in spite of the Melbourne triumph, I sense that Len is still pursued by his own personal demons. He will never be completely content until the series has been won and he has exorcised his two personal tormentors, Lindwall and Miller. Not for a moment does he relax his own bottled-up intensity. He frowns on 'sleeping with the enemy' and counsels against our going into the Aussie dressing-room after a game to fraternise with our affable on-field opponents. In Melbourne, however, he could afford to be magnanimous. After the game he threw wide the door of the English dressing room.

The champagne flowed, flooding well into the night. Even 'George' abandoned his usual beverage of beer for the despised 'soda-pop'. I soon tired of the celebrations and after lunch K.V. and I went to an afternoon picture show. Tonight, as I write, I remember that I have forgotten my promise to go to the broadcasting box to do an interview with Alan McGilvray, the Aussie broadcaster. I wonder if Alan will ever forgive me!

Thursday January 6th.

An unexpected sabbatical: a day off earned by our finishing the Test a day early. We have won ourselves time to look around Melbourne and go to a party in the evening. How I must have enjoyed it! I fell asleep on our host's lounge room floor!

The final scoreboard at the M.C.G.

Tyson's typhoon . . . by HUGH MORREN
A TYPHOON STRUCK AUSTRALIA EARLY TODAY— CAUSING THE TEST WICKET—
SS AUSTRALIA
-TO BE WELL WATERED!

Chapter Nine

A Bush Interlude

Friday January 7th.

TODAY WE ARE BOOKED ON A mid-day flight to Tasmania and are thus spared the usual hassle of early morning packing and George Duckworth's nagging directive to get our 'suitcases outside the door at seven'. Our D.C.3 took off from Essendon airport, reaching Hobart three hours later. Air travel in Aussie is wonderfully easy. Essendon airport, for instance, is only seven miles or a half-hour drive from central Melbourne.

The Hobart airfield is also conveniently situated a few miles from Tassie's capital city on the southern bank of the broad and beautiful Derwent River. On the drive into Hobart we enjoyed a picturesque introduction to one of the oldest cities in Australia. Hobart Town, and its satellite of Port Arthur, were, in the early days of colonisation, regarded as the most secure penal settlements in Van Diemen's Land, isolated from the mainland by Bass Strait and from northern Tasmania by a narrow isthmus of land. As one approaches Hobart from the east the town appears to nestle at the foot of the 'organ pipes' flank of Mount Wellington: a peak which, even in the heat of an Australian summer, is sometimes capped with snow. Hobart's harbour is one of the deepest in the world and, during the Second World War, the largest troopships such as the Queen Mary and Queen Elizabeth were able to tie up at Constitution Dock alongside Salamanca Place. The sandstone buildings of the city and nearby Richmond gave us the best glimpse of antiquity that we have experienced since leaving England.

But 'old' is not always 'best', as we soon found out when we booked in at Hadley's Hotel and sampled its dining room and room service! I am not selected to play in our Hobart game, which is against a Combined Eleven made up mostly of Tasmanian players, and bolstered with the mainland internationals: Alan Davidson, Neil Harvey, Les Favell and Richie Benaud. One of the anomalies of Tassie cricket is that although the island is home to some of the oldest clubs in Australia - sides such as the Break O' Day Eleven dating back to the early nineteenth century - it has never had the population base to field a competitive Sheffield Shield side. Over the years, it has produced outstanding cricketers: players such as Jackie Badcock and Lisle Nagle. But they had to migrate to the mainland to carve out international careers for themselves. Consequently, when Tassie plays overseas touring teams, it usually needs reinforcements.

In the hierarchy of Aussie cricket, the Apple Isle enjoys the same status as that of minor counties in England.

Saturday January 8th.

The pocket-handkerchief North Hobart Cricket Ground has stood astride of its hilltop overlooking the Derwent estuary for more than a hundred years. Its double-decker, weatherboard pavilion is antique, draughty, uncomfortable and cold. The walls of its small rooms are lined with photographs of moustachioed nineteenth century and stiffly formal twentieth century teams. From its upper storey one can look seawards, down the Derwent towards the South Pole, or up-river in the direction of the mountainous west coast wilderness with its horizontal forest. On its inland boundary a low single-decker stand provides spartan glassed-in spectator cover and houses - of all things - a Totalisator Betting Shop! The reason for the latter's presence becomes evident only on a closer examination of the Oval. For, enclosing the playing area - which incidentally doubles as an Australian Rules Football Ground during the winter months - is a greyhound track which hosts regular race meetings. The antique North Hobart Oval must rank as one of the world's first multi-purpose sporting complexes!

The supply ships which service Australia's Antarctic base at Mawson are headquartered in Hobart and ply north to south and back again with an infrequent but clockwork regularity, governed only by the seasons. Slightly upriver from the North Hobart hilltop ground lies Government House, to which the M.C.C. were invited - *de rigueur* - within hours of our arrival. The height of the cricket ground above sea level exposes it to the full force of the Tasman gales and the often inclement Tasmanian weather, which is similar to that of a cool England summer - and its attendant showers! As a result, the wicket for today's game looks very green and promises to provide some sport for the batsmen.

Wickets may differ around the world, but it seems that newspapers are remarkably alike. The *Hobart Mercury* is no exception. When I opened it this morning, I discovered that, at the civic reception at the Hobart Town Hall to which the touring team had been driven directly from the airport, I appeared very bored - despite the many complimentary things that were said about my recent performance in Melbourne. I suppose one cannot please all of the people all of the time!

Our recent triumph in the Third Test makes us a tremendous draw-card wherever we play and the ground was filled to overflowing for each of the three days we played in Hobart. More than 20,000 spectators attended the match, breaking all previous Tasmanian records for a first-class game. The local captain, Emerson Rodwell, won the toss and, not being inclined towards chivalry, batted first. His innings of 70, plus 82 from the enterprising Harvey, made up most of the Tasmanian 221 total. For the most part, the batsmen struggled against the parabolic swing and pace of Bedser, Loader and Bailey, who between them monopolised the wicket-taking. I spent a restful day watching the cricket, during which time I met up again with Jim and Shirl, two acquaintances from the trip out on the Orsova.

Sunday January 9th.

The touring party spent the morning at Guy Rixes' place: a restful interlude which culminated in an excellent barbecue lunch. As usual, our social invitations were extended to the press gang and most of them tagged along. They certainly enjoyed themselves - too much so apparently! For, after having tucked in to a succulent steak and several 'bangers', Splinter Woodcock of the *Times* was suddenly taken violently ill. At first we were under the imp-

ression that after so many years of steak-less, wartime austerity, Johnny had overdone the 'tooth' bit. But it turned out to be far more serious. He was carted off to hospital where the doctors diagnosed him as the proud owner of a couple of stomach ulcers! Poor Splinter! He was never 100% for the remainder of the tour. We used to invite him into the dressing room so that he could at least watch the games and do his job in gastric comfort.

This afternoon we drove to the top of Mount Wellington. A first-class sealed road gives access to the summit, skirting the base of the geologically remarkable 'Organ Pipes' and slanting upwards from left to right. The mountain is about 3000 feet high and, at the top, a perfectly flat plateau furnishes a wonderful viewing plat-

Hobart from Mount Wellington.

form. At our feet the 'Organ Pipes' sheered away, opening a breathtaking, panoramic vista of the southern ocean, the islands of the Derwent estuary, the valleys, mountains and Hobart Town. It was one of those moments in one's life which remains indelibly recorded in the inward eye. The air was icy cold and the wind pierced to the bone and we were glad to descend once more to the comparative warmth of the lowlands.

Monday January 10th.

We may be 2-1 up in the Ashes series, but there was not very much in our batting performance today to suggest that we deserve that lead. Admittedly, the Hobart pitch was more suited to a club than a first-class match; but the continuing failures of Reg Simpson and

Vic Wilson with the bat, on top of Bill Edrich's poor form, do not augur well for a good score in the approaching Adelaide Test. So miserably did we perform in our first innings in Hobart, that when our eighth wicket fell, we were still 22 in arrears. It was left to a ninth wicket stand of 40 between K.V. and Big Al to take us into a slender 21-run lead. Against a home-grown opposition which is 80% Taswegian and well below first-class standard, this was a great disappointment. The most annoying feature of this Combined Eleven game is the way in which our batsmen and bowlers have played into form players who we are likely to encounter in the next Test. Harvey enjoyed a good match, scoring 129 runs; Davidson helped himself to four cheap wickets and Benaud completed a

P.B.H., Kipper and 'Ger' at a model prison in Port Arthur.

Looking towards the Island of the Dead.

sound double of 81 runs for once out and 2/79 in the M.C.C.'s first innings.

Most of these observations are based on hearsay and the scorebook. I had the day off and spent the morning with John Arlott browsing through the second-hand bookshops of Hobart. The afternoon was spent with P.B.H., Kipper and Geoffrey Howard on a visit to the former penal settlement of Port Arthur, sixty miles to the south, across the narrow Eaglehawk isthmus. Few escapees attempted to swim across the sea channels either side of the isthmus. It was said that they were patrolled by sharks! I must confess to a degree of disappointment in Port Arthur. To begin with, the final 30 miles of the trip down was over bumpy bush roads which left me 'all shook up'. When we finally arrived, we found an almost deserted ruin of stone cells and buildings with no-one to explain their history. The structures were solid and strangely elegant, fashioned as they were from the local stone. I could appreciate that the only way out of Port Arthur was, as it was explained to us, across the narrow straits which separated the prison from the settlement's cemetery on the Island of the Dead. It is, however, a little over the top to describe the 120-year-old Port Arthur ruin as 'historic' and 'ancient'!

Tuesday January 11th.

I resumed active duty today; but only as twelfth man on the last day of an all-too-brief three-day match which finished more with a whimper than a bang. When the Combined Eleven

The team at the Camerons' homestead.

batted a second time, they meandered along. The local skipper, Rodwell, dithered so long over his declaration that, when it finally came, he had smothered any hope of a result. Neil Harvey and Benaud both made a token gesture of forcing the pace; but all to no avail. When the closure finally came at 6/184, the Skipper rejected the improbability of scoring 164 in 100 minutes out of hand. He demonstrated what he thought of the ludicrous challenge by promoting Keith Andrew from number nine to opening the innings with Reg Simpson. I remained an unused twelfth man; Hutton left his batsmen to their own devices. Not one message did I relay to them - even at the drinks break!

Poor old Jim McConnon! Today his abysmal tour became a total disaster. Fielding a hard off-drive from Harvey,

he broke the little finger of his bowling hand. Harold Dalton took him to the hospital for an x-ray. There he was told that he would be out of action until the last two weeks of the tour of New Zealand. Completely shattered, he packed his bags for the last time. He is homeward bound. He will travel on to the U.K. when we next hit the mainland.

Wednesday January 12th.

This morning we were packed, in the lobby of Hadley's Hotel, and ready to leave bright and early. We were scheduled to travel by road 120 miles north to Launceston where we are to play in a three-day game against Tasmania beginning tomorrow. By the time we reached the outer Hobart suburb of New Norfolk we were very aware of just how dry the countryside was. The weather on the Apple Island over the Christmas holiday period has been cold: cold but dry. The locals say that the island is in the grip of a drought. We motored until about eleven o'clock, when we stopped to visit the Camerons'. We met and made friends with Don and his wife when we sailed with them on the Orsova. They own a 'modest' farming property in the Tasmanian midlands - a mere 60,000 acres! This apparently is as nothing when compared with that of Don's brother and neighbour. He owns 100,000 acres! A wonderful buffet lunch was laid on the wide verandah of their low rambling homestead and we, together with several of the Camerons'

family and friends, did the meal ample justice!

I am in a totally foreign world. Middleton and cotton mills seem so distant from outback stations. But even amongst this comfortable munificence of gravelled weedless drives and wide, sweeping manicured lawns fringed by glorious flowering shrubs, I miss the Lancashire folk. The Camerons even have their own river, flowing not a stone's throw from their homestead. Reg Simpson took Sam Stott (one of our supporters travelling with us - and dubbed 'the well-known Lancashire businessman travelling incognito') for a row in a dinghy moored to a small wharf. Somehow (I don't know how), Reg contrived to break an oar and it

Sam Stott, the well-known Lancashire businessman, travelling incognito, gives Denis a ride on the Camerons' river.

took us ages to get the row-boat back to the shore! The rest of the trip into Launceston - pronounced Lonston - was a sleepy interlude.

Thursday January 13th.

A brilliant dawn was followed by a brilliant day. But that is more than can be said of the cricket played today against a totally home-grown Tasmanian side. It was six hours of what tennis buffs call 'unforced errors'. But, *mirabile visu*, at long last, it provided us with a glimpse of what our batsmen were really capable of. 'Long Tom' Graveney capitalised on the Taswegians' fielding errors to register his first century of the tour. He went stroke for glorious stroke with Hutton and Compton to notch a dispiriting 134 runs. Dispiriting, that is, for the Tassie bowlers! Our first day occupation of the crease produced 427 runs for the loss of seven wickets. In addition to Graveney's major contribution to that total, Len, Compo, Vic Wilson and Johnny Wardle each scored half-centuries in their own, widely-differing and idiosyncratic ways. Denis in particular was in his most innovative and inventive mood pulling some remarkable strokes out of the bag.

Friday January 14th.

Most of today's proceedings concerned the locals' rather ineffectual batting. They did not make a very good fist of dealing with Scrubs Loader's inswing. The Surrey bowler has not had much opportunity to display his bowling wares on this tour. But seldom has such a gifted paceman had to play a supporting role on an M.C.C. tour. Loader is a remarkable swinger of the ball: one of the few bowlers capable of bowling inswingers to the right-hander from around the wicket! He can transform his normal fast-medium outswingers into slow off-cut with little or no perceptual change to his action, which is usually concealed behind a sideways approach to the wicket. His bouncer is lethal and its clear intent is to pin the batsman against the sightscreen! His inexplicable wide range of pace has, from time to time, raised the suspicion of a 'kink' in his action. He can certainly generate a great deal of speed for a man who is of a very slender build.

In twelve parsimonious overs, Loader conceded only 22 runs, captured six wickets and the locals were dismissed for 117 in the space of just 43 overs. It was then that the Skipper sprang the first of two surprises. Even though we were leading by a substantial 310 runs, he did not enforce the follow-on - choosing instead to bat a second time. Rumour had it that Len's decision was based on a wish to keep a healthy slice of the game for the spectators' consumption tomorrow: a Saturday and a day on which a large crowd is expected. Then came the second shock: he sent me in to open the innings with Reg Simpson! He was obviously keeping the best batsmen back for the next day!

Saturday January 15th.

Hutton's unexpected decision to send me in at number one proved an inspired tactic! I top-scored with 27 in our second innings total of 6/133! Laugh that one off, those of you who doubt my batting talents!

We declared at lunch-time and, having been promoted in the batting order, I was now demoted in the bowling pecking order. It was left largely to Loader, Appleyard and Wardle to winkle out the Taswegians a second time in two sessions of play. But the Skipper's desire to prolong the entertainment almost led him to miscalculate. Maddox and Hyland added 60 in 15 profligate and loose overs from Compton and Cowdrey, who conceded 100 runs between them. I came on to bowl right on cue, and combined with Scrubs to knock over Hyland, Rodwell and Richardson. Wardle then chipped in with three wickets to win the game by 243 runs, claiming his last victim 15 minutes before time was called. Spinner Wardle's six wickets in the game was an encouraging sign in the lead-up to the Adelaide Test.

The Tasmanian game was more notable for the islanders' hospitality than the standard of cricket played. I am very sorry that we did not have the opportunity of seeing more of the picturesque island, particularly its north-western districts around Burnie, Stanley and the Knob. It is a region

My visit to a Consolidated school in Launceston.

strewn with English-sounding towns like Ulverston and Sheffield - and largely given over to dairy farming and logging. Cradle Mountain National Park is one of Australia's most famous beauty spots. The West Coast of the island is swept by the Roaring Forties, which blow across the Southern Ocean unchecked by any land-mass. They flatten the trees until they are parallel to the ground and people can walk on their canopy. The region is wildly beautiful and almost inaccessible by land. The west coast abounds in crayfish - the Aussie lobster - which the local fishermen catch and fly off remote beaches by light plane, bound directly for Tokyo tables.

The one excursion I undertook in Launceston was a visit to a Consolidated School. This is a school for pupils drawn from an extended farming community and offering a curriculum largely made up of agri-cultural subjects. Since I am a teacher by profession, it was assumed that I was interested in pedagogic affairs - and indeed I am. I left the school impressed by its airiness and pleasant ambience - and its relevance to vocational training.

Sunday January 16th.

It seemed that dawn had only just broken when we left Tasmania this morning. Perhaps not - but it was ridiculously early. At Launceston airport we discovered that we were to fly in one of Ansett's brand-new Convair planes, which are propelled by modern jet turbines. The air-hostess demonstrated the smoothness of the plane's flight by placing a glass of water on a window ledge. The vibration of the engines did not cause even a ripple on the surface of the liquid! Our pilot was English, on secondment to Ansett and instructing his Australian counterparts on how to fly the Convair.

By midday we were on the ground at Essendon airport, and were immediately whisked off to lunch at the Windsor. By 4.30p.m. we were airborne again - this time in a D.C.3 and heading for Mount Gambier in South Australia. We arrived slightly late, having to fly into a strong headwind. Mount Gambier turned out to be one of the most hospitable places we have encountered in our journey around Australia. Its inhabitants mastered the social art of catering for every minute of our stay, yet still allowed us our own space.

Monday January 17th.

An uncommitted day which Woozer, Bob Appleyard and I spent fishing on the River Glenelg, which flows into the ocean just a few miles south of the Mount. Fred Kraihe, mine host of the South Australia Hotel - the team's headquarters in the town - drove us down to Nelson, a small fishing village, crouching in the shadow of the volcanic cliffs which border the estuary of the Glenelg. Fred took us upstream in his boat and we fished for bream, baiting our hooks with whitebait. A prehistoric silence hung over the sheer river banks which rose to a height of about 100 feet on both sides. The cliffs were of igneous rock and over the millennia the river had scoured out a deep bed for

Nelson on the River Glenelg
- Jack Hobbs once convalesced here.

itself, laying bare stratum after stratum of red and black basalt. The whole countryside is volcanic in nature, the surface soil being rich and fertile volcanic ash. Fred told us that land around the Mount sold for about 200 pounds an acre - by comparison with the five shillings an acre one paid for dry land in Tasmania. The soil was ideal for viticulture, which is a major industry around the Mount. The locally produced full-bodied Koonawarra red wines are famous all around Australia - and beyond.

The bream refused to bite and we returned, empty-handed and with wet bums, to the local pub. As we sat down to lunch, the Nelson publican announced he had something to show us. He produced an old, tattered hotel register from the early twenties, and there inscribed as a guest during one Aussie summer was the name 'J.B. Hobbs'. Apparently, the former England opening batsman fell sick during an M.C.C. tour and after he recovered, he convalesced at this tiny pub in out-of-the-way Nelson!

After lunch Fred took us along to visit the Princess Margaret Rose Caves: an extensive underground complex of high caverns, cared for by its remarkable custodian, Jock. Jock lit our way, through its narrow entrance at the top of the river cliff-face, into a veritable Aladdin's fairyland of stalactites and stalagmites. Bob Appleyard maintained that they were not as impressive as those at Cheddar. I thought it remarkable that such caverns in such a remote part of Australia should not have been more publicised and commercialised!

The Blue Lake, Mount Gambier.

And so we returned to the Mount bearing two fish - netted, not caught! True anglers would have been ashamed of us! On our return car trip we overtook a couple of Aussie youngsters walking along the dirt road. Just before we reached them one of the lads bent down and picked up what seemed to be a length of thick rope. Holding it by one end, he cracked it like a whip and then draped it over a spike set in a roadside telegraph pole. Fred provided the explanation; 'The lad's just killed a brown snake. Broke its back!'

Back in the city we took the opportunity of visiting the lakes for which Mount Gambier is world renowned. The town itself is situated on the slopes of an extinct volcano, which in time immemorial blew its top leaving a crater which, as it filled with water, created four lakes. The biggest of the four is the Blue Lake which is found in the main crater. Its depth is said to be immeasurable and, for some unexplained reason, as the seasons pass, its waters change from a brilliant light blue colour to a deep purple. The Leg of Mutton lake is so-called from its unmistakable configuration, while the names of the Valley Lake and Browne's Lake leave no room for imagination.

Tuesday January 18th.

The South Australian Country Eleven were in a hurry. After losing the toss, they only spent four hours in the field. But in that short space of time their bowlers went for 328 on an easy-paced wicket. Skipper for the day, P.B.H. led the way with 62; but he was outscored by Reg Simpson who showed a welcome return to form with a sound

68, which suggested a possible recall for the Fourth Test. Denis and Long Tom notched 53 and 44 respectively. Before close, Brian Statham bowled opener Fuller, but Bennett and Hanna survived the remaining 70 minutes of the day.

The M.C.C/South Australian Country Eleven game was specifically staged at Mount Gambier as part of the celebrations to mark the town's promotion to the status of a city. Having gained its 10,000th inhabitant, it let its hair down and staged a civic ball in its community hall. Local bye-laws, however, forbade the consumption of alcohol within a hundred metres of municipal buildings. Therefore the new citizens of Mount Gambier set up their own bars - scores of them - in the boots of their cars, which were parked at the exact correct legal distance from the dance hall! It was the most confused ball I have ever attended. But it was good fun and we formed many friendships with people whom we were to meet again in the course of the Fourth Test in Adelaide.

Wednesday January 19th.

Nineteen Country eleven wickets fell in today's play, which, astoundingly, began 40 minutes late because of the weather - and ended 20 minutes early because of our opponents' inability to occupy the crease. First Bailey and Bedser separated the two overnight batsmen. Then they handed over to Appleyard, who dismissed all but one of the remaining South Aussies at a personal cost of 26 runs. P.B.H., in no mood to be generous, asked the locals

to bat again. This they did - and in an even more hurried fashion than in their first knock. When the score was 3/27, George Statham took the ball and clean bowled the next six batsmen without conceding a run! It was a remarkable demonstration of the Lancashire paceman's philosophy 'The batsman misses…I hit!' The Mount Gambier side were dismissed for 45 and we won by an innings and 177 runs. Statham's figures for the match were 12 overs, six maidens, eight wickets for 19!

A few beers with the hospitable people of Mount Gambier and then we were on our way. We were transported to the railway station by motorcade down the main street, escorted by the Blue Lake Girl Pipers! To the cheers of a crowd of a few hundred we climbed into our sleeping compartments for our overnight trip of a couple of hundred miles to Adelaide.

Chapter Ten

Adelaide and the Fourth Test

Thursday January 20th.

IT WAS ONLY 6A.M. WHEN WE rolled into Adelaide station this morning. It had been a bumpy, sleepless night. I threw back the cotton sheet which had covered but not warmed, only to discover that I was covered with a film of grey dust which had seeped in through the wooden lattice shutters of the windows as our train had lurched and chugged its way through the drought-stricken bush. The Adelaide station with its long platform is just across the River Torrens from the Central Oval; but we were more intent on getting a good breakfast and a decent shower than looking at the cricket ground. We piled into the waiting Holdens and headed for Glenelg-on-Sea. We are staying at the Pier Hotel again: a long way from our workplace, but at least cooled by a blessed and constant sea breeze. For the past few days, Adelaide has sweltered in century temperatures, which so heated the Mount Gambier stone of the city buildings that just to walk down Rundle Mall was an oven-like experience.

Showered, changed, fed and fresh, this afternoon we went up to the Adelaide Oval and flogged ourselves at the nets. It was just what we needed after a few days of comparative idleness, low-pressure cricket and travel. The practice facilities at the Oval are superb: four fast and true nets at the rear of the red-roofed George Giffen stands, cheek by jowl with the changing rooms and a spacious oval for fielding practice. The only problem is the proximity of the net area to the North Adelaide boundary. Not infrequently, batsmen loft their drives 50 yards over the fence, out of the ground and into the surrounding parkland.

We always look forward to playing at the Adelaide Oval. The staff is especially hospitable. The little caterer Johnny Leith goes out of his way to keep us happy; and men like Roly Vaughton, the former State wicket-keeper and baseballer, are wonderful company. It really is remarkable how South Australia turns out such versatile sportsmen; athletes like Vic Richardson who are just at home on a cricket field as they are on a football oval or baseball diamond!

As expected, Brian and I are being rested for the Test match and we are not playing against South Australia tomorrow.

Friday January 21st.

Last night was sultry, only slightly cooled by the sea breeze, which, however, was not strong enough to

Inseparable room-mates - myself and K.V.

blow away the mosquitos. Not much sleep for us - but then I don't have to play today. My room-mate Keith does, and he must not be feeling bright-eyed and bushy-tailed this morning.

This M.C.C side is a wonderfully happy mob to tour with. We are imbued with a wonderful sense of camaraderie. Take this morning for instance. At 8 o'clock, we were just about ready to pile into our Holdens and head for the Oval when I discovered that I had forgotten to bring my usual supply of handkerchiefs - always useful for mopping the brow on hot days. I knew that K.V. was still upstairs in our room. So from the lobby of the hotel I shouted up the stairs to the first storey: 'Keith, grab a couple of handkerchiefs from my case will you?' 'O.K.' came the response from the upper regions. And a few

moments later, Denny Compton trotted down the broad staircase of the Pier and handed me my hankies! How often does one see a senior member of a team put himself out for the most junior!

In spite of the fact that it is ten miles from the city, Glenelg is still a convenient and relaxing place to stay. Travel is no handicap. The Town Hall square is the terminus for a wonderful tram service which plies regularly and at a remarkable speed between the Adelaide town centre and the Glenelg City square. Close by is Holdfast Bay beach on which the first free settlers of South Australia disembarked in the early nineteenth century. 'Crow Eaters', as South Australians are nicknamed, take great pride in the fact that their ancestors were willing migrants and not felons and convicts transported from

The Town Hall square, Glenelg.

'The Old Dart'. The colony continued to attract new settlers even in the mid-nineteenth century, when many Germans fled the European wars and unrest to make their homes in the Adelaide Hills around Hahndorf and establish the vineyards of the Barossa Valley.

The single-decker Glenelg trams are brown-painted monsters with the company name emblazoned in yellow on their sides. At rush hour two carriages are linked to cater for the extra customers and - while they progress down the Glenelg High Street at a decorous pace in the early part of their trip and finish their voyage at a similar rate in the city CBD - they rattle along at spanking pace in the parklands between the sea and the city. At nine and five o'clock, it is far quicker to travel into the city by tram, than it is to negotiate the traffic on the Anzac Highway.

The trams end their inward journey in Victoria Square which is also the home of that unique Adelaide institution: the Cowley's all-night caravan pie stall. One cannot claim to have tasted all the delights of Adelaide unless one has eaten 'a pie-floater' - an upside-down meat pie swimming in a bowl of pea soup and doused with tomato sauce and vinegar - at 3a.m. outside the Adelaide G.P.O.!

The Glenelg beach is a wonderful location to keep fit. During our stays in Adelaide I often began the morning with a jog along its shore-line, pushing off from the abandoned jetty, partly demolished during a violent storm, and trotting along for a couple of miles and back again - just to get the blood singing along the veins.

The shingly beach is a wonderful soccer field and the team often kicks a ball around on it when we have a few spare moments. Some of the 'boys' are very good footballers. Brian Statham, for instance, has a powerful backheel. He places his right foot just in front of the ball and to its right; then, swivelling powerfully on his right toes, he hits the ball with his heel, usually sending it about 20 yards to his left - wrong-footing his opponents! The manoeuvre produces a loud thud, which is quite the equal of the sound produced by a full-blooded kick!

We shall soon see just how good we are as footballers. The press has challenged us to a game on the beach next Sunday. It looks like a sporting stay in Glenelg. I have also been invited to play in an evening bowls game at the Holdfast Bowling Club, just along the sea-front.

P.B.H. assumed command of the team for the South Australian game, and, losing the toss to Pancho Ridings on a very hot morning and, with the prospect looming of a superb pitch, feared the worst. But he reckoned without the new-found confidence which we have derived from our Melbourne Test triumph - and which now underscores everything we do. The superb bowling of Alec Bedser, Peter Loader, Bob Appleyard and Johnny Wardle was far too much for the South Aussie batsmen, despite the presence of Test men Les Favell, Graeme Hole and Gil Langley and the experience of Neil Dansie, Col Pinch and Phil Ridings. Our fielding was disappointing, but even though we grassed opportunity after opportunity, we still managed to 'roll' South Australia for 185, with only Ridings and Langley putting up any show of resistance. Bedser took two key wickets for 41, Loader and Wardle three, and Bob Appleyard two.

Our batsmen began in a similar hesitant fashion as their opponents. Bill Edrich, Tom Graveney - promoted to open the innings - and Vic Wilson all failed to exceed 25 and we slumped to be 3/55 at close of play.

Saturday January 22nd.

A timely red-letter day for our batsmen, right on the threshold of the Fourth Test. Nightwatchman Johnny Wardle stayed with Kipper Cowdrey until the score reached 91, when the Yorkshire spin-bowler was caught behind by Gil Langley off the bowling of Gregg.

Most of the remainder of the day was monopolised by the artistry of Denis Compton, Colin Cowdrey and Peter May. Kipper was bowled by the diminutive left-handed spinner Chucker Wilson for 64 with the score at 183; but his departure only made way for the real fireworks of the innings. Denis Charles Scott conjured up memories of his two hundreds in one Test on the same ground in 1947. He tore into Ridings' bowlers. All of them suffered as Compo occupied centre stage for 285 minutes to record our highest individual score of the tour - 182 - and add 234 with Peter May for the sixth wicket. May's contribution of 114 helped to

hoist the M.C.C. total to 451: our best of the tour. Compton may be in the autumn of his golden days, but the spark of genius still glows, illuminating the seemingly impossible stroke and playing shots which are so late that they appear to be afterthoughts.

After a couple of hours practice in the morning, I saw the beginning of the Compton epic - but then accompanied the Skipper, George, Godfrey and The Boil to the Cheltenham race meeting. I won £50 but, in retrospect, I think that I would have profited more from watching Compton's innings. It is not often that you get the opportunity of watching a genius at work.

On the way back from the races, we called in at the Legacy Camp in the Adelaide Hills to meet the children who spend their holidays there. It gave them a thrill. Legacy is an ex-servicemen's organisation which looks after the kids whose fathers were killed in the two World Wars.

Handed over most of my race winnings at the Saturday Night Club! You can't win!

Sunday January 23rd.

Today was the day of the Great Soccer Challenge Match: the M.C.C. v The Gentlemen of the English Press. The battle - and at times the game resembled no-holds-and-no-dirty-tricks-barred, open warfare - took place on the beach alongside the Pier Hotel. Initially it was an admirable venue for the early morning encounter. The sand was firm and the sea-breeze provided an admirable coolant. But as the game progressed, the half-length pitch was dug up by the constant pounding of forty-four frenzied feet, the Admiral's refereeing lost something of its authority, and tempers became over-heated. What we failed to realise was that while the playing surface looked smooth and sandy, beneath it was shingle and abrasive. Bill Edrich was playing on the right wing and when a long pass was pushed ahead of him, gamely set off in pursuit, ploughing his way through the now loose sand. As his feet sank deeper and deeper into the beach, his progress became more and more laboured, until he finally stumbled forward full-length, ploughing head first into the pitch. When we pulled him upright he was bleeding profusely from one side of his face where the shingle had ripped the skin off his cheek. He was not seriously hurt, but he was not going to be a pretty spectacle when he took the field again on Monday. Shortly afterwards the soccer match was abandoned as a no-result.

This afternoon I joined Peter May and a couple of the lads on an outing to Victor Harbour: a seaside holiday resort fifty miles to the south of Adelaide. Our hospitable guides were Bill Warren and Justin Franklin and their respective families.

Colin Cowdrey is the most virtuous of the touring party. He attended *matins* at the Adelaide Cathedral and read the lesson.

Monday January 24th.

When the South Australians began their second innings, 266 runs in arrears of the M.C.C.'s highest total of the tour, they were soon in trouble against the Surrey pace duet of Loader and Bedser. With the sun on his back, Big Al was close to his fittest of the trip and his best bowling form. He soon had Favell and Dansie back in the hutch and when Col Pinch ran himself out, the local team found itself 3/18: a total which soon became 5/29 when Loader chipped in with two wickets. Phil Ridings and Trowse put up a 67-run stand for the sixth wicket, but after a spin interlude from Bob Appleyard and Johnny Wardle, Peter May brought back Scrubs Loader to trap Trowse leg before wicket and bowl Osborne and Gregg. With Wardle claiming the wickets of medium-pacer Horsnell and slow left-arm spinner Wilson, the home team were dismissed for 123 and went down to defeat by an innings and 143 runs with a day to spare.

Tuesday January 25th.

The extra day's rest, courtesy of our expeditious despatch of South Australia, could not have come at a better time. The South Australian sun is stoking up the furnaces below the Adelaide pavements. The heat just bounces off them and hits you in the face. The sandstone buildings are heat banks, storing up the 101 degree temperature like glowing coals.

Fishing in the Glenelg River.

We are glad for Al, Peter, Bob and Johnny - glad that they are not out in the middle of the Adelaide Oval, as they should be, sweltering in the torrid conditions. Taking advantage of the sea breeze and the cool morning beachside conditions, we went for a long pre-breakfast run, south towards MacLaren Vale, though certainly not as far! The team decided to profit from our day's holiday, leave net practice and hard training until the two days preceding the Fourth Test, and play golf. We did not want to go too far to play and opted to play the Glenelg course; a sandy but lush eighteen-holes, just a drive and a low iron along the beach road, and quite close to the airport. I cannot say that I played with distinction; but I did witness the best golf stroke played on

the tour. The foursome in which I was playing had finished its round and we were relaxing over a beer in the lounge of the nineteenth hole, situated at the top of a high bank overlooking the eighteenth green.

Down the eighteenth fairway marched the Yorkshire twosome of Wardle and Appleyard, in the company of two club members. Johnny had laid up his approach iron some 40 yards short of the green. A left-hander at golf as well as at cricket, he pulled out his wedge to play a chip shot - which he hooked and hit far too hard. His ball sailed straight towards the club house, passing over our heads and landing with a tremendous clatter on the concave metal roof above us. That, we thought, was the end of Johnny's round! Not a bit of it. A few minutes later the whimsical Yorkie marched around the corner of the clubhouse and passed in front of the lounge window - carrying a long ladder on his shoulder! He propped the ladder against the side of the building, pulled an iron from his golf bag and slowly climbed the ladder, passing out of our vision as he clambered on to the roof! We heard the scraping of his studded boots on the iron roof - then nothing! Suddenly there was a loud clang above us, as though an iron golf club had struck the tin roof! A golf ball sailed into view and plopped on to the green a metre or two from the hole! 'E'en the ranks of Tuscany could scarce forbear to cheer.' We broke into loud applause, little knowing that Johnny had struck the roof with his club and then thrown the ball on to the green! What a Yorkshireman will do to win the money!

Wednesday January 26th.

Australia Day. To the accompaniment of the national anthem, flag-raising ceremonies took place today all over Australia to mark the country's National Day. For us, the preparation for the deciding game of the series began in earnest. If Australia could claw back the Adelaide Test, they could square the rubber - and possibly go on to win it by defeating us in the final game in Sydney. Early morning work-outs on the beach were succeeded by a day's hard labour at the nets, interrupted only by lunch. Hard work it may have been, but it was also a pleasure to play cricket in such surroundings. Through the

tunnel which passed under the stands and connected the net area to the concourse in front of the Father and Son Stand one could look eastwards towards the gates named after South Australia's favourite sporting son, Vic Richardson. Beyond, one could make out the squat, low lines of the Lofty Ranges which sandwiched Adelaide against St.Vincent's Gulf. The spire of St Peter's Anglican Cathedral squinted over the red, yellow and black scoreboard, as though keeping a close moral eye on those spectators who, during matches, drank at the bar on its ground floor. At the city gate end of the Oval, the River Torrens, dammed to plenitude, flowed gently the length of Memorial Drive and through the parkland adjoining North Terrace, giving the appearance of a defensive moat around the City of Colonel Light, its surveyor and founder.

After our victory in Melbourne, the selectors are not contemplating any changes to our successful team. George Statham is still troubled with the big toe of his left foot. Constant friction between the toe and the front of his boot has torn off his toe nail. He is now bowling with his toe sticking out of the hole which he has hacked in the boot's toecap to ease the pain. Knowing George as I do, I have not the slightest doubt that he will soldier on.

Don Bradman, Jack Ryder and Dudley Seddon, the Australian selectors, seem undecided about the final composition of the home team. In the past few days there has been a lot of panicky chopping and changing to the home side's final line-up. Two games after scoring 153 in Brisbane's First Test, the Aussie vice-captain, Arthur Morris, has copped all of the blame for Johnson's failure in Melbourne and has been given his marching orders. Victorian opener, Colin McDonald, replaces him. The local lad Graeme Hole has also been dropped and Les Favell - originally named in the side ahead of Morris - suffered a similar fate on the morning of the match. Morris was then resurrected at the last moment and N.S.W. opener Jimmy Burke was called up into the twelve. The major blow to the home side's hopes is the withdrawal of the match-winning fast bowler Ray Lindwall, after pulling a muscle in Queensland's game against Victoria. His replacement is the left-handed speedster Alan Davidson. The diminutive Victorian 'keeper Len Maddocks is also retained after his sterling batting display in Melbourne, but his inclusion has caused much indignation amongst the supporters of Gil Langley, the local hero. What confusion!

Thursday January 27th.

Alec Bedser is well acquainted with the hard 'yakka' of bowling on the Adelaide Oval. He knows just how unrewarding it is to pound the ball down on its unresponsive featherbed strip, beneath a blazing sun and in the merciless heat which South Australia can turn on day... after day... after day! In the southern state it is not unusual for temperatures to top the century mark for a week at a time. And observing 'Sod's Law', such heatwaves usually coincide with the Adelaide Test. Alec remembers one occasion in Adelaide in 1947 when he had to bowl for most of one day in 102 degree heat. After his last over, he was completely befuddled and had to be led from the ground by his team mates. Not knowing where he was, he stumbled up the steps through the Father and Son Enclosure, past the Press Box and into the England dressing room. There the team physiotherapist took him into the showers, sat him down on a wooden chair, fully-clothed and still wearing his boots, and turned on the cold tap. It took almost three quarters of an hour for the big Surrey bowler to come round from his heat exhaustion!

On previous visits to Adelaide, Alec has also found it almost impossible to get a good night's sleep in non-air-conditioned city hotels. After a week of torrid days and hot nights, bedrooms in such pubs become sweatboxes. Alec asked his friends, the Warrens, for help and they invited him to stay with them in their weekend home, high in the Lofty Ranges, where the evenings are ten degrees cooler than in the city. Alec still takes refuge there, on hot nights. Our present sojourn in Adelaide is tempered by the ocean breezes which waft around and cool the Pier Hotel at Glenelg. There is no need to 'head for the hills' but it was great, however, to be taken by the Warrens and Alec for a day's excursion - just an hour's drive - to the Warrens' place in Lofty Ranges. While the Adelaide Oval dressing rooms are hot, they are also comfortable and airy, well equipped with a massage table for Woozer Dalton, a fridge for cool drinks, ample fans, easy access to the nets down a metal stairway at the rear of the changing area and a spacious viewing area for the players overlooking the Oval from square-leg.

Since my successes in Sydney and Melbourne, a couple of pressmen have been hounding me to write a column for their papers. I have already agreed to contribute to the *Empire News* for a tenner a week; and now my Middleton team-mate, John Kay, has put the hard word on me to do a piece for the *Manchester Evening News* for a similar amount. I hope there is no conflict of interest.

Net practice was flat-out as usual. We look as if we should be hitting our peak tomorrow. I feel great! A quiet night before the big game.

Friday January 28th

Another scorcher. After a gentle loosening run along the beach, we left for the ground, relaxed but keen. Most of the 35,000 spectators who attended the first day of the game were already inside the gates by the time that we disembarked from our Holden fleet at the Memorial Drive or River Torrens gates, wended our way along the concourse in front of the stands and climbed to the dressing room. As we were sipping our pre-match cup of tea, a loud cheering reached our ears. We went to the viewing area of the dressing room and looked down on the Member's gate in front of the George Giffen Stand. The cheering was a welcome for Gil Langley, the deposed Aussie wicket-keeper and local hero, as he made his way towards the Aussie dressing room!

Right up to the toss, no-one seemed absolutely sure about the final composition of the Australian team. It was only when Ian Johnson tossed with the Skipper that it was revealed that Favell had been dropped and Morris re-instated in the opening bat position. McDonald was given the nod to partner Morris, Jimmy Burke replaced Hole and Davidson was added to the fast bowling strength of the home side. With the temperature hovering around the century mark, Johnson struck the first blow for Australia by winning the toss and jumping at the opportunity to bat first on an excellent batting pitch. When lunch arrived McDonald and Morris were still together with 51 runs on the board. The only excitement came when Morris offered a difficult chance to Hutton's left hand at slip off the bowling of Statham. It looked like being a hard day for our bowlers!

Responding to the Skipper's nursing us in short spells, George, Trevor and I hung on like bulldogs for the remainder of the day, restricting the home side to 161 for the loss of four wickets. After 110 minutes of perseverance, I struck the first blow for England by having Morris caught off his gloves by Godfrey. McDonald, after being missed by Compo off a dolly at mid-on, tried to hit his way out of frustration and edged Appleyard to May at slip. I came back into the attack to have Burke caught at short-leg and, after tea, Brian and I alternated at the River Torrens end as Trevor kept the cork tight on the scoring bottle from the Cathedral crease. The Boil's fine spell was rewarded with the wicket of Harvey caught at slip, but Benaud and Miller held the fort until close of play. Nonetheless we were not unhappy with our position at the end of the first day's play.

Saturday January 29th.

There was no extravagant expenditure of energy this morning - either trotting along the beach or bowling at the nets. The mercury is still high and we are still a little weary from yesterday's exertions. In spite of this, we are still pretty upbeat - we did well on the first day of the game. A warm-up at the nets got us ready for the resumption of hostilities. With the need to conserve our energy for the second new ball a paramount consideration, Len only bowled 'George' and me for a couple of overs before tossing the ball to Bob Appleyard and Johnny Wardle. The result was immediate and indicative of what was to follow. 'Applecart' got the ball to bite, cut and bounce and he picked up the wickets of both Benaud and Miller in the space of two overs. An Archer six-hit off the Yorkshire left-arm spinner was the signal for the Skipper to beckon Trevor and me to the bowling crease. Immediately I had Archer caught in the slips and Davo was caught behind by a strangely listless and fallible Evans. Godfrey is an enigma; sometimes his athleticism is breathtaking and you would swear that there is not a better keeper in the world. No-one else could have taken the leg-side catch which he conjured up to dismiss Neil Harvey in the Melbourne Test. As a plus, the Kentish dynamo

keeps us all on our toes with exhortations to 'stick to the ship lads!' Yet when his interest lapses, he is strangely lackadaisical. Sometimes he misses straightforward chances - but he is so good at hiding such chances that no-one on the field knows.

Johnson should have been run out with the score standing at 270, but Appleyard hurled the ball high over Godder's head, with both Maddocks and the Aussie skipper at the same end. The error cost us 92 runs - which in the final analysis meant we had to bat a second time. Eventually the home side staggered to a 323 total against bowling which wilted in the heat. Brian flagged as his big toe began to bleed; he must have been in pain. Subsequent redemption came in the shape of our best opening stand of the series. Len and the battle-scarred W.J. were still together at stumps with 50 runs on the board.

Sunday January 30th.

Yesterday evening I dined with John Arlott and some friends, one of whom is Max Harris. Max is the proprietor of a gourmet restaurant in the city, where he serves wonderful food and - as one would expect of any of John's friends - magnificent South Australian wines. Max is a writer and distinguished poet. As a student at Adelaide University he became involved in what was known as the 'Ern Malley affair'. He and a group of his fellow undergrads published what the South Australian police and justice department regarded as obscene material in a student magazine. The group were arrested in a park for offensive behaviour, at which stage it seemed that the authorities had mounted a vendetta against them. The students were then held up to ridicule when their magazine printed a volume of avant-garde poems allegedly written by a certain Ern Malley. Malley's existence was authenticated by 'family members' and the publishers hailed his verses as masterpieces. It was then that the spurious authors of the poems revealed their true identity and said that they had cobbled the poems together from telephone directories and various disparate and very unpoetic sources!

Dinner was in an elegant Adelaide hills home, overlooking the fairy-lit wonderland of the city. Our host was dressed in a loose shirt and legionnaire pantaloons, and seemed very pre-occupied with psychology. When he discovered that I was the brutal fast bowler who, he had read, was committing Test match mayhem on inoffensive batsmen, he asked me if my mother or father had abused me when I was young. The only excuse he could find for my violent behaviour towards my fellow-man was that I was suffering from an inverted Oedipus complex! It proved to be a lively dinner party with stimulating intelligent conversation!

Today a group of prominent Adelaide sportsmen took most of the M.C.C. party to the Barossa Valley, where they visited the Hill-Smith, Pewsey Vale vineyard and the Lindsay Park horse stud.

Monday January 31st.

Australia struck two quick blows at the outset of the third day's play. Bill Johnston swung one in late to flatten Bill Edrich's off-stump, but not before W.J. had helped Hutton to assemble England's best opening partnership of the series. This bonus was squandered, however, when 1/60 became 2/63; a Benaud leg-spinner found the edge of P.B.H's bat and Archer at slip scooped up a spectacular slip catch, low and to his right. Though we had lost Peter's invaluable wicket, there was still reason for Appleyard and Wardle to smile - just a little! It did not escape their keen Yorkshire notice that Benaud had turned the ball quite appreciably - and quickly! And it was only the third day of the game!

Len and Kipper then took command and were one short of a century partnership when the Skipper was deprived of his first hundred of the Test summer by the atrocious luck which has dogged him from the moment he stepped ashore in Perth. Big Bill Johnston served up one of his rare long hops; Hutton seized the moment and, moving on to the back foot, hit a full-blooded pull. Davidson, fielding at short-leg, sensed trouble was heading his way and turned his back on the stroke. The ball hit him squarely between the shoulder blades and ricocheted slowly upwards for the fieldsman to do a left turn and complete a now easy catch! Poor Len! He looked so completely in control that it seemed inconceivable that he should not transform his 80 into three figures!

Fortunately Compton and Cowdrey carried on his good work and at close of play England were well placed, 93 runs behind with seven wickets in reserve.

Tuesday February 1st.

This morning Keith Miller lived up to my high opinion of his superlative all-round talents. He shared the second new ball with his gifted fellow all-rounder and New South Welshman, Alan Davidson, and, together, they swung the ball to such good effect that our eight remaining batsmen added only 111 more runs. Strange, how that supposedly unlucky 'Nelson' figure of 111 keeps cropping up in this series. We dismissed Australia for 111 in its second innings at Melbourne!

How I admire Miller! He has such a wonderful attitude towards life. Once during the tour, he saw me looking worried and asked after the cause of my anxiety. He then helped me to put matters into perspective by enquiring if I could remember what I was worrying about a year previously. When I answered that I couldn't, he made the wonderfully perspicacious observation which put everything in true proportion: "Then why were you worrying then - and why are you worrying now?"

Nugget began the batting rot by trapping his kindred spirit and good mate, Denis Compton, l.b.w for 44, after two hours of intense concentration. Then Davidson ended Cowdrey's five-hour 79 when he persuaded him to flash at an angled outswinger and keeper Maddocks did the rest. Fortunately The Boil did his stuff and dropped anchor for 38 runs,

and, with Godfrey chipping in with another 37 and Johnny Wardle slashing a further 23, we finished with a lead of just 18. I made a complete fool of myself, prodding and probing without producing a positive stroke. I am always troubled by the sun when I bat in Adelaide. It seems to shine at the most inconvenient angles. The 18-run lead was not enough - or so we thought - but our opinion changed before the end of the day.

It was at this vital stage that Len showed his true Yorkshire 'nous'; and after today's events there can be no doubting his shrewd leadership qualities. As we took the field for the second time in the game, the Aussie batsmen braced themselves for the usual fast, ferocious, full-frontal attack from our shock troops. But Brian and I only got a couple of overs! Then Len took the ball, examined it to see how much shine was left on it - and tossed it to Bob Appleyard! It was a courageous tactic, especially after the previous successes of our pace attack. But it was a move which subsequently proved to be hailed as a stroke of genius. Bowling into the bowlers' footmarks, Appleyard made his medium-paced off-cutters kick and turn - to the complete discomfiture of the left-handers Morris and Harvey! Arty got a delivery which stopped on him and he pushed a catch back to the bowler. Burke only survived briefly before being rolled by a beauty. Harvey followed him back to the pavilion, bowled by a delivery which pitched in line with his leg-stump and clipped the off bail as he attempted to glance it! In 10 overs, Appleyard conceded only 13 runs and took three wickets, leaving Australia 3/69 when the umpires called time.

Wednesday February 2nd.

'George' and I followed our usual routine this morning and went for a jog along the beach. We chatted about what Len's tactics would be when the match resumed, little realising that he was about to place his hopes on our shoulders - and call for one last supreme effort! Between breakfast and leaving for the ground I lay on my bed and read the local broadsheet, the *Adelaide Advertiser*. To a man the pundits in the press and broadcasting boxes were unanimous: Appleyard with his fast off-spinners was the danger man as far as the Aussie batsmen were concerned. The scribes little knew the devious workings of Len Hutton's mind!

As we stepped down from our Holdens in front of the South Australian Cricket Association offices and entered the gates of the Adelaide Oval, the 90 degree heat hit us in the face. It was warm just to walk. But I did not think I would be doing much bowling today. Not with a wearing wicket and Bob Appleyard raring to go!

Warm-up practice behind us, Len led us on to the field. He picked up the comparatively new ball left on the turf in front of the pavilion, examined it carefully, and gave it a polish. Everyone was expecting him to give it to Appleyard. But having bowled Appleyard instead of Brian and I earlier, he now tossed the ball - not to

Appleyard, but to Statham! At the same time he indicated to me that I should be bowling at the River Torrens End. It was the psychological master-stroke of the captain of a side which had established a fast-bowling supremacy over its opposition. Half a dozen overs later, George had bowled McDonald and Miller and had Maddocks l.b.w. I provided support by trapping Benaud l.b.w., having Archer caught behind and Johnston taken by Appleyard. After an hour's maximum effort Brian and I were still bowling and still Len gave no hint of an approaching rest. At lunch we had bowled without respite for the full session of 90 minutes, taken a joint six wickets for 34 runs, and Australia were 9/103. Not bad on a turning wicket! My groin ached, but still Brian urged me on. 'Come on. Just another wicket to go.' He himself was bowling with his bloodied big toe protruding from the hole which he had hacked in his left boot. We did not quite finish the task Len had set us. It was left to Wardle to claim Davidson's wicket l.b.w. in the first over after lunch, setting us just 94 runs to win the Test match and the series.

What ensued was a classical demonstration of the truism that a cricket match is not over until the last ball is bowled. We began our run-chase badly. It was all due to that man again! Not the comedian, Tommy Handley - but the very serious Keith Miller! A beautiful inswinger sliced its way through Bill Edrich's defences and crashed into his stumps. One wicket down for three became three for 18 when Cowdrey nicked an

Hutton and Edrich go out to bat at Adelaide for the second time - 94 needed for the Ashes.

outswinger into the hands of Archer at slip and Hutton followed suit, picking out Davidson at the wider slip as his preferred catcher. Len came back to the pavilion in despair. His life's ambition was to beat Australia 'on its own midden'. And here we were within a heartbeat of achieving that goal - and we were throwing our chance away! As Denis Compton picked up his bat to go out to join battle with Nugget, The Skipper paced the dressing room, muttering: 'The buggers have done us again!'

'I'll show you who's done who!' riposted a defiant D.C.S.

And he did! But not before Peter May had been dubiously caught by Miller at cover off the bowling of Johnston for 26, when we were 45 runs from victory. Diving to take the catch, Miller placed his body between the ball and the line of vision of both the umpire and P.B.H.

'Did you catch it?' asked Peter.

When Nugget nodded, Peter walked. From our spot in the viewing box we could see that the ball bounced out of Miller's hands and hit the ground. He maintained that he had held it long enough for it to be deemed a fair catch. We begged to differ. It was the most unworthy thing that I ever saw Keith do on the cricket field. 'Barnacle' Bailey hung on and Compton played the strokes, until we were four runs from victory. Falling l.b.w. to Big Bill Johnston, Trevor was replaced by Godders, who refused to bow to the gravity of the situation and immediately hit the winning boundary. He departed crowd-chased and waving his bat aloft - and England had won a series in Australia for the first time since Bodyline. His duodenal ulcers forgotten, John Woodcock of *The Times* - the convalescent guest in the team's viewing box - almost went through the roof as he jumped to his feet, cheering and jubilant! Even Len permitted himself a smile!

Then the celebrations began, firstly with the champagne in the dressing room and then in the South Australian Cricket Association Committee room. Then it was back to the Pier Hotel where, after a brief stop for mafficking

Adelaide - the crowd in front of the dressing room after the Ashes victory.

with our supporters - rugby league 'great' Arthur Hughes, Sam Stott, still travelling incognito, and Spen Cama et alia - we were off to a party at the Warrens'. I spent most of that celebration under the grand piano asleep, and consequently missed the spectacular failures of Bill Edrich's egg-trick. W.J. was still in the limelight when I returned to the Pier Hotel in the early hours. He was atop a smooth marble pillar in the colonnaded lounge, having swarmed up some 20 feet to win a bet. How he got down, I never found out! This morning the manager, Geoffrey Howard, told us that we had drunk 56 bottles of champagne just at the hotel!

Chapter Eleven

Dear Old Pals

Thursday February 3rd.

ARTHUR HUGHES LOOKED dreadful this morning at breakfast. And he is still celebrating! Keith and I spent the morning in town shopping. We ran into Keith Miller and Neil Harvey in Rundle Mall; apparently they are on their way to have morning tea with one of Nugget's many friends! The rest of the day was peaceful preparing for our trip to Melbourne, where we shall be playing a country and state game. Several of the team are travelling overnight to Melbourne on the 'Overlander'. The remainder is following tomorrow by air.

Friday February 4th.

Rising at an obscenely early hour, we were in the Windsor Hotel, Melbourne by lunch-time. We settled in for a fortnight's stay. With only three state and country games to play plus the final Test of a dead series, the pressures of travel and cricket have lessened considerably. Originally we intended dropping our heavy luggage at the Windsor and taking the train up to the coal mining town of Yallourn in Gippsland, where we are to play our next game. But the General Motors agency have very kindly loaned us four or five Holdens so that we can drive the

two-hour, ninety-mile trip at leisure. I am not in the team to play in the Victorian Country eleven, but I chose to accompany the side because I have arranged to meet up with the Jenkins. Alan and Rita's practice is quite close to Yallourn at Maffra: a dairy farming area and the headquarters of the Nestlé Company. They tell me they have a charming partner, Dr. Silvani. They migrated from Tyneside ten months ago and I think they find life much more rewarding Down Under than under the National Health Scheme.

About 6.30 in the evening the M.C.C. motor cavalcade drove into Yallourn. The complement of our car consisted of Reg Simpson (driver), Tyson (co-driver - though I do not own a car), and Andrew and Edrich (backseat and reckless drivers). Reg did a marvellous job, driving at dusk through the Pentland Hills, along narrow unlit roads through a confusion of leafless, grey ghost gums. Dinner at the local hotel was an excellent, hearty meal, after which we were encouraged to pop along to see the local open-cut brown coal mine, which operates 24 hours a day.

It is enormous: more than a mile long and 300 feet from top to bottom! Brobdingnagian robots slide slowly along horizontal rails set in the flanks of the man-made valley of the open-cut,

Alan Jenkins and myself at Yallourn.

slicing and scooping out gigantic slabs of peat-like fibrous brown coal. They look like the machines from Mars, described in H.G. Wells's *War of the Worlds*. Apparently this seam of brown coal lies beneath a layer of topsoil just 15-feet thick. It was discovered by an old prospector and developed by German migrants whose original factory is still standing. Amazingly it stretches for 40 miles far into the distant Great Dividing Range and contains enough coal to provide fossil fuel to supply Australia for 1000 years! The entire mining operation is completely mechanised and one seldom sees human movement in the cut. When the mine is fully developed, it will entail moving the town of Yallourn to dig out the coal beneath it. Brown coal is coal which has not completely formed. To use it, the peat-like substance has to be moulded into briquettes for domestic use. Research is being conducted into commercial gasification possibilities.

Saturday February 5th.

Last night I stayed with Alan and Rita in Maffra. Alan had driven down to Yallourn in his trusty Ford Prefect to meet me. After we managed to shake off the crushing hospitality of the local cricketers and escape from the hotel, we got on board the little saloon and set off. At the outset of our journey, Alan told me that Maffra was 'just down the road'. He meant 'just down the road' by Australian, not English, standards. It took us a good hour's motoring to get there - and having been led to expect it to be closer, I kept anticipating it around the next corner! It was 9.30p.m. when we finally arrived. It was the first time I had met Rita and we had a long chat well into the night to get acquainted. This morning we made an early start to get to the match before the first ball was bowled.

We were not expecting luxurious facilities at the ground, but we were taken aback at just how primitive they turned out to be. To be brutally honest, while the pitch for the game was quite good, the general match facilities were absolutely dreadful. Because of the twenty-four-hour excavations going on less than a mile from the oval, the air was thick with coal dust and everything we touched seemed filthy. The press were housed in a primitive tarpaulin tent and their desks were planks resting on what seemed to be barrels. The flies were both enormous and present in plague proportions. Scrubs Loader swallowed one of them half-way through his run-up, choked, and had to leave the field. He reckoned there was enough meat on it to last him a week!

The 'Ger got a game - scored nought not out - and did not get on the field after that. In his younger days he kept wickets in a handful of first-class games and he was a regular for London Banks. Surprisingly, K.V. did not keep, allowing Godfrey to don the gloves. Equally surprisingly, the Victorian Country Eleven opted to bat first after winning the toss - thus depriving the Saturday crowd of the opportunity of

The Press Box at Yallourn. Seated from the left are John Kay, unknown thought to be John Batty, Ray Robinson, Jack Fingleton.

The 'Ger makes his tour debut.

seeing the tourists' batting stars. This gave Alec and Scrubs the chance of having a good work-out after a week of comparative inactivity during the Fourth Test.

We only fielded three regular bowlers - but they proved more than enough for the country players to handle. Wardle, bowling his 'over-the-wrist' stuff, had all of the opposing batsmen bamboozled and took 12/91 in the game. His 5/46 in the first innings, together with Loader's 4/29, limited the country eleven to a 182-run total. At the close of the first day we had reached 0/130, with Hutton and Simpson giving us the best opening we have had on tour.

The memories of the Brisbane Test are now just faint and bitter echoes of the past. Ironic how past failures fade into nothingness and players begin to find their true form when the tour is drawing to a conclusion! Johnny Wardle, for instance, is now bowling his wrist spin as well as he bowled his more orthodox finger-spin in Perth. He has learned to disguise his true turning intentions by beginning the swing of his bowling arm behind his body. This action seems to give him more lateral shoulder-swing, more drag on the ball and consequently greater spin as he releases it. Whatever the truth of the matter, Wardle is now a match-winner. Our tragedy is that it has taken him nearly four months to reach that status.

Wardle's Yorkshire colleague, Apple-yard, revealed in the Adelaide Test that he is a great bowler. Well over six feet in height, his bowling arm comes right over the top, producing disconcerting bounce. He cuts rather than spins the ball at genuine medium-pace. Indeed his speed is such that, for his county, he often takes the new ball at the opposite end to Fred Trueman. He well knows how to employ the shine and run the ball late towards the slips. Opposing batsmen therefore have to decide which is Applecart's off-cutter and which is his outswinger. And they do not have much time! His action is all arm and open, but it is sharp enough to hurry most batsmen's strokes. The relationship between Appleyard and Wardle is oddly out of place in members of the same team. It almost amounts to a bitter rivalry.

Scrubs Loader is also proving a late developer of the tour. His control is now immaculate. His slower ball is mystifyingly subtle, his swing is almost in the Lindwall class and his bouncer is as unexpected as it is physically dangerous - some say because it is suspect. The trouble is that he is his own worst enemy. He loses his temper at the slightest provocation. And with the loss of his rag goes his control. Big Al is now over his fitness problems and back to his best. What can one say about such a great bowler? His inswinger is back. His leg-cutter has returned. His control is now immaculate. He is the Bedser of old - Before Shingles! It would not be an unwarranted selection to slot him in to the England line-up for the Fifth Test in Sydney.

On the batting front, Reg Simpson is middling the ball sweetly. Surely, he too, deserves consideration when the selectors sit down to choose the team for Sydney? He must have a chance ahead of W.J., who has not reached the half-century mark in a first-class game since his second innings in the Brisbane Test?

Sunday February 6th.

Yesterday evening K.V. returned with Alan and me to Maffra. We had dinner with the Jenkins and then we went to visit the Pennyfathers. The Pennyfather family is country aristocracy. It used to own a large station just outside Maffra. Everything about the Pennyfathers seems large: Mr. Pennyfather himself; his family; his homestead and his wealth. His holdings are much diminished. He now works his farm with only one hired hand - and he is down to his last half-million pounds. One of the gentlemen whom we met at the Pennyfathers has just returned from a ten-month trip to Europe: a family holiday which cost him £20,000! The wealth of the Australian squattocracy is absolutely staggering - at least to a lad from a Lancashire mill town!

The Maffra area is divided into small farms, many of which were settled by ex-servicemen returning from the two World Wars. It is the greenest spot we have visited in Australia and the land is rich and productive. Irrigated land in Gippsland is priced at about £250 an acre. The daily output of milk from the farms around Maffra alone is 75,000 gallons! Small wonder that the Swiss dairy company, Nestlé, has made its headquarters in the town!

Alan and his family have settled in famously in this little community. It is a completely different lifestyle for a man educated in the English Public School system, at St. Bees in Cumberland and Durham University, and growing up in north-eastern England. Rita - a real

Keith and myself at Yallourn - the contented tourists.

Geordie - has had to adapt too! No doubt the family's bush location is going to mean some radical changes to the education arrangements for their children, Caroline, Andrew and Stephen. They must also miss their English families and friends. As the local GPs, they run the town's cottage hospital and they are on call 24-hours a day.

Alan has involved himself in local affairs since he first arrived in Maffra. At first he turned out each weekend for the Maffra cricket team. He told the skipper that he had opened the batting for Durham University and was sent in first. What he did not realise was that cricket on a concrete wicket in the Australian bush is a vastly different game to that he played with the Durham Medics. The bounce of the pitch is more pronounced and the outfield is only mown once a month. Alan was brought up on school and varsity wickets and schooled in the principle of keeping his strokes on the turf. In his first game for Maffra, he played in classical fashion and his drives sped all along the floor - until they hit the long grass just off the square. Then they stopped dead! As a result, all that Alan had to show for his efforts after an hour's batting was a couple of singles! His skipper, who was batting at the opposite end, came down the pitch.

'Yer playin' good Doc. But 'ittin' it along the deck is gettin' nowhere. Yer'v gotta 'it it inter the air!'

Thereafter Alan found it rather difficult to get time off on Saturdays!

We spent today visiting the Great Gippsland Lakes, which are about 40 miles to the east of Maffra and about 200 miles from Melbourne. The lakes are contiguous, narrow inland water-ways which are about a mile wide, run parallel to the ocean and stretch for many miles along the coast. A narrow ridge of sand-dunes some 20 yards across and 20 feet high separates the lakes from the sea, making them ideally safe for boating. On the ocean side of the dunes is a long beach, the name of which - 90 Mile Beach - gives some idea of its extent. There is one man-made entrance and exit between sea and lake, at a spot which, unsurprisingly, is called Lakes Entrance. The tides race through this narrow channel of water at an alarming speed, and govern the advent and egress of the fishing fleet based at Lakes Entrance.

This morning was the first time in my life when I have been awoken by silence: an utter stillness unbroken by even the sound of birdsong. By 9.30a.m. we were on our way, heading

On the Great Gippsland Lakes with the Jenkins.

K.V. and his crew on the Great Gippsland Lakes.

for Bairnsdale and thence to Paynesville, a little village on the lakes, where we got on board a large motor launch moored there and owned by our host for the day: the Maffra publican who rejoiced in the cricketing name of 'Dick Pollard'. Dick was a remarkable man, with a great thirst - as he demonstrated by opening the bar as soon as we embarked. Dick's taste for beer once led to his asking a receptionist for a glass - even though he was checking into a hospital!

It was extremely hot, but the sea breeze made our voyage to Lakes Entrance - broken only by a stop at Metung - very pleasant. At Lakes Entrance we had a picnic lunch and visited the Gilder family. John Gilder was one of the crew of the launch. And thereby hangs a tale.

Fred Gilder, his father, was up at Oxford with Douglas Jardine - of Bodyline fame. John told the tale of how, during that tour, Jardine took time off to pay a visit to his father's station for a couple of days' shooting. During his fellow dark-blue's stay, Fred Gilder took Jardine to witness a bush cricket match: a game played on a bouncy 'cement' pitch and rough outfield. A ferociously fast bowler - an Irishman called Lannigan - was playing in the game. Jardine was persuaded to face a couple of balls from him, one of which almost decapitated the England skipper. It is strange to think that the Bodyline crisis was almost averted - before it began - in a little Gippsland village, by an Aussie 'Larwood from the Bush'!

We had a swim then headed home, trailing fishing lines. The boat trip back from Lakes Entrance was choppy and I was a bit sea-sick by the time we moored again in Paynesville and transferred to Alan's little Ford Escort. The road back to Maffra was littered with dead rabbits and, in one instance, a large and very deceased wallaby.

It being our last evening with the Jenkins, Alan and Rita had a few friends in for drinks. Keith and I were introduced to a host of people. It is utterly impossible to remember all of their names, but I do recall Graeme and Jill McKinnon and the Silvanis: the local dentist, his wife and the Jenkins' medical partner. We dined out but were in bed by midnight - a long day behind us and an early start ahead of us on the morrow.

Monday February 7th.

Rising early we were on our way to Yallourn at 7a.m. The weather cooled while we were out on the lakes yesterday and today it remains overcast. Back at the ground, the local lads had conjured up some extra canopies to provide additional shade for both the players and the press. The flies still pestered me, in spite of the fact that one of our hosts had gone to the trouble of searching out a fly net to cover my head.

When the game resumed, we batted on and piled on the runs until we declared at 8/307: the highlight of which total was the manager's 0 not out and a colourful 17 from Godders batting in a green sun-hat! The Victorian Country Eleven's second innings disintegrated in the space of

23.5 overs, Wardle claiming 7/45 in a paltry total of 99. The end result was an easy M.C.C. win by an innings and 26 runs.

This evening I shared a room with Big Al, to be ready to depart early for Melbourne in the morning. We tried to get into the local cinema - but it was a case of 'no room at the inn'. So we spent a hilarious evening playing 'hookey' at the home of the hotel receptionist.

Tuesday February 8th.

It was raining when we motored back to Melbourne today. We passed through a damp Latrobe Valley, skirting the towns of Moe and Morwell whose enormous power stations are fed on Yallourn's brown coal and supply most of the Melbourne metropolitan area and the state of Victoria with electricity.

When Len Hutton and Godders walked into the Windsor Hotel this morning they were pleasantly surprised to be greeted by their wives: Dorothy and Jean. Lord's has apparently relaxed its embargo on wives touring with their husbands. Mrs. Hutton and Mrs. Evans have just flown in. Not having previously met them, I was introduced.

The rain has set in and no practice was possible today. It is a practice much to be desired - since I have not picked up a ball for nearly a fortnight. But one cannot do anything about the Melbourne weather. It was a day for shopping and the cinema.

Wednesday February 9th.

We again awoke to sombre grey skies and incessant rain. Time passes slowly. Reading and the cinema seem the only remedy to crushing boredom. It is even a welcome diversion to sign the autograph books of the enthusiasts who seem to be everywhere in the lobby of the Windsor. We went to the ground, but there was no hope of net practice; it was flooded - although the square was completely swaddled in a huge rectangle of tarpaulins. So it was back to the hotel and after lunch, a stroll down Bourke Street and another visit to the flicks. Fortunately we have found an excellent restaurant and this evening we were the dinner guests of a Baron, no less, at Claridge's: a gourmet's haven which also provides entertainment in the form of singing waiters. Good food, a glass of wine and music lit up an otherwise drab and damp evening.

Thursday February 10th.

More and yet more rain. We shall certainly remember Melbourne. And the forecast is no better for tomorrow. We dined again at Claridge's and then went on to the theatre, courtesy of Denis Compton, who obtained a few tickets from his friends and English neighbours, John McCallum and Googie Withers, who are appearing in

UNSAFE BEHIND THE IRON CURTAIN. *Frank Tyson obliges every junior inhabitant of Yallourn, a Victorian open cut coal centre, with his autograph. He signed over 2,000 autographs before sailing, spent many hours on board signing photographs, and then spent much of his time off making Australia's children happy with some 4,000 further signatures. Tyson, having helped to win the rubber at Adelaide, wasn't playing at Yallourn. He was there to look on. And the kids were there to look on at Tyson.*

Signing autographs at Yallourn.

the show. The show was called *Simon and Laura*, and the unanimous team verdict was 'very good' - especially the first act. All this social activity is rendered more permissible - and consequently more enjoyable - by the fact that Geoffrey Howard has told me that my services will not be required in tomorrow's game against Victoria.

Friday February 11th.

Today was the first scheduled day of the match against Victoria. But our total Friday cricket activity consisted of going down to the Melbourne Cricket Ground. There was absolutely no hope of any play on the first day of the match. The meteorological office tells us that the eastern Australian seaboard is totally enveloped in a deep depression. The endless rain in Melbourne bears out its forecast. Ian Johnson, the Victorian and Australian skipper, is still incapacitated by the injury which kept him out of the Adelaide Test and the all-rounder, Sam Loxton, has stepped up to the plate. Sam is an ebullient character, a complete cricketer and a member of Bradman's 1948 undefeated team which toured England. He is leading a strong side which includes Test men, McDonald, Harvey, Loxton himself, Maddocks, Johnston, and top-spinner, Jack Hill. Unfortunately they got no opportunity to display their skills; they had to remain in the dressing rooms for the whole of the day playing cards, reading and filling in time as best they could. There was never a suggestion of

the curator even beginning to lift the covers off the pitch

Saturday February 12th.

At long last our game against Victoria got under way on the second scheduled day of the game. The rain finally stopped, but the atmosphere remains heavy and humid. Beneath its topcoat of waterproof covers, the wicket is bound to have sweated enough to offer swinging and seaming encouragement to George, Scrubs and The Boil - as well as providing some spinning assistance to Wardle and Appleyard. And so it proved to be.

Loxton won the toss and Victoria elected to bat. That was the home side's first mistake. The surrounds of the centre square were slippery, viscous, black Merri Creek clay and treacherous underfoot. In spite of this handicap, our bowlers outdid themselves - so much so that McDonald, the two Harveys, Lindsay Hassett's nephew John Shaw, Kendall and Maddocks were all back in the hutch within the space of 39 runs. It was left to Loxton and the left-handed spinner Dick to salvage some respect-ability from incipient ruin. Even so their 53-run stand could only patch together a mediocre total of 113. In reply, tonight at close we have lost Bill Edrich's wicket for 90, May and Simpson each being 33 not out.

Today, the control and speed of Statham, Bailey and Appleyard yielded each of them three wickets for 23, 22 and 14 respectively. The M.C.C. bowlers were right at the top of their form. I doubt whether any batting side in the cricket world could have withstood their combined might.

Sunday February 13th.

Today was a rest day - but it really did not matter. The rain bucketed down all day. This is our last stay in Melbourne; and if today is any indication of what the weather is usually like here, I cannot say that we are sorry to be leaving. I have been all the more miserable because I have not heard from Margaret. I have written to her twice but I have not received a reply from her since Adelaide and I am at a loss to know what has happened. I mooched around the hotel all day. It was not even worth setting foot outside.

Monday February 14th.

We were supposed to have resumed the Victorian game today. Some hopes! The weekend rain has left the ground under water. There is disaster all around the State. Melbourne telephones are completely inoperable and there has been one drowning in a swollen river. Team bad news came with the announcement that The Boil has broken a finger of his right hand while fielding. We can only hope that he will recover before the start of the Fifth Test.

Tuesday February 15th

Today was the same story as on previous days. Heavy and sporadic showers continually drenched the M.C.G. and there was never any hope of a resumption of play. The game was abandoned as a draw and we took the opportunity to pack early at the ground, before returning to the hotel to get ready for our usual overnight rail trip to Sydney.

Chapter Twelve

Sydney's Fifth Test

Wednesday February 16th.

THIS EVENING WE WERE OFF ON our final train trip, back to the Harbour City, changing as usual at the border town of Albury. Reg Simpson was in high spirits and the trip was made more interesting by two intruders who insinuated themselves into the Tyson-Andrew compartment. Apparently there had been a double booking. Confusion reigned supreme, necessitating our calling the conductor. Then Admiral George Duckworth joined in. Finally we got some peace, but not before I received a tumblerful of water straight in the eye!

Keith then decided to explain to me why he insisted on sleeping on the upper bunk. It had something to do with there being less movement up there, away from the carriage's centre of gravity. It was all Greek and engineering theory to me!

At 7a.m. we arrived in Sydney's Central Station. I was rather apprehensive. I had written twice to Margaret but without reply. It transpired that she never received the mail. I can only presume that the letters had been intercepted - by whom is only a matter for conjecture!

We are staying at Usher's Hotel once again. It is very much more convenient, being in the centre of Sydney

Thursday February 17th.

A game of cricket at last! Tomorrow I am in the side to play against New South Wales. It will be the first time in a fortnight that I have stepped on to a cricket field. And the weather in Victoria was so bad that there has not been a chance to net or practice since we left Adelaide. When the M.C.C. left England with what many people thought a top-heavy touring party of 18, the selectors little knew how difficult it was going to be to give every player chosen a fair go. I really feel sorry for men like Reg Simpson, Vic Wilson, K.V., Scrubs and even Alec Bedser. Their omission from the Test team has severely limited their chances of proving themselves. And they are all Test performers who are now striking top form - ironically at the end of the trip! I have been lucky. My performances in the Sydney and Melbourne Tests created early opportunities for me, without which I would probably have ended up in the ranks of the supernumeraries - as Len said I might at our Orsova conference at the beginning of the trip.

As a result of my lay-off, I am not feeling very fit. There has not even been much chance to go running! Moreover, the approaching game is a tough re-introduction to competitive

Reg Simpson had plenty of time for relaxation on tour.

cricket. New South Wales is one of the strongest teams in the Sheffield Shield competition - and it is captained by the most imaginative and aggressive of captains - K.R.Miller! This morning the England practice was conducted at full throttle. In the light of subsequent injuries to Scrubs and myself, perhaps we overdid it. The fast bowlers, however, could not pull out all of the stops; the nets were too lively. Sydney wickets this season have the reputation of being green and quick. This is not surprising when the home team has in its ranks pacemen of the calibre of Miller, Pat Crawford and Alan Davidson. The teams for this game have been determined as much by availability and injury as by merit. The State team was unable to include its

regular opening batsmen, Watson and 'Arty' Morris, who have been chosen for the West Indies tour in March and are nursing stiff arms as a result of inoculations. Batsman Brian Booth and leg-spinning all-rounder Peter Philpott replace them in what is a very young New South Wales line-up - six players being under the age of 25.

Friday February 18th.

There was rain in the air as the two captains tossed for innings. Miller, however, scorned the odds and the elements, won the spin and decided to take first strike. It proved to be a costly mistake. Briggs, who in statistical terms is one of the most consistent batsmen in Sydney District Cricket and, indeed, in

Australia, became the caught-behind victim of a Bedser leg-cutter off the first ball of the innings. The big Surrey bowler is now back to his most formidable form - as he went on to demonstrate by having Burke caught at slip in the same over and then trapping Benaud, pouched by Wardle. I chipped in by having Simpson caught by Graveney at slip and when Loader imitated my example to claim the wicket of Miller, New South Wales were staggering at 5/26. It took a courageous stand of 86 from the two international ingénues, 'Percy' Philpott and 'Sam' Booth, to take the home side into three figures and eventually enable them to reach 172. Booth is an interesting study of moving elegance. He has a lot of time in which to see and play the ball; yet he appears to be constantly on the move as he executes his strokes. Without him the Sydney side would have been in big trouble. He remained undefeated on 74 at the fall of the last wicket.

Then it was that Len committed his cardinal blunder of the match. Still searching for a solution to our opening-bat problem, he fiddled with our batting order and permitted the Sydneysiders to get back into the game. When we went in to bat shortly before close of play, Len asked Vic Wilson to open with Reg Simpson. I thought at the time that it was a big blunder. And so it proved to be. Nugget produced a Miller Special; an inswinger which cannoned into the stumps and ended Wilson's opening ambitions before they started. It was patently unfair to ask Vic - a middle-order aggressor - to take on the new ball

in the hands of experts like Miller, Davidson and Crawford. Scrubs was pressed into service as nightwatchman. Another mistake! Miller proceeded to crunch into Loader's thigh. Softened up by Miller, the Surrey bowler was then knocked over for a duck by Davidson and we finished the day at 2/4.

Saturday February 19th.

A good Saturday crowd crammed into the S.C.G. expecting fireworks and a good contest. They got both. We began just as unconvincingly as New South Wales had on the day previously. Our first innings performance was no better than that of New South Wales. Davidson swung the ball prodigiously and Pat Crawford troubled most batsmen with his bounce. A month earlier, the Sydney side 'rolled' Victoria for 86 on this very ground - Crawford, Miller and Davidson capturing 19 wickets between them. They have the best fast attack in the Sheffield Shield and have already wrapped up Australia's domestic championship. Reg Simpson became Davidson's first victim of the morning, caught by Briggs at slip. In quick time we lost P.B.H. - caught behind off Crawford for three - and Kipper, who edged Davidson to 'keeper Lambert after scoring a dozen. We were in big trouble at 5/35. For a while Long Tom played the role of the little Dutch boy, sticking his finger in the dyke, and together with Len, who had come in at number seven, jockeyed the score along to 94. Then Graveney, chasing his thirty-sixth run, flashed once too often, edged and became wicket-keeper Lambert's third victim of the innings. Hutton played as only Hutton can when his side is up against it. At the other end, Godders with the impertinence of a perky London sparrow, picked up 40 cheeky runs before being bowled by Crawford. Johnny Wardle slashed a quick 16 and was then caught in the outfield by Crawford off Treanor. My partnership with Alec failed to blossom and I was run-out. Hutton fell an unlucky two runs short of his fifty when he edged the quickish leg-spinner Treanor and was superbly caught by the 18-year-old Bobby Simpson. What a prodigy this boy is! He is equally brilliant with bat, ball and in the field. With the pressure off the Test matches, Hutton obviously felt he could relax in this game and drop himself down the order. It was a supreme piece of irony that he was called upon once more to save the team: to be the glue which held our later

HAVING SEEN IN THE NEW YEAR, ALL WE WANT NOW IS AN OPENING BAT IN AUSTRALIA TO SEE IN THE NEW BALL.

Goody. the bowler's hit my bat

innings together and finally helped us to tie the New South Wales first innings total of 172.

But, important though Hutton's innings was, injury factors turned out to be more crucial to our hopes of winning the match. Loader's nightwatchman heroics rendered him so lame that he could not bowl after lunch on the third day. Look what a mess just taking our eye off the ball for a moment has landed us in!

Sunday February 20th.

The end of the series and the tour is rapidly approaching. I am going to find it a wrench to leave Margaret. She seems to sense this and we are spending as much of our free time together as possible. She has a job at a pharmacy on the Manly Corso, but I am afraid her employer is not seeing much of her.

Today K.V. joined us as we drove around the harbour in 'Hinemoa', Margaret's car. Sydney is a veritable Pandora's Box - there is always some new treasure to unearth: some new landmark to see, some new restaurant such as Doyle's Fish eatery at Watson's Bay to sample. There are even resid-ential golf clubs such as the Royal Sydney to stay, eat and play at. One of the journalists, who is something of a snob, loves spending his time in the Harbour City at the Royal Sydney - a club with reciprocal rights with his own club in England. Each morning before cricket, he rises early and plays a round. In the evening he returns to a gourmet meal at the club. We did hear that he blotted his copybook on this trip. He

apparently left his clubs in the club captain's locker, and when asked to remove them, he proved difficult! The upshot was that he was requested to remove himself from the club completely!

They tell me that the Harbour bridge is constantly being painted - no sooner do the painters finish one coat than they have to start another. I wonder how much paint that takes? The city itself is a living history book. I loved strolling through Hyde Park and on the Domain, alongside Government House and Mrs. Macquarie's Seat. St. Mary's Cathedral and the New South Wales Parliament House may not be on the grandiose scale of European cathedrals or Westminster. But they are graceful and beautiful. Less aesthetic is the pub of the male chauvinists in Woolloo-mooloo's dockland where it is said that the services of Ladies of the Night are auctioned at closing time! Just up the hill in King's Cross, no auction is necessary! It is just a straightforward sale!

I learned yesterday that a Botany Bay Sports Goods manufacturer, Stokes McGown, are making and marketing an autographed cricket ball - 'The Typhoon' - in my honour! Needless to say there will be some profit in it for me! The ball should swing, since it is only a two-piecer. I shall take some home and try flogging them around the clubs. The price is very reasonable and hand-stitched balls in England cost a fortune.

The Sydney Harbour Bridge.

Monday February 21st.

Today we had a glimpse of what might have been if our fast bowlers had not seized the psychological advantage and won the Second Test at Sydney. Keith Miller turned on an outstanding performance as skipper. We began to appreciate the magnitude of the Australian selectors' mistake when they passed over the dynamic leadership qualities of Miller and made Ian Johnson and Arthur Morris captain ahead of him. Keith is not a favourite of Bradman - and Bradman is all-powerful at the selection table. Nugget at the helm would have posed a real problem for us in the Sydney, Melbourne and Adelaide Tests. Looking back, our overwhelming loss in Brisbane and its ringing confirmation

of Ian Johnson as skipper did us a favour. Miller is never short of ideas - never frightened to take a gamble - and ever willing to seize the initiative. I think that Len is slightly in awe of him. A fast bowler who alternates bouncers with wrong 'uns does not meet the Yorkshire expectations as to what a paceman should be. Unpredictable skills and fearless individuality are out of place at Headingley.

Today Lady Luck was on the side of Miller and New South Wales. On Saturday evening I told Woozer Dalton, our physio, that my left calf muscle was aching. Ever an alarmist, Woozer thought that I had torn it slightly and, with the Test match just a few days away, advised that I should rest the injury until next Friday.

Consequently, I did not bowl in the game after lunch today. With Scrubs also *hors de combat*, we are down to two regular bowlers in Bedser and Wardle. They responded magnificently, sending down a combined 47 overs before Len gave them some respite and experimented with Vic Wilson's medium-pace. In the New South Wales first innings, Wilson surprised everyone by taking two wickets for one run. This time the Sydney batsmen refused to flatter him. He did not escape as lightly - four of his overs going for 42 runs!

The fact that 'Farmer Vic' was so expensive was due to Miller's directive to his batsmen to go for the runs. Opener Briggs did not get much of a chance to follow orders. I knocked him over before he had scored - thus completing his 'pair'. With the withdrawal of Loader and me, Hutton's bowlers were now conserving energy by operating off short or shortish runs and the scoring was brisk. It began to drizzle and the ball became a bar of soap, as Burke and Simpson added 159, refusing to leave the ground and concede their advantage. Len therefore approached the umpires complaining about the conditions - then led the side off. His action left the two batsmen standing all by themselves out in the middle of the Sydney Cricket Ground in what was quite heavy rain. Simpson, who was only two runs short of his century, was so angry that he completely lost his cool. When play resumed after a short break, the inexperienced 18-year-old swung wildly at Johnny Wardle's first ball - a

wrong 'un - and was stumped by a country mile. How the crowd howled their disapproval!

Benaud and Miller continued the Burke-Simpson run-fest, each scoring a half-century. Miller declared the home side's innings at 8/314 shortly after tea. Once more, Hutton opted not to open the innings and, in my opinion, this decision lost the game. The left-handed Wilson failed again, this time being bowled by Davidson for 4.

**Keith 'Nugget' Miller
- an inspirational skipper.**

Tuesday February 22nd.

The victory equation for the M.C.C. was simple. We needed just under 300 runs in a full day's play with most of our wickets intact. The task Miller had set was achievable and quite reasonable. Most of our batsmen got a good start and if they had gone on with the job we must have won. Unfortunately they did not. And once more the man who took the key wicket was Keith Miller. Nugget produced the unplayable ball which rattled Peter May's stumps after P.B.H and the Skipper had added 77 for the fourth wicket. Reg Simpson managed 24 before being caught at slip by The Claw - Davidson - off Benaud's leg-spin. Graveney also fell to Benaud l.b.w. for 28 - and Cowdrey was caught by Simpson off his fellow evangelist, 'Sam' Booth, after he had scored 33. Hutton succumbed to Burke - 'of the shot-putting action' - caught at slip playing for the turn which was not there. How on earth Burke gets away with his action without being called for throwing, I shall never know! Godders completed a valuable double with a defiant innings of 39, before falling to a Miller catch off a Davidson away-slanter. It was left to the leg-spinner Treanor to mop up three tail-end wickets as we fell 45 runs short of our target. One of the most decisive aspects of this New South Wales victory was the excellence of its young close-to-the-wicket catchers. One would have to travel many a country mile to encounter 'slippers' as mobile and as sure as Simpson, Philpott, Benaud, Booth and Burke. Catches certainly went a long way towards winning this match!

Wednesday February 23rd.

Our undeserved reward for losing to New South Wales was a two-day holiday. With the series decided, all the pizzaz seems to have gone out of this tour. The weather did not help; for two days Sydney was enveloped in a permanent overcast with sporadic horizontal rain slanting in on a strong easterly wind. We can only seek fitness; thus training was a chore and a damp uninspiring affair. It looks as if our honorary memberships of the City Tattersalls, the New South Wales Leagues and Commercial Travellers' Clubs, will come in handy.

Before the first ball has been bowled in this Final Test of a dead series, the Aussie selectors have written it off and begun their preparations for the approaching tour of the West Indies. They have nominated Queenslander, Peter Burge and New South Wales opener Billy Watson - two debutant tourists - in the team for the Sydney Test, plus the comparatively inexperienced South Aussie, Les Favell. In my estimation these changes, added to the exclusion of Morris, makes their batting line-up suspect. This weakness will be further exacerbated if wicket-keeper Len Maddocks does not recover from the bruised finger he has picked up since Adelaide. For our part, we are suffering from the injury hang-over of our New South Wales defeat. The Boil's broken finger, a legacy of the Victorian game, is still red, inflamed and angry-looking. Knowing Trevor's fixity of purpose, I am sure that he will play if it is humanly possible. But the broken finger is in his bowling hand and it will test his pain threshold severely. Kipper is suffering from tonsillitis and a broken nose, sustained while fielding in the Adelaide Test. And Woozer will keep insisting that the strained muscle in my left leg has not fully recovered. I can hardly feel the so-called injury. Long Tom Graveney has been named as the replacement opener for Bill Edrich. His promotion is well earned and not before time. Bill has only held his place in the team thus far because of his senior status.

Thursday February 24th.

Jupiter Pluvius seems to have made his permanent home in New South Wales. The meteorologists tell us that the downpours, which even now persist in the Sydney region, are the worst experienced in the last fifty years. The wine-growing area of the Hunter Valley is the worst affected and floods are causing millions of pounds worth of damage. There have already been quite a few deaths by drowning. Less importantly, the weather is completely ruining our final stay in this beautiful harbour city. Today, only a cursory work-out was possible.

Friday February 25th.

Raincoats - not cricket flannels - are the order of this, the first scheduled day of the Test. When we entered the green painted gates of the S.C.G., the only indication that a game of cricket should have been going on inside were knots of hopelessly optimistic spectators, grouped beneath the shelter of the turnstile roofs, hoping against hope that the rain would stop. As we drove around the rear of the Members' stand, we could see that The Number Two Ground to our left was completely under water. When we reached our dressing room in the left-wing of the pavilion, we discovered that the main oval was in a similar condition: it was a vast lake with an island of tarpaulins in the centre. Not even the players' viewing balcony was sheltered from the storm. A near gale was blowing off the sea, ten miles to the east. It whipped unrelenting slanting sheets of rain over the Hill, on to the ground and into our faces, as we stood on the viewing area exposed to its blast - but not for long. Looking towards the Pacific Ocean I could not perceive any break in the cloud cover. Rain! Rain! And more rain! After lunch we retreated to our hotel.

The day was not a complete loss, however. Alan Jenkins had taken a few days off from his Maffra practice and had come to spend the last week of our stay in Australia with the team. He is staying at the Kinneir where Margaret and I dined with him tonight. Alan is a wonderfully level-headed influence. It is great to have this tall, calm, blond presence with us as Margaret and I approach our emotional parting.

Saturday February 26th.

Stack's had our Holden cars on the doorstep of Usher's Hotel promptly at 8.30a.m. Off we went to the S.C.G. But it was the same old story of - 'Is your journey really necessary?' It was raining with even greater intensity than on Friday - if that is possible. Rain! When will it stop? Yesterday's pattern was repeated and the flood on the cricket ground showed no sign of abating.

We had a hilarious Saturday Night Club meeting. Then Alan, Margaret and I dined at the Chequers nightclub. The American comedienne, Ruth Wallis, was on stage and Alan insisted on buying me an album of her songs, *Ruth Wallis Goes Romantic*, which she autographed. It fitted our mood perfectly. We had a lovely night!

Sunday February 27th.

The rain is not selective. It falls even on rest days. Today a party of us went fishing from a boat on Middle Harbour, followed by a barbecue picnic at Clontarf. But the rain put a damper on the venture. We finished the day with no fish and wet bums. At one stage we thought our luck had changed and we had hooked into a monster fish. But it transpired that we had cast our lines across the anchor line and were hauling in the hook!

Monday February 28th.

The rain is still falling, conjuring up visions of Noah floating down the Parramatta River in his Ark. I don't know where all this water is coming from! The Hunter River is flooded. Newcastle is deluged. The Hawkesbury has burst its banks. Crops, vineyards and the work of years have been swept away. And the death toll continues to rise. Today is the last day of the month. I wonder what February's rainfall has been! No play was possible and it was not worth leaving the hotel.

Tuesday March 1st.

Hooray! The rain has finally stopped! And what a mess it has left. Everything is dripping. Every pavement is wet. Every drain is flowing. And every patch of turf is soggy. Instead of a thirty-hour Test match, we can only look forward to a game of thirteen! The M.C.C. finances will suffer drastically and our tour profits are estimated to have been reduced by £8,000. That would pay the tour wages of ten of our eighteen players!

The ever-faithful Stack's Holdens were on the hotel doorstep at nine prompt to pick us up and splash their way through the puddled and sparsely populated Sydney streets to the Moore Park ground. As was to be expected, there were not too many eager spectators panting to get into the S.C.G. when our cars drove through the main gates and drew up in their allotted parking spaces. As we entered the dressing rooms the ground staff was beavering away in the centre of the ground, feverishly attempting to restore The Oval to a state at which some play would be possible. But to be truthful, with only three days remaining for play, it is hard to envisage this game coming to a definite conclusion.

The curator's men laboured all of the morning, sopping, sweeping, mopping, squeegeeing and using every device, usual and unusual, orthodox and unorthodox, to clear the water off the tarpaulins, and down the drains at each corner of the square. When they finally cleared the covers and laid bare the pitch beneath its hessian underclothes, it was revealed - affected by the deluge, but still playable. The teams took an early lunch. And the ground authorities announced that a start would be possible at two o'clock. The captains went out to toss. Johnson won and, being unwilling to gamble on the way the wicket would play, asked Len to bat. Australia excluded Ron Archer from their side, which is pretty unjust -

he is currently heading the home bowling averages with 13 wickets at 16 each. Sir Donald and his co-selectors must be pretty keen to give Watson and Burge a run with the bat!

The Skipper's batting contribution to the match was completed after the fourth ball. He took six runs off Lindwall's first three balls; then he glanced an inswinger to leg slip where Burge grasped a juggled catch. That was Australia's last success for 182 runs. On a damp pitch which played slowly but truly, Tom Graveney and P.B.H. dominated the strong Aussie attack of Lindwall, Miller, Davidson, Johnson and Benaud. The fact that the ball came on to the bat slowly did not bother the batsmen in the least. In two and three quarter hours of uninhibited driving, the two batsmen scored at a run

TYSON PHOTO-FINISH MAKES THE AUSSIE FAN YELL 'NO BALL!'

YOU simply cannot keep England's Lancashire-born fast bowler, "Typhoon" Frank Tyson, out of the news. Three big question marks surround his appear-

Fifth Test

ance in the fifth Test starting on Friday.

1.—Will Tyson be fit to play? He has a slightly pulled thigh muscle.

2.—Will Tyson be dropped to give Alec Bedser a last chance to play in a Test in Australia?

3.—Will Tyson be "sacrificed" to avoid any risk of giving the Australians a chance to scream that Tyson persistently bowls no-balls by foot-drag over the crease?

The answer to No 1 comes from England's manager,

Geoffrey Howard. He says: "Tyson's prospects of playing are not unhopeful." That's so far as his injury is concerned.

Answer No. 2. Tyson will play if fit. Bedser will have to find another place, possibly the injured Trevor Bailey's.

Answer No. 3. Look at the three pictures above. Australians claim they *prove* that Tyson is guilty of bowling no-balls. They say he did it eight times in an over.

Judge for yourself, but make allowance for the camera angle.—CHARLES BRAY.

a minute and, when Long Tom finally gave Ian Johnson a return catch, he had scored the reputedly unlucky total of 111. It was his first hundred against Australia - but the style with which it was scored made it worth waiting for. Yet I cannot not suppress the gut feeling that it is strange how Tom often 'comes good' when the pressure is off. Previously, I had always regarded him as Lindwall's 'bunny'- particularly when the ball was pitched well up to him. But then, who is not 'Lindy's bunny' when he slots his yorker on the right spot? Len always looks askance at rubicund players like Tom. They seem to enjoy the game too much. He prefers the intense pale-faced men who look as if they have just come up the shaft from the mines!

Kipper played for Johnson's turn and was caught behind off the first ball he received. Then May was taken at slip by Davidson off a Benaud leg-spinner, after three hours of uninterrupted concentration. When the players retired to the pavilion for the night, the scoreboard read 4/196, last man 79.

Wednesday March 2nd.

Today those pundits who thought that we would be playing for the draw, happy with our current two match advantage in the series, got a big shock. From the moment that Compo and The Boil stepped on to the still damp S.C.G., they were clearly after a 4-1 victory in the rubber. Denis played himself in very deliberately, spending twenty minutes over his first run. After lunch, with Trevor in support, he cut

loose, employing his dazzling array of strokes to such good effect that 62 runs flowed from his bat in just under an hour and a half. He was caught and bowled by Johnson just 16 runs short of his century, after his fifth wicket association with Bailey had yielded 134.

Godders advanced our total by 10 and was then caught off Lindwall, setting the stage for the most unlikely piece of cricket drama I have ever witnessed. With Ray needing just one more wicket to become the only fast bowler to capture 100 wickets in Anglo-Australian Tests, Bailey - The Boil- The Barnacle - the constant thorn in the side of Australian bowlers - deliberately missed a straight ball. He virtually kicked it into his stumps to ensure Lindy got his century of victims. Then he walked down the pitch to congratulate his most inveterate opponent! Apparently Trevor laboured under what turned out to be a misapprehension that Lindwall was going to retire and this match would be his last against England! Bailey's 72 occupied a lengthy three and a quarter hours and included only four boundaries. But there is no gainsaying its value and Bailey's guts, handicapped as he is by his still tender broken finger.

Bailey's dismissal prompted an immediate mid-afternoon declaration from Hutton with the score standing at 7/371. With the pitch a little firmer and quicker than on the previous day, George and I set about the Aussie batsmen with a will. But McDonald and Watson stood firm. We had to wait for Wardle's fourth over before the little

New South Wales' opener played on. I returned to the bowling crease and rattled Favell's stumps just after he had broken his duck. Overnight, Australia was 2/82, with McDonald 45 and Harvey 12.

With only one day's play remaining it seems unlikely that we can force a decision in this Test.

Margaret and her mother, Pat, saw the day's play, but I still have the impression that I am not a favourite in that quarter.

Thursday March 3rd.

It seems that Johnny Wardle has discovered yet another Achilles Heel of the Australian batsmen: they do not play left-arm wrist spin at all well.

This morning, wickets fell at regular intervals in Australia's first innings. When he had added one to his overnight score, I bowled an off-cutter to the left-handed Harvey. It stopped, straightened and presented me with the easiest of return catches. At this stage of the game our fielding was right out of the top drawer. Kipper ran out Miller in smart fashion and with Wardle setting knotty problems about the direction of his turn, sharp catching got rid of Burge for 17, Benaud for seven, Maddocks for 32, McDonald for 72 and Davidson for 18. When Compo ran out Ian Johnson - attempting the run which would have saved the follow-on - the home side was still 150 runs behind. I rather gained the impression that Johnson thought that his team was safe from the indignity of being the first Australian side to be asked to bat twice in succession since the Oval in 1938. He was wrong. He was one short! And Hutton took delight in informing him of his miscalculation and asking Australia to bat again. None of the newcomers in the Aussie batting line-up had scored runs;

At this stage there were only two hours remaining for play and only a bowling miracle would enable us to bowl out Australia again in the allotted time. Astonishingly, we came very close to achieving that miracle. Brian Statham and I were rationed to five overs each, with me bowling off a three-pace approach to save time. I showed that I was still fast enough to knock the bat out Watson's hands - but George did even better, having Watson caught at slip by Graveney. Then the Skipper called up Johnny Wardle, who had already bowled 24 overs in the day and taken 5/79. In spite of his weariness, Johnny obliged once more, having Favell caught at slip, catching Harvey off his own bowling and rattling Miller's stumps.

But it was too little too late, and Hutton relinquished his pursuit of the improbable, indicating his abandonment of the impossible by introducing himself and Graveney into an all leg-spin attack. And wouldn't you know it? Graveney picked up McDonald's wicket caught behind! In this way the game 'died to a fall', with the two-hour Australian second innings producing only 116 runs but rewarding us with a bonus of six wickets. Wardle's marathon bowling effort occupied most of the last day and encompassed 46 overs, seven maidens and yielded eight wickets. He finished the day by amusing the small crowd and giving them an impression of how tired he felt - bowling the last ball on his knees! But it was another Yorkshireman who had the best bowling figures of the innings. Hutton bowled Benaud as he swung wildly, trying to hit him out of the ground. Len finished the series top of the bowling averages with the analysis of one wicket for two runs!

To my dying day I shall remember Sydney: the airiness of its streets, the attractive girls floating through its shops in wispy dresses, the beauty of its harbour, the wonderful times which I spent there, the thrilling cricket I played there and the people I met there. One of the happiest moments of the tour was my meeting with my boyhood hero, Harold Larwood, at his modest home: 7 Leonard Avenue, Kingsford. He gave me a few photographs of himself and his family: mementos of greatness which I shall always treasure.

The sequel to the Fifth Test was harrowing. Margaret was my first great love; indeed she was my first real girlfriend. In matters of the heart I was naïve until I met her. The fact that her family thought little of me and did little to encourage our liaison made our affair both difficult and awkward. We had, however, fallen heavily and, when we had to part, we were confused, anguished and at a loss to know where we were heading. Would we meet again? We did not know. If we were to see one another again, how was it to come about? We were young and did not know what the future held for us. We agreed to keep in touch - but could

we guarantee that some influence would not intervene? God knew!

The evening of March 3rd was one of the worst nights of my inexperienced existence. John Arlott, the journalist and broadcaster, befriended me in the course of the tour and, that evening, invited Margaret and me to a farewell dinner. It was farewell to Australia - and, heart-wrenchingly - farewell to Margaret, who never stopped weeping throughout the meal. The South African broadcaster, Charles Fortune, and his wife were in the party. Mrs. Fortune, God bless her, took Margaret under her wing. She provided the motherly influence Margaret needed. I was a boor and drank a Lethe draught of forgetfulness. We were leaving for New Zealand on the half-past midnight plane. Tour regulations dictated that I travel to the airport in the team bus. But Margaret drove out to Mascot and the anguish began all over again. Our agony was prolonged when it was announced that Christchurch airport - our destination - was fogged in and TEAL flight 576 - our plane - would be delayed for three hours. I proceeded to get higher at the airport bar, which was opened for our benefit? At 3a.m., one final tearful goodbye and I left Margaret in the compassionate hands of Lindsay Hassett, the former Aussie skipper-turned-journalist. The final memory I had was of Margaret's blond head cradled in her arms on the rails of the embarkation gate. Shall I see her again? I must.

There were other leave-takings. We had to say farewell to Compo and Big Al, who were not accompanying the

Margaret with a koala - would I ever see her again?

side to New Zealand. Their return to England was a sensible precaution which did no more than reflect their general state of health and fitness throughout the tour.

The flight over the Tasman Sea was physically and mentally rough. I sat next to Johnny Wardle, who had added his little contribution to our departure by temporarily delaying it. At ten in the morning we landed at Christchurch airport. One of the finest Test Series ever played, an Australian tour and the greatest cricketing experience of my life was over! And England won!

Chapter Thirteen

New Zealand

Thursday March 3rd.

JUST OVER THREE HOURS AFTER leaving Margaret and Mascot airport, the chequered tablecloth of the New Zealand countryside is spread beneath our aircraft's wings: grey white basalt mountains, boulder-strewn river beds and sheep pasture stretch as far as the eye can see. These are the Canterbury Plains. The first difference we noticed between Australia and the 'Land of the Long White Cloud' is that everything is so green. Our watches tell us that it is seven o'clock in the morning; but the three hours time difference between Sydney and Christchurch mean that the local time is ten. The aircraft had been descending for the past half-hour. Now it banked into its final approach, flattened and lowered its flight path - dropping the last few feet of its journey, and jolting and screeching as its tyres made contact with the asphalt of Christchurch International Airport.

Old friends were at the airport to greet our senior players - Len, W.J., The Boil, Reg Simpson and Godfrey. Kiwis Tom Lowry, Walter Hadlee, John Reid and Bert Sutcliffe are well-known to many of the England side from their previous encounters on both English and New Zealand cricket grounds. To a man they are delighted with our victory in Australia. New Zealand is a nation of anglophiles - especially when it comes to the common ambition of beating the Aussies at cricket.

The austere buildings of the airport are a drab introduction to the land which I have only known previously as the provider of succulent Canterbury lamb chops. But the unfavourable first impression which I gained of New Zealand quickly dissipated, changing to absolute delight as our motorcade moved into the verdant countryside which lay between us and Christchurch. This is a beautiful country!

The original 1840 settlers of Christchurch built a town exactly like the one they left behind in Hampshire: a country town through which flows the River Avon. As in England, the stream abounds with trout. It is the first time I have ever seen a trout stream flowing through the centre of a city! To be honest there is little of the city about Christchurch. It is more of a conglomeration of linked parks like Hagley - a hive of cricket activity at weekends - interspersed with scattered buildings of obvious English origins. Presiding over the settlement is the lofty spire of its neo-Gothic cathedral. The town's public school, Christ's College, is perhaps more English than many of its English counterparts. Scholars are still compelled to wear straw boater hats! Strangely, the French were the first Europeans to settle at Christchurch, on the coast across the Port Hills in what has become Lyttelton. The Viscount Cobham, the President Designate of M.C.C. and ex-skipper of Worcestershire, is a former Governor-General of New Zealand; his family name of Lyttelton is the same as that of Christchurch's port. It reflects a long association between the Cobhams and this far-distant outpost of the British Commonwealth.

Arriving at our pleasant country-style hotel, we settled in and rested. How we needed it! The locals have a strange way of serving beer here. They dispense it by means of what looks like a petrol pump! It helped with the general search for détente after the Australian series.

Friday March 4th.

Lancaster Park, the setting for tomorrow's game against Canterbury province and our preparation for the Dunedin Test, is a dual purpose rugby and cricket ground. It has a pleasant atmosphere and a very good wicket. This morning was devoted to practising for tomorrow's encounter with Canterbury: a side not to be taken too lightly since it contains half a dozen national representatives, some of whom, like the left-arm spinner Tom Burtt, are very experienced. The weather is pleasantly fine and it is quite a relief to escape the heat of Australia.

After lunch we heard that the salmon were running in the Waimakariri River - commonly referred to by the locals as 'Why-kick-a-moo-cow-when-a-moo-cow-can't-kick-back'. We are told that

watching the run and the anglers at work was worth the effort. It was more than worth the effort - it was positively terrifying! After an hour's drive in a northerly direction, we halted in the open countryside, parked the car in one of the few remaining spaces of a grassy parking lot half a mile from the Waimakariri and traversed the bushland which separated us from the scene of the action on foot. There we found about a hundred fishermen crowded shoulder to shoulder along the grey shingle bank of the river, just where it rushed with roaring speed into its turbulent estuary and thence the ocean. Looking seawards down the stream we could see thousands of large silver fish approaching from the ocean, curvetting in and out of the torrent, swimming steadily upstream. They made seemingly little headway against the current and towards their spawning grounds high in the distant Southern Alps; yet they never ceased in their efforts until they finally disappeared into smoother waters upstream. The anglers were armed with what appeared to be quarterstaffs which they plied with a will, constantly casting thick lines, at the end of which were silver spinners. They were not using bait and the lures were no more than enormous hooks attached to small metal reflectors to catch the fishes' attention. There was not delicate playing of the salmon; they were just hooked and hauled in! This was food culling pure and simple. How on earth the anglers avoided being impaled on the flying hooks of one of their neighbours, I shall never know! Yet no-one seemed concerned or even threatened!

A quiet night of recuperation after our departure from Australia.

Saturday March 5th.

Today we began our first match in New Zealand. Not regarded as a top-line Test side, the Kiwis are nonetheless dogged opponents and number some fine players in their ranks. The left-hand batsman Bert Sutcliffe has two centuries to his name against England: 101 at Manchester in 1949 and 116 in Christchurch in 1951. All-rounder John Reid notched 135 against South Africa at Cape Town in 1953/54 and skipper Geoff Rabone reached 107 at Durban in the same year. John Hayes and Bob Blair are both dangerous medium-fast bowlers, while beanpole Tony Mac-Gibbon is an experienced medium-pacer who can evince lift from the most docile of wickets. Guile is provided by schoolteacher-cum-leg-spinner Alex Moir, while there is stock medium-pace aplenty in the persons of Reid and Cave. Tom Burtt is a left-arm, orthodox spinner of world-class ability; but unfortunately he is on the brink of retirement from first-class cricket.

The weather held fine as Canterbury preceded us to the wicket and managed a shaky 140 in its three-hour first innings. Test contenders - openers, solicitor 'Tubby' Leggat and Matt Poore - both got starts but could not go beyond the 35 mark. Wardle completely bamboozled the Kiwis with his 57 varieties of wrist spin and returned figures of 4/46. Loader shouldered most of the fast bowling responsibilities and captured 3/34 with his clever assortment of swing, well-suited to New Zealand conditions. Then it was our turn with the bat and Long Tom Graveney continued the wonderful form which he had exhibited towards the end of the Australian series. His 101 in only 95 minutes combined elegance with power - yet surprisingly did not establish complete dominance over the Canterburians. That was left to the tail-enders - and at long last I found some batting form. I hit an unbeaten 62 in an hour. I enjoyed myself hugely, twice slogging Burtt for six and hitting nine fours. 'George' Statham and I added 75 for the last wicket and the M.C.C. finished 162 runs in the lead on a total of 302.

Sunday March 6th.

Today we enjoyed a wonderful introduction to the New Zealand countryside. Peter Arnold - a team-mate of K.V. and I in the Northamptonshire side - hails from Christchurch and today his dad and his friends, the Mercers, took us into the mountains shooting! Big Boy stuff! Shooting with .303 rifles and hunting deer! I am afraid the 'huntin - shootin' part of the trip was completely wasted on me. I have no heart for slaughtering beautiful animals - and I have always abhorred rifles ever since I was forced to shoot one at the range during my National Service spell with the Royal Signals. It was a most unpleasant experience. The recoil of the gun hurt like hell, and my three bullets evinced no signal from the markers that I had even fired, let alone hit the target. I later found that I shot at the wrong

Above: The Hunting Party.

Below: K.V. and I high in the mountains.

Above: Mount Olympus.

Below: K.V. - only shooting at a bottle!

K.V. - The Deer Hunter.

one! To cap it all we had to march 10 miles in full pack, back to our lines in Catterick, through freezing slush and snow! Never again I thought! It was therefore with some reluctance that I agreed to shoulder a firearm once more. But how could I refuse Mr. Arnold's kind invitation? I swallowed my scruples.

Our drive to the granite killing fields on Mount Olympus, overlooking the Rakiai Gorge, was a steep test, even for a car. Nor had our climb finished when we got out and unpacked the large amount of gear which was apparently needed for any self-respecting hunting expedition. Then it was a case of onwards and ever upwards. We kept a weather-eye open for any deer which might be unfortunate enough to run across our path. We stopped for hot tea - very welcome at this cold altitude. Lunch came and went and still we had not sighted a living creature. Then, excitement! Something moved a hundred metres to our right! K.V. and I assumed the prone position, ready to fire. There in front of us, a large rabbit raised its nose skywards and sniffed almost disdainfully. Well it was better than nothing! It was decided that I should take the first shot. Sighting my prey with great care, I fired. The explosion nearly burst my eardrums and its echo bounced off the rocky hills for what seemed an eternity. I looked at where the rabbit had been. It was still there! Still sniffing! Still aloof! My shot had passed under the rabbit's belly, raising dust! The animal just hopped into the air, came down in the same spot and resumed its sniffing! What a .303 bullet would have done to such a small creature, if it had found its target, I shudder to think! Thankfully it didn't, and before Keith could loose his shot,

Brer Rabbit hopped down a burrow and disappeared! And that ended the action for the day! Except, that is, for a few welcome beers at a pub on the way back to Christchurch. In retrospect, I have to concede that K.V. and I had an unexpectedly enjoyable experience, even though most of our shooting was at bottle targets. Up in the Alps, we enjoyed the god-like thrill which comes from drinking in fabulous scenery. Surely there can be no more beautiful spot on earth.

Monday March 7th.

Canterbury showed much better form in its second innings. The rotund 'Tubby' Leggat was in a particularly obdurate mood; he batted well for four and a half hours, he and Matt Poore putting on 67 for the home side's first wicket. At 98 Leggat survived an absolute 'gaper' to Johnny Wardle at short leg - off me! I could not believe my eyes when the catch went down! That is twice that Johnny has dropped easy catches off me this trip. The mistake unnerved Tubby and, striving for the coveted century, his ambition over-reached his running speed. He called Sammy Guillen for an impossible single - and experienced the batsman's worst nightmare: 'run-out 99!' Wicket-keeper Guillen is an unexpected player to find in the Canterbury team. He kept wicket for West Indies in five Tests against Australia and New Zealand in 1951/52 before deciding to emigrate to and settle in Kiwiland - somewhere, I detect the hand of a woman in that move!

Tuesday March 8th.

The rest of the Canterbury batting was undistinguished, only four players reaching double figures. The result was that the Christchurch team was dismissed for 206, leaving us just 45 runs to score for victory. This was duly accomplished before lunch by virtue of the umpires extending the morning session by 25 minutes. The jovial Tom Burtt enjoyed a long, last loud hurrah. Playing in his final first-class game he scored an unbeaten 30 and hit his fellow slow left-arm bowler, Johnny Wardle, for 24 in an over, which included two sixes and three fours. He will be expelled from the molly-duker's union! But it could not have happened to a nicer fellow. We duly knocked off the required runs, losing the wickets of Andrew, Cowdrey and Wilson en route. Poor Vic Wilson! He bagged a pair - bowled MacGibbon, and bowled Hayes - in his penultimate game of the tour.

Wednesday March 9th.

Today the team travelled just under 200 miles south towards the Antarctic, the southern extremity of South Island known as the Bluff, and Dunedin, the setting for the First Test. The only major outpost of civilisation between us and the South Pole is the city of Invercargill, the home of big, succulent oysters. We tasted a few!

We could be in Scotland. Family names begin with 'Mac'. There is a highland burr in the speech of the natives; and all around us a persistent Scottish mist covers Glen and Ben with a grey Hibernian pall. Place names have a north-of-the-border ring to them: Invercargill, St. Kilda Beach. The very name of the provincial capital - Dunedin - is Edinburgh spelt back to front. And Dunedin's gloomy weather could be discovered any day of the week in the Western Hebrides. The town itself is neatly squared between two hills and along the shore of an ocean inlet - sheltered from the savage Tasman gales which sometimes batter this region. The Carisbrook Ground, the scene of the Dunedin Test, is better known as a rugby union ground rather than a cricket oval.

Thursday March 10th.

Today we had our first peep at the Test pitch. It looks slow and it seems unlikely to produce any assistance to our faster bowlers. It may therefore be impossible to reproduce the fireworks of our Australian successes. Now we shall see just how fast Brian and I really are! The weather looks threatening and we shall be extremely lucky to get through this match without rain. Practice today was perfunctory. The outfield and wickets were damp. Carisbrook is uncomfortable and only provides the basic dressing room facilities of a football ground.

Today, out of the blue came a message from a certain Mr. MacFadyen. He turns out to be Alan MacFadyen, my former O.C. in Headquarters Squadron 4. Training Regiment, Royal Signals during my national service at Catterick Camp. We controlled the movements and billeting of men transferring in and out of the Regiment - and we were not very good at it as I recall. In fact I remember one occasion when the

The City of Dunedin.

Military Police picked up a couple of our problem soldiers, who were A.W.O.L. on Glasgow station - before we realised they were absent!

Alan emigrated to New Zealand where he has established his own transport business at Gore in the Southland Province. We have arranged to meet and he has promised to see what he can do about arranging some trout fishing for K.V. and I on the rest day.

Friday March 11th.

Today began gloomily - dull and overcast with the promise of rain to come. It did not do justice to the first day of Test cricket ever played at Carisbrook. The wicket looked green, but it turned out to be wet, slow and placid. The Skipper won the toss and defied the maxim 'when you win the toss, think about bowling, then bat'. He asked Geoff Rabone, the Kiwi captain, to bat. The press box believed that Hutton had played the three-card trick on the home side: they thought that he had persuaded the New Zealand batsmen - usually a free-stroking batting lot - that the pitch and our attack were full of devilry. There is no doubting Len's mastery of cricket psychology. He knew that the reputation of George and I had preceded us across the Tasman. He was equally aware of the fact that New Zealand's complete lack of success in Tests against England would make them apprehensive.

So it proved to be. Rabone played each delivery with the suspicion he would accord to a ball which swung

George and I warm up before the start of the Test at Dunedin.

each way before pitching, and spun in each direction after bouncing. He occupied the crease for three hours and was rewarded for his patience with a mere 18 runs. With only three runs on the board he lost his partner Chapple, bowled by a Statham ball which kept low and hit the base of middle stump. Sutcliffe followed his captain's example in subordinating attack to grim defence, and boring the 10,000 spectators out of their socks. They must have been relieved when lunch came after 25 overs and 90 minutes which produced only 11 scoring shots and one Rabone straight drive for four.

In the afternoon, the home team's lethargy got them into trouble. Sutcliffe started off as if he was about to lift the tempo of the game. He helped two leg-side deliveries from Bob Appleyard over the boundary on the full. Prodded into attempted imitation, Rabone advanced down the pitch to Wardle's wrong 'un, changed his mind, played defensively and, for his hesitation, was stumped! Quite a surprise! George then hit John Reid's off-stump and at tea New Zealand were 3/72.

After the interval the rot really set in. In the space of eight balls I bowled the timid McGregor and Watt without conceding a run - then pressed home our advantage by yorking Cave. Sutcliffe sensed that, if the home team were to achieve a respectable total, it was down to him. He hoisted his own fifty in 200 minutes and helped his side to the century mark in four and a quarter hours. Then it all unravelled with rapid finality. Brian bowled Alex Moir and Bob Blair before Bailey, brought on to keep things tight, had MacGibbon caught behind.

Meanwhile Sutcliffe - clearly a class above the other batsmen - was trying to conjure up runs out of thin air. But with fieldsmen stationed on the boundary to counter the ploy, he paid the inevitable price and was caught in the deep for 74, having scored all but 51 of his team's 125 run total. The left-handed Sutcliffe is good-looking in every respect. With finely chiselled features and wavy hair

he is film-star material; moreover he has the air of a fine player about him. His batswing is straight and vertical, his footwork is crisp and incisive and his courage is there for everyone to see as he moves into position directly behind the line of the ball. Statham was the most successful of the England attack, returning figures of 4/24 off 17 niggardly overs; I contributed 3/23 off 19, thanks largely to the negativity of the Kiwi batsmen. Those figures sum up the whole of Friday's 271 minutes of batting sloth.

Saturday March 12th.

England's first innings reply was only marginally better than its opponents' score - in content, composition and pace. But there is no questioning the drawing power of an M.C.C. team. In spite of yesterday's snail-play, a record crowd of 16,000 hardy souls was drawn to this most austere of cricket grounds. Can it be that the grim game played here today is the same as that we played at the beautiful Adelaide Oval? It is hard to believe. The New Zealand bowlers sent down ninety-two overs today - from which we scored 209 runs at minimally more than two an over - and lost eight wickets in the process. This is hardly thrilling fare.

Tom Graveney was at his elegant best when he opened with Hutton; the Gloucestershire batsman helped himself to all but 11 of the first 60 runs coming off the bat. Then the Skipper feathered a catch to Colquhoun behind the stumps off John Reid. Most of us who followed got a start to our knocks - but few went on with the

Colin and Reg in the 'Long Arm of the Law' during the Test at Dunedin.

job. Peter May was 'castled' by a MacGibbon seamer, while Kipper was on the wrong end of an l.b.w. decision in favour of Reid. Umpiring in New Zealand is in the same developmental stage as the Kiwis' batting! The slow-medium Harry Cave bowled his 'floaters' with an immaculate conception and execution, knocking over Graveney and Reg Simpson. He was well supported by John Reid who had the rare distinction of trapping The Boil l.b.w. for a duck. Then he bowled Evans for a similar no-score, leaving us eight wickets down and only 31 runs ahead. Fortunately for us, Johnny Wardle proceeded to entertain the spectators as only he can, advancing down the pitch to pace and spin alike, swinging cross-battedly, slogging and scrambling another 52 eccentric runs. I hung around to help out with 16; but I fell to MacGibbon and the new ball on the stroke of time with our score standing at 209 and Wardle unbeaten on 32.

The clouds which hovered over Carisbrook on the first two days of this game do not augur well for its future. Apparently, when the wind comes from the rainy quarter the result is a downpour so heavy that in some parts of the South Island they measure the rainfall not in inches, but in feet!

Sunday March 13th.

Another sunless day. Alan MacFadyen took the opportunity of taking us out to fish. Apparently there are some monsters to be caught in Lake Wakatipu near Queenstown and close to an abattoir where the trout feed on the offal effluent released into the lake.

That is too far to go and so we had to be content with a modest river close to Dunedin. We hoped for rainbow trout but were told that the stream contained only brown trout - and caught neither!

Monday March 14th.

Awoke this morning to the ceaseless drumming of rain on the window panes of our hotel room. Since the Carisbrook Ground is low and level, it must be a lake by now. And so to another day without play - spent reading, playing cards, or going to the cinema.

Tuesday March 15th.

I don't know where all this rain comes from! After the deluge which spoilt the Sydney Test and now this wash-out, I am beginning to think that some Australians and Kiwis must have gills! This is like playing cricket in Bradford! Again a day on which not a ball was bowled.

Wednesday March 16th.

When I opened my eyes this morning, I fully expected to hear the sound of falling rain once more. But instead of the room being dark and gloomy, it was bright and sunlit! Good weather had returned! And it continued glorious summer as we breakfasted and made our way to Carisbrook, where, *mirabile visu*, the ground was bathed in brilliant sunshine. The outfield was still damp, but even the most optimistic amongst us could scarcely have hoped that the pitch would remain completely unaff-

ected by the two-day downpour. Yet such proved to be the case. The wicket rolled out seemingly firm and hopefully true. We still had two wickets of our first innings to fall - but since we had lost so much time to the weather, the Skipper declared at our Saturday night total of 8/209, to maximise our bowling opportunities.

Our lead of 84 seemed inadequate when New Zealand opened its second innings with its two most successful batsmen of the first innings - Rabone and Sutcliffe. Skipper Rabone went early, l.b.w., playing back to a Wardle 'chinaman'. But Sutcliffe and Chapple, completely untroubled, advanced the total to 67 at lunch. Then suddenly the wheels fell off the home side's innings. Second ball after the interval, Chapple called Sutcliffe through for a second improbable run off a leg-glance. Changing his mind, he sent him back, and Sutcliffe was still yards from safety when May's superb throw from fine-leg arrived. Chapple immediately compounded this error of judgement by losing concentration to be bowled by Statham. Bob Appleyard thereupon cleaned up the 'Wee McGregor' and Les Watt, before Hutton recalled me to the attack. I was fully aware of the slow reaction of the Kiwi batsmen to real pace and kept the ball well up to them, letting the wicket do the work. In quick succession over went the stumps of Cave and MacGibbon, up went the umpire's finger for Moir and finally Reid played on. In six overs I claimed four victims for seven runs. Finally, Wardle, recalled to the bowling crease to clean up the ruins of

New Zealand's second innings, bowled Blair and we were left with 49 to score for victory.

Tea was due and taken. But Rabone stretched the match regulations and the bonds of Anglo-New Zealand friendship by claiming the ten-minute interval between innings - in addition to the twenty-minute tea break. But even this irregular half-hour hiatus only deferred the inevitable. We were still left an ample one and a half hours to win the match. Perhaps Rabone was praying for rain! If so, Jupiter Pluvius let him down - for once!

When our innings bolted out of the starting gates, we raced to 22 in the first 15 minutes and it appeared that we would only need one-third of the time available to reach our goal. But one should never under-rate the fighting spirit of the Kiwis! They shocked us into caution by claiming the wickets of Hutton, caught behind for three, and that of May, bowled by a quicker one from the lanky MacGibbon for 13. But Graveney's fluent driving settled the Kiwis' hash. He sped to an unbeaten 32, clinching the issue with a delicate leg-glance. Amazingly we had won the Test by eight wickets in only three days' play!

Tonight New Zealand announced its team for the Second Test in Auckland. It contains only three changes: Tubby Leggat, after his 99 in Christchurch, comes in for Murray Chapple at number one; opener Matt Poore strengthens the batting line-up replacing Les Watt, and fast bowler John Hayes gets the nod over Bob Blair. An interesting inclusion is the elegant young left-hander, John Guy as twelfth man.

Tom is applauded from the arena after his unbeaten 32 had sealed victory in the Test.

A victory smile from Colin.

Thursday March 17th.

Today we flew northwards the length of South Island, passing Christchurch on the starboard side of the aircraft - then across Cook Straits to land in Wellington on the southernmost tip of North Island. Wellington is the political capital of the Dominion and the home of New Zealand's Parliament, which is housed in the building whose unique shape has earned it the nickname of 'The Beehive'. The city itself is a harmonious blend of sea and mountains, with many of its attractive suburbs perched on precipitous hills overlooking the Straits to the west and the almost land-locked harbour of Port Nicholson to the north-east. The river Hutt decants into this bay, draining an extensive catchment area stretching towards the Alps. The suburbs of Lower and Upper Hutt are populous and popular. Port Nicholson is a shallow treacherous stretch of water, often whipped up to a heaving fury by the ferocious winds which inhabit the region. Not for nothing is this city known as 'Windy Wellington'. Those travellers who opt to cross the Straits to the South Island by the ferry to Picton are well advised to stock up on sea-sickness pills. The airport is a collection of grim grey buildings which services both international and domestic travel. We settled in to our homely hotel and had a quiet evening.

Friday March 18th.

Cricket's Wellington headquarters is known as Basin Reserve, for reasons which are immediately obvious as soon as you set foot in the ground. It is very central to the city, being situated almost at the end of the main thoroughfare. The playing area slopes down from the pavilion, like the concave side of a shallow basin, levelling out as it approaches to within 50 yards of the wicket area. The colour and topography of the pitch are disconcerting - at least they would be if I were a batsman. From the dressing rooms in the pavilion it looks as if someone has painted a broad slash of green diagonally across the middle of what is an otherwise yellowish pitch. The greenness of the grass in that locality is attributable to the former presence of a drain which bisected the ground - and which still exercises a moist and lively influence on the bowling done there. The confidence of our batsmen has not been boosted by locals who say that when the ball pitches on the side of the ditch closer to the bowler, it keeps low, and when it bounces on the upward slope, it takes off like a rocket! It looks as if there is going to be a high time in the old town tomorrow! No high scoring is anticipated.

Nor are our opposition to be dismissed lightly. Wellington holds the Plunket Shield. The side is well led by John Reid, a skipper who advocates the Keith Miller dictum of 'Attack!' They field aggressively and well, and include the international talents of Reid himself, Lawry, Miller, Dempster, Blair and Morrison. It is said that the left-arm spinner, Dempster, would

The Basin Reserve, Wellington.

be an automatic choice for the Test team if he could get leave from business to play.

Saturday March 19th.

Have we solved our opening-bat problem? It would seem so, for today, Tom Graveney, going in first, scored his third century in four consecutive matches. Not bad, when you consider that the next-highest score to the Gloucestershire batsman's 102 was that of acting-skipper Peter May, who spent 50 laborious minutes over 22 unconvincing runs. The provincial bowling was first-class, with Bob Blair, probably smarting at his omission from the Test side, working up a full head of steam to capture 4/50. He was well supported by fellow quickie Morrison with two wickets, the nippy

Reid with 1/51 and the accurate Dempster with three victims. Smart catching supported the hostile bowling and with wickets falling steadily throughout the morning, we could only muster a mediocre total of 207.

But if the Wellington attack was excellent, for England the Yorkshire duet of Wardle and Appleyard was superb! The local batsmen were no match for their accuracy, bounce, seam and spin.

Sunday March 20th.

A rest day, spent largely sight-seeing and window shopping for the home market. Greenstone seems to be the favoured local stone for jewellery. Wellington has the atmosphere of a large provincial English town. The 20-

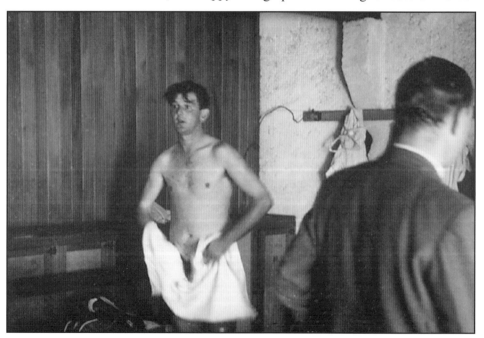

Tom changes after yet another ton.

mile tourist trip along Marine Drive slides along a narrow coastal terrace around Oriental Bay to Evans Bay, across an isthmus and past the airport, then to the Merimar Peninsula - providing spectacular views all the way. A cable car climbs from Lambton Quay to Kelburn, where one finds the Botanical Gardens, the floral beauty of Begonia House and the Lady Norwood Rose Gardens - and some breathtaking views back over the city and harbour. In case you should think life is dull in Wellington, just remember that the city is situated on a major geological fault-line and earthquakes and tremors are not uncommon.

Monday March 21st.

This morning our two Yorkshire bowling surgeons continued their clinical dismemberment of the Wellington batting. Wardle and Appleyard hustled the local players from the crease almost as quickly as they could walk to it. The tall Appleyard made the ball lift and cut back disconcertingly off the suspect wicket. From his 20 overs the batsmen could glean only 36 runs for the loss of three of their number. They could make absolutely nothing of the direction of Wardle's spin and in his 15.4 overs, he pocketed five victims at a cost of 42 runs. Wellington scraped together 127 unconvincing runs and trailed by 80 on the first innings. Reid fought out a gutsy innings of 31, two better than Beck and 11 more than Barber. Only four of the Wellington batsmen reached double figures.

Life did not become easier when we batted a second time. The pitch had not improved - and John Reid was right on target with his skiddy medium-pace. He bowled both of our openers, Graveney and Simpson, so there was no salvation coming from the direction of Gloucester in this innings! However, Peter May chipped in with 41, his highest score in New Zealand to date. When he was seventh out, three wickets fell on 194, and, with Bob Appleyard failing a sprint test, to be run out for zero, we were all out for 201. Reid returned the admirable figures of 5/65 in 20 overs.

Tuesday March 22nd.

Our moderate second innings score means that Wellington are still very much in the game. They need 282 to win - not a lot in a day's play. But if they score that number of runs on the now unpredictable Wellington wicket, it will be the highest total of the game - and we will have to bowl atrociously.

In fact the task was 187 runs too hard for the champion Kiwi team. Appleyard ran amok. He conceded one run per over for 21 overs - 13 of which were maidens - and took six wickets. He and Wardle bowled all but three overs of the innings - the left-hander capturing the remaining four wickets for 46. Only three of the Kiwis reached double figures, opener Smith top scoring with 26. They were all out for a paltry 94.

Brian Statham and I were both rested for the Wellington game. This gave the Royal Aeronautical College of

New Zealand the chance to ask George and me to collaborate in a trial to discover just how fast we bowl. They set up an experiment which involved painting a metal coating on a ball. The Kiwi boffins then asked us to bowl this ball into a sonic beam projected by a dish the length of a cricket pitch. As the ball passed through the beam, it gave off a high-pitched whistle. The duration of this sound was recorded, measured and translated into miles per hour by a complex equation. The half-dozen balls which I delivered were calculated as travelling at 89m.p.h. George's speed was reckoned at 87m.p.h. There were just a couple of matters which complicated and cast suspicion on the experiment. It was a damp cold day and both of us bowled in a couple of thick sweaters! We did not even bother to change into our whites. We just slipped on our cricket boots and, without a warm-up, bowled at considerably less than full pace - on to a pitch which had been saturated by overnight rain - which had made the run-ups very greasy! Still - anything for the sake of science!

Wednesday March 23rd.

With a New Zealand record of three matches and three wins behind us, we left 'Windy Wellington' - Kiwiland's equivalent of America's 'windy city' of Chicago - and travelled northwards towards Auckland, where we are to play the Second Test. Each mile we advanced, there were more faces of indigenous Maoris in the streets of the towns through which we passed. The weather was warming up. Below ground, too, the temperature was rising, for we were approaching the volcanic centre of North Island at Rotorua. We took time out to visit Lake Taupo and Rotorua. In the Whakarewarewa Thermal Park, we saw the Pohutu Geyser jetting skywards with clockwork regularity from the midst of steaming white-coated rocks. Nearby, boiling mud pools bubbled, emitting sulphur-dioxide gas which filled the air with the stench of rotten eggs. In the town hydro, tourists lolled in the stone baths of hot mineral-rich thermal water - good, we are told, for the treatment of rheumatism. In Ohenemutu Village we were given a guided tour by a real live Maori princess, who regaled us with the legend of the Maori Princess Hinemoa: Oh Margaret! Where are you?

We were treated to a concert of poi demonstrations - 'those tiny balls on the end of strings' - and Maori songs. The meanings of the elaborate carvings on the pantry and assembly huts were explained to us. No need of winter central heating in this little settlement; the huts were warmed by the thermal steam rising through the floorboards. Down the highway are the Waitomo Caves: and in them - a dazzling floodlit display of stalactites and stalagmites. Crossing from the caves to the Glow-worm Grotto nearby, I was frustrated in all my efforts to photograph the tiny phosphorescent insects - not enough light! A subsequent visit to the Rainbow Springs gave K.V. and I the experience of hand-feeding rainbow trout!

Above: The Pohutu Geyser.

Below: Players group at The Pohutu Geyser, Rotorua.

The Skipper rubs noses with a Maori princess.

Thursday March 24th.

Auckland is a spectacular harbour city. It lacks the completeness of its land-locked Sydney counterpart, but, in terms of natural scenic variety, is the equal of its Australian rival. The horizon, as one looks seawards from the quayside, is broken by the outlines of several islands and headlands like Rangitoto and Waiheke. Auckland is really two harbours rolled into one; on the north-western side of the isthmus, on which the city is built, lies the sheltered yachtsman's haven of Waitemata Harbour, home to the Royal Yacht Squadron. The south-eastern side of the same narrow neck of land is washed by the much rougher Manukau

Harbour, land access to which is through a most beautiful, forested and mountainous national park. The main thoroughfares of Auckland either skirt the harbour or descend quite a steep hill towards it. The main quayside is a bustling terminus for ferries to the commuter islands and a menu-ful of restaurants. Auckland houses present an unusual appearance. Being in an earthquake zone, many are of wood to obviate danger and make them easier to rebuild. Some residences, being built on the side of hills and steep shelving blocks, are on long wooden legs, which support the overhang. One can imagine that we are back in Brisbane.

Our hotel in Auckland is the Station. It is not far from the ferry terminal and is one of the strangest I have stayed in. It, too, is built on the side of a steep hill. One walks into its lobby and reception area from a street, level with one of its higher floors. Most of its rooms are built on the floors beneath. They are accessed by lift from either the higher public rooms or the ground floor, which opens on to a street at harbour level, 50 feet below the registration area! Confusing isn't it!

The strange construction of the Station Hotel lent itself to a rather childish prank on the part of K.V. and I. We were sharing a room on the fifth floor and one morning, just as we were preparing to leave by coach on an excursion from the harbour-side hotel lobby, we noticed the press boys accompanying us assembling five storeys down from our room. It was an ideal opportunity to settle a couple of scores. Almost under our window stood the diminutive and bespectacled Harry Gee, a rather serious agency journalist, and a fastidious dresser. This morning he was impeccably dressed in a light suit which had obviously just been pressed. The creases in the trousers were knife-edged. He was engaged in an animated conversation with a colleague and oblivious to what was going on above his head, where Keith and I were making our preparations. First we ensured that the lift, which was next to our room, was immobilised on our floor with its gates pushed back and the door to our room wide-open, ready for a speedy getaway. I filled a large paper bag with water from the washbowl tap in the room and, after gauging the trajectory of our 'water bomb', hid in the nether darkness. At a given signal from Keith, I took a couple of quick steps to the window, launched the missile and, even as it left my hands, spun on my heels and headed for the exit and the lift. The water bomb beat us down by a short half-head. As Keith and I stepped from the lift, creating the illusion that we had not had the time to drop the bag and be on the scene so quickly, the roar of anger from the press corps had not yet died down. The bomb was dead on target. Poor little Harry Gee copped the main blast, but others around him did not escape a dousing. A puerile prank really - but what the hell! We had won the Aussie series, and we were entitled to let off a bit of steam! Of course we had to wait for Harry Gee to change again for the trip - and the team had to pay for his dry cleaning. But to the end of his days, I doubt whether Harry ever knew who threw the Auckland Station Hotel water bomb!

Our first view of Eden Park, the venue for the Second Test, did not promise the aesthetic satisfaction suggested by its Garden-linked name. It is, in reality, a barren rugby ground with a cricket square in the middle. An austere concrete stand flanks one touchline without quite extending to the full length of the cricket arena. The stand is situated on the square-leg - or cover, depending on how you look at it - boundary, and houses the team changing rooms, access to which is gained by a tunnel, typical of a soccer arena. Directly facing this ugly construction and on the other side of the playing area, a hill slopes upwards from the boundary to a cluster of houses which stand outside the ground 50 feet above and fifty yards back, marking the full extent of the ground. This is the Auckland Hill: the equivalent of baseball's bleachers - and the home of the Kiwi barracker, a formidable vocalist. The Test pitch was mown in the centre of the oval, and parallel to the rugby touchlines. It is covered with a coarse grass and looks hard and bouncy! Bob Appleyard lick your lips!

To the left of the footy stand is a low block of administrative offices, alongside which is another smaller stand, at right angles to the first, facing on to the ground and almost behind the bowlers' arm. This miniature viewing area separates the main oval from Eden Park's number two practice ground, which is the setting for today's preparations for tomorrow's contest.

In the nets at Auckland preparing for the final onslaught.

Friday March 25th.

A lovely day for cricket: sunny with a light breeze, and the wicket promising both runs and wickets. A capacity crowd of 20,000 was in the ground when Rabone won the toss from Hutton and immediately opted to bat. New Zealand was in trouble as early as my second over, when the Canterbury opener, Tubby Leggat, fell l.b.w. to one that kept low. Matt Poore showed poor match temperament when he drove injudiciously at the third delivery he faced, edged and was caught by Godders. From a precarious 2/13, the rescue and rehabilitation of the Kiwi innings became a hard, uphill slog. Fortunately for the home side, it had just the men for the task: Bert Sutcliffe and John Reid - the two class batsmen of the Land of the Long White Cloud. Their association yielded 63 runs and was ended by Statham on the tick of lunch. It was at this inopportune moment that Sutcliffe, looking to reach his half-century before the break, finally tired of the fast short-pitched barrage to which he had been subjected and attempted to pull a Statham delivery which reared. He only succeeded in spooning the ball to Bailey at mid-on, and New Zealand went to the interval at 3/76. Sutcliffe's defiant contribution of 49 contained eight fours.

I lunched as usual on the Woozer Dalton special: the easily digested concoction of a raw egg beaten up in orange juice. But Woozer had another anxiety as far as I was concerned. I jarred the heel of my left foot in the morning session and now it was badly bruised. It was decided that I should field but not bowl in the afternoon session.

John Reid assumed the mantle of New Zealand's aggressor after the departure of Sutcliffe. At the other crease, skipper Rabone presented a dead bat to almost everything served up to him, crawling to a personal tally of 29 in two and a half hours. Reid's powerful driving forced Tom Graveney to retire to the pavilion nursing a bruised leg, and, with the Wellington skipper and Rabone still together at tea, the home could lay claim to having won the honours of the session.

After the interval, however, the pendulum swung back in our favour as Wardle first had Reid caught in juggling fashion by Statham at mid-off - and the catcher then claimed the wicket of Rabone caught behind for 29. Bob Appleyard made himself very unpopular with his Yorkshire team-mate Wardle, by dropping pace bowler MacGibbon off him - twice! Then, to rub salt into Wardle's wounded disappointment, he personally accounted for Cave, Mac-Gibbon and Colquhoun to finish the day one ball short of a hat-trick. New Zealand, after the early heroics of Sutcliffe and Reid, ended proceedings on an inadequate 8/199.

Saturday March 26th.

The weather yesterday was just too good to last. And last it did not. Saturday's play was constantly inter-rupted by rain squalls which had the players in and out of the pavilion like the miniature figures on a Swiss clock. Although the weather was unkind, it did not deter the spectators; 10,000 of them were in the stands and on the grassy hill to watch the first ball of the day bowled. They were drenched by the early morning rain and became progressively more and more dumbfounded by their team's batting failure.

Bob Appleyard failed to complete his hat-trick. He did not get another opportunity - or indeed another ball - as George Statham first removed Alec Moir l.b.w. and then bowled Hayes in the space of four deliveries. New Zealand was dismissed for a nicely rounded 200.

When it came our turn to bat, the Skipper was still feeling the effects of an infection which had plagued him last week and dropped down the order. He sent Reg Simpson and Tom Graveney in to open. Reg outshone the in-form Graveney, quickly moving to 23 against the accuracy and movement of MacGibbon and Hayes. Long Tom, handicapped by his leg injury, rarely produced any of his fluent drives, and was ill at ease when Hayes dropped the ball short. With the total on 21, he followed a Hayes outswinger, edged and was caught by Rabone at third slip. This greatly pleased the crowd which by now had increased to 23,000. With the score at 56 and the going getting slower with every ball, Reg's habitual impatience got the better of him. He decided to demonstrate his contempt for spinners - inopportunely, in the last over before lunch. Advancing down the wicket to the leg-spin of Alex Moir,

who had been brought on for the last over before the interval, he presented the bowler with the easiest of return catches.

During the break, half-an-hour of heavy rain drenched the crowd once more. Small wonder they were vociferous and restive. Play restarted on time with P.B.H. and Kipper making the most of the bowlers' difficulties in gripping the wet ball and running up on slippery approaches. The two amateurs also had problems themselves, since the ground was so heavy that it was almost impossible to find the boundary via the turf route. Peter, ever the classical player who seldom used the aerial path, hit seven threes! Both varsity men benefited from dropped catches and departed in quick succession, after a third-wicket partnership of 56. Moir bowled Cowdrey with a good leg-spinner - quite an achievement against such a good player of spin. Hayes thereupon knocked May over, bringing Bailey and Hutton together just before tea with the score standing at 4/117.

The Essex all-rounder blocked as his captain unleashed some exquisite drives to take the score to 145 - at which stage the skies darkened and the heavens opened once more, forcing both teams off the field. No sooner were they in the dressing room than the rain stopped! The crowd hooted and jeered, but half an hour passed before the covers could be removed and the umpires brought the players out once more. Hutton and Rabone, it appeared, had been unable to agree on the resumption. Further delays were caused when the noisy crowd erupted in an attempt to distract the batsmen. Bailey and Hutton added only three more runs before the umpires called it quits for the weekend. We were still 52 runs behind the New Zealand total with a long tail to follow the not-out batsmen.

Tonight was the last meeting of the Saturday Night Club. I shall miss it.

Sunday March 27th.

A day spent sightseeing around Auckland and on the Harbour. The weather is still damp and overcast.

Monday March 28th.

This day will go down in the annals of cricket as unique. Never has a Test match ended so abruptly - so unexpectedly - and so decisively. Bailey and Hutton resumed in bright, sunny conditions, but The Boil had added only three to his overnight score when he edged the boomeranging Cave and was caught by the keeper. He had supported Hutton for more than two hours of hard graft. Godders and Johnny Wardle did little for our cause, both failing to trouble the scorers and both being caught by Reid at slip off Moir. At 7/164 we were in deep trouble, still 36 behind and no recognised batting to come. I walked to the wicket just before lunch, and half-way to the middle the Skipper met me.

'Stick around for a while, Frank,' he said. 'We may not have to bat again!'

In the light of subsequent events, those words amounted to necromancy and fortune telling! I can only presume that having already batted for two hours

or more, Len was more awake to the problems of the pitch and conditions than his dopey team-mates. I did as I was told and 'stuck around'.

Lunch having been taken, MacGibbon and Hayes availed themselves of the second new ball. MacGibbon got one through Hutton's defences and ended our 37-run association. His had been a fine defensive innings which lasted 195 minutes and yielded the England top score of 55. (Little did I know it at the time, but this knock was to be Hutton's farewell to Test cricket.) We were only one run ahead: a situation which was only minimally improved, when Hayes had Bob Appleyard caught behind with the total standing at 218. It was only thanks to a spirited last wicket stand between George Statham and I that our lead was stretched to 46 before he too was 'caught Reid bowled Moir'.

At three o'clock on the dot, New Zealand began its second innings and in the forty minutes which remained before tea, lost the wickets of Gordon Leggat, Matt Poore and John Reid in scoring 13 runs. Hutton surprised everyone after the interval by introducing Johnny Wardle into the attack. A 'chinaman' tempted Sutcliffe into trying a big hit. He missed and Wardle hit. Now Hutton played his trump card, replacing me with Appleyard. Obviously with an analysis of 2/10 off seven overs I was too expensive! Appleyard responded to the invitation to bowl by taking three wickets in four deliveries - and four wickets at a cost of seven runs! With eight wickets down for 22, The Skipper asked George and I to finish off the New Zealand series, the Aussie rubber and the tour Down Under. I was, however, as the French say - *de trop*. With his fourth ball Brian trapped Rabone l.b.w. His eighth removed Hayes' middle stump! In just over a session's play, New Zealand, a full member of the Test club, had been dismissed for 26 - the lowest Test score ever! Hutton had been right. England did not need to bat a second time; we won by an innings and 20 runs with more than two days to spare. Coincidentally, Arthur Gilligan, the skipper who had led England when New Zealand scored its previously lowest Test score of 112 against that country on the same ground in 1929/30, was present when Hutton's side established the new record.

Twelve thousand stunned Kiwis staggered out of Eden Park and made their way home, well in time for dinner. It was almost a re-enactment of the Melbourne Test three months earlier, when 60,000 Aussies who had come to see their side win the Third Test, saw them beaten in one pre-lunch session and retired utterly bewildered and crushed to eat their meals in the Fitzroy Gardens!

There were the usual celebrations after the game. But they were rather muted in recognition of the lesser status of the New Zealand series.

Tuesday March 29th.

Celebration-lagged and champagne-logged, we are more than ready for England, home and beauty. Since we put a decisive end to the Second Test two days early, we were able to move our departure for home forward a couple of days. Today we took off in a Pan American Constellation and headed for Fiji, where we landed at Nadi airport - can we call it that? - where we were housed in what appeared to be a large shed, as our aircraft was refuelled. Then it was off again into the wide blue yonder, heading north-eastward. It was dark when we landed on a small atoll in the vastness of the Pacific. Canton Island is a mere speck on the map and God knows what happens to aircraft that mess up their navigation! If the Nadi Airport is basic, Canton Island Airport is positively primitive! Just a galvanised iron hut! Having taken on board another quota of fuel, we took off once more and this time made it as far as Hawaii. Since we crossed the International Date Line during this leg of the trip, we landed in Honolulu on the same day that we took off from New Zealand! Disembarking from the aircraft, we were garlanded. Then, still unsure about whether it was morning, afternoon or evening, we passed through immigration and headed for a beachside Waikiki Hotel, a good meal and a sound sleep. The French windows of our hotel room opened on to the beach and we could just stroll out on to the sand and into the surf. But this was nothing new after Australia! Indeed it was not as good as Surfers' Paradise!

Wednesday March 30th.

There was only time for the briefest of tours of Honolulu. We are booked on flight 26 of United Airlines, due to

Waikiki Beach in Honolulu, Hawaii.

depart at quarter to ten this evening. San Francisco is only an overnight flight away.

Thursday March 31st.

Landing in the Golden Gate City we were whisked away by Californian cricketing enthusiasts to a luxurious golf club, overlooking the Pacific, where the amenities include steam rooms, restaurants and barbers. Breakfast and then to our hotel. We are due to spend a couple of days in this lovely part of America and we should be able to see yet another corner of the world. It is amazing where cricket takes you!

Sunday April 3rd.

Left San Francisco by United flight 500 at 5.15 in the afternoon. Thus we travelled into the night and over the Rockies without being able to appreciate their beauty.

Monday April 4th.

Landing in New York, we were met by England's 'Lucky Mascot', Henry Sayen: our most ardent Yankee supporter who barracked so successfully for us in Sydney as he had in '53 in England. Sadly sickness forced Henry to return to America before we clinched the series. But here he was in New York, ready to share our victory and show us the town. He had come up

Garlanded players in Honolulu.

from Princeton, where he and his family now live and where he attended university. We dined at his Union League Club before ascending to the top of the Empire State Building to have a good look around 'the Big Apple'. A musical comedy rounded off the evening - after which most of the team headed back to Idlewild Airport - destination London.

Tuesday April 5th.

Henry very kindly invited Trevor Bailey and I to join him and his family for a day at his Princeton home, to meet his two sons and eight grandchildren. We took the train to the University town and spent the night with the Sayen family. Today The Boil chatted about cricket to a group of Princeton alumni, who gave a very good imitation of listeners who knew what he was talking about! The former Yankee fast bowler kindly showed us around his old college - which could cater so admirably for cricket but sadly doesn't - wished us well, took us to Idlewild and deposited us on BA flight 522 for London.

Chapter Fourteen

Envoi

SO IT WAS THAT I CAME HOME - almost 29 weeks to the day after I first stepped from the foyer of the Great Western Hotel in Paddington on September 15th 1954, took a cab to St. Pancras, entrained and then embarked on the S.S.Orsova at Tilbury. Early on the morning of April 7th 1955, my mother, my family and friends were at Heathrow Airport to greet me - back to a world which would never be the same. The Great Party was over: a party which lasted 203 momentous days and was crowned by a memorable England victory Down Under. England's 3-1 triumph was its first win in Australia for 22 years. In the space of its seven months in the Antipodes, Hutton's touring side played seven Tests, won five, drew one and lost one. In all, we played 21 first-class matches, won twelve, drew seven and were defeated in only two. We played a total of 28 games, winning 17 and drawing nine. My personal contribution to the tour was 39 Test and 64 first-class wickets at a cost of 17.25 and 17.81 runs respectively.

The tour had its ups and downs. Its nadir was undoubtedly our disappointing loss by an innings in Brisbane's First Test. But at least we were a side with enough character to admit to our shortcomings, remedy them, bounce back, extract our revenge and hit our top form in Sydney, Melbourne and Adelaide. If the tour proved nothing else, it showed that English cricket had guts. To me, beating Australia 'on its own midden', was the fulfilment of the teenage ambitions which I dreamt about as I practised my run-up on the balconies of Queen Elizabeth's Grammar School.

I suspect that my skipper in Australia, Len Hutton, was possessed by the same magnificent obsession. In 17 years of international cricket he had never returned victorious from Down Under. When he finally did, was it coincidence, I wonder, that Len chose to retire from the game in the following summer?

Why did we win the rubber? Personally, I cling to the romantic belief that our success revolved around the fact that we were a united team of Happy Warriors:

Whose high endeavours are
an inward light,
That makes the path before them
always bright.

We played together both on the field and off. Trevor Bailey later confirmed this impression when he told me that the 1954/55 tour was the happiest he ever shared. Years afterwards I learned that there was some dissatisfaction in the ranks, particularly on the score of selection. That, I suppose, was inevitable. One cannot keep all of a team happy, all of the time. Hutton was the prime target of these complaints - especially when he chose to pass over Bedser for the Sydney Test - and insensitively communicated the Surrey man's omission by posting a team list on the dressing room noticeboard! Reg Simpson also aired his grounds for complaint to some; he was not happy, that with his record of success as an opener in Australia, he was not chosen ahead of Bill Edrich or Trevor Bailey for the number two slot.

I got on very well with Len. But he was not everyone's cup of tea. He forfeited the sympathy of some senior men in the team by his reluctance to play in the Melbourne Test. Racked though he was with fibrositis, it was his responsibility to lead, and men such as George Duckworth, Geoffrey Howard, Bill Edrich, Denis Compton, Godfrey Evans and Trevor Bailey did not relish having to go to his bedroom on the morning of the game to persuade him to play. Nor did Peter Loader - along with other junior bowlers - enjoy being called to a briefing by the Skipper, a couple of days out of Tilbury, to be told that, when the serious business of the tour started, we would probably be relegated to mere support trundlers for the established Test bowlers.

Len's enigmatic, dry sense of humour was not to everyone's taste. It was wasted, for instance, on Keith Andrew, who enjoyed the odd game of golf. He bridled, therefore, when he asked Len for permission to play a few

holes and was told that at his age he should be following his captain's example and eating, drinking and breathing cricket - not playing golf! Keith's riposte was to enquire how the Skipper had managed to get his golf handicap so low! In spite of these differences of opinion, the general mood of the team remained friendly and sunny. Indeed, the strength of the touring party lay in the willingness of individuals to subordinate their personal whinges to the general good of the side.

In one respect, Hutton's leadership was beyond reproach - unless, that is, your sympathies lay with the Australian cause. There was no questioning the Yorkshireman's tactical acumen. It would be extravagant to claim that he never made a strategically wrong decision during the whole seven months of the tour. But I think that it would be safe to say that his errors were few and far between. He regulated his field placements with meticulous exactitude; he changed his bowlers at precisely the right physical and psychological moment; he was, eight times out of ten, spot on. Most people regarded his winning the toss in Brisbane and asking Australia to bat first as the bloomer to end all bloomers. The ensuing innings defeat seemed to support that viewpoint. But what other choice did Hutton have after the tour selectors handed him a side with no spinners and four specialist fast bowlers? After that, his biggest hope of dismissing Australia cheaply lay in exploiting the early life which the Queensland game indicated was there

Leaving Australia after a job well done.

for the seamers on the first day at the Gabba. Hutton got that decision wrong. The pitch turned out to be a featherbed, our catching turned out to be butter-fingered, and all of our luck with sickness and injury turned out to be bad!

Perhaps too, there was a case to be made against Hutton's tinkering with England's batting order in the post-Adelaide phases of the tour. His anxiety to find a satisfactory opening partner led him to try hammering square pegs into round batting holes. It was motivated by a desire to lessen the responsibilities which lay heavily on his own shoulders and - more import-antly - weighed heavily on his own mind. But it was most unfair on the square pegs. I felt for the failures of Wilson, Edrich, Cowdrey and Bailey when they were press-ganged into opening the innings. It did not reflect well on the original 18-man selection of the touring party that not once during the tour did England field an estab-lished and successful pair of opening batsmen. Had we possessed a regular pair of openers we might have avoided our two defeats of the tour.

But Hutton got it right on the final day of the Adelaide Test. On that occasion many pundits forecast that, with the wicket taking more and more spin, Len would place his trust and the winning of the game into the fingers of his fellow-tykes, Bob Appleyard and Johnny Wardle. The England skipper, however, held another point of view. He chose to press home the psychological advantage established by Brian Statham and I in the Sydney and Melbourne Tests. Speed not spin mopped up the Australian second innings resistance, leaving us just 94 runs for victory in the Test and series.

Having opened England's batting for almost eighteen years, and having confronted the pace blitzkrieg of Lindwall and Miller for most of that time, Hutton had first-hand experience of the psychological ascendancy that genuine fast bowling exerts over irresolute resistance. Now that he had authentic quick bowlers in his side, he knew how best to use them. He rarely slackened the fury of his fast assault; and he paced England's over-rates according to the attacking capacities of his dominant pace attack. His rationale was that it did not matter if his quick bowlers bowled only 12 overs an hour - provided they took a wicket every seven overs! As an ex-bowler, I incline to the viewpoint that excitement in cricket comes just as much from the rapid fall of wickets as it does from an avalanche of runs.

In Australia in 1954/55 Len agreed; he insisted on quality pace bowling, not a quick succession of indifferent overs. Sometimes, when he detected a slackening in my pace and deduced I was wearying, he would wait at first slip until I reached the end of my run-up and was just about to turn and begin my approach. Then he would hold up his right hand, like a policeman on point duty. Having halted proceedings, he would then walk slowly the length of the pitch and my run-up, approach me and enquire in a confidential manner: 'Are you alright, Frank?' Having been reassured I was fit and ready to proceed, he would then say, 'That's alright then' and walk slowly back to his slip position! End of rest period!

The Aussie side complained long and loud about Hutton's tactical use of his fast bowlers and England's slow over-rate. Alan Davidson expressed the opinion of many of the home batsmen when he said that in bowling a miserly 65 overs a day, England's pacemen restricted Australia's diurnal ration of runs to 200 - whereas the Australian bowling rate of 90 overs a day allowed England to score 300 runs. This, Davidson maintains, placed Australia in a defensive mode - except in Brisbane where the home team passed the 600 mark, and could indulge in the luxury of stroke-making in the latter part of its innings. It is Alan's contention that thereafter England's slow over-rate compelled the home side to grind out their runs against a daily quota of overs of pace, making batting an uphill struggle.

To argue that a slow over-rate forces a team on to the defensive is a load of rubbish. The factor which compels batting sides to defend is the loss of wickets. England may have had the opportunity to score 300 runs in a day off the Aussie bowling, but, in fact, only passed that score in an innings once in Adelaide and once in Sydney when the rubber was dead. In every other innings we were bowled out for under 300. Similarly, Australia, after Brisbane's 8/601 score, only exceeded 300 once - in the first innings of the Adelaide game - for the same and good reason that they were bowled out!

A few figures explain the superiority of England in the rubber. England bowled 554 overs in the series, of which the quicker bowlers sent down 404.7 or 73%. By comparison Australia delivered 758 overs with the fast men sending down 529 or 69.72%. Not a great difference in this comparison. England's pace bowlers took 57 wickets at a strike rate of a wicket every 58 balls and an average of 27.14. It should be noted that without the Brisbane Test, our strike rate would have been vastly improved. Australia's faster men took 59 wickets at a strike rate of a wicket every 72 balls and an average of 25.11. These figures show that the Aussie quick bowlers took more wickets than ours - but at a greatly inferior strike rate - albeit a better average. Simply put we took a wicket 2 overs more frequently than Johnson's side.

Another consideration worth examining is the clear superiority of the England slow bowlers in the rubber. Appleyard and Wardle sent down 149.6 overs or 26% of England's total overs. They took 21 wickets at a strike rate of one every 57 balls (better than the faster men) and an average of 21.57 (much better than the quickies). Compare these figures to the Australian stats. Johnson and Benaud captured 22 wickets at a strike rate of one every 83 deliveries and an average of 28.18. They did this in spite of the fact that they did 30.% of the bowling and had much greater opportunities. In both instances of strike rate and average, the England figures were superior to the Australian.

Setting to one side the crucial batting contributions which Wardle and

Appleyard made to the first Sydney Test, a very good argument can be mounted that the England slow bowlers were just as influential in determining the destination of the Ashes as the more acclaimed faster men. The key is to compare the frequency in which the two sets of bowlers took their wickets - and not the time taken to bowl overs.

The best example of Hutton's tactical intuition, however, came my way in the Second Test against New Zealand in Auckland: the final match of the tour. Len batted at number 5 and had most of his eventual 53 runs on the board when I came to the crease at number 9, with the scoreboard showing 7/164 and England still 36 runs behind the Kiwis' first-innings tally of 200.

'Stick around for a bit, Frank,' said Hutton,' we might not have to bat again!'

I stuck around, scored 27 not out and helped England to a total of 246. Len finished with 53. Then England bowled Geoff Rabone's side out in its second innings for 26: a still existent record low for Tests. So Hutton was proved right! England did not have to bat again! But how could Hutton possibly have known that we would bowl New Zealand for so few runs? Fifty years after the event, no international side has remotely descended to such a nadir! Hutton must have been fay!

By his own high standards, Len had a poor tour with the bat. He averaged only 24 in the Tests and not one of the three centuries which he scored came in Tests. The same could be said of Compo, who topped the tour's first-class averages, batting virtually on one

leg; his highest score in the games that mattered was only 84. It was hard to see the logic in the selectors retaining Bill Edrich for the first four Tests against Australia when his form scarcely justified his inclusion. He managed only 180 runs in eight knocks and finished the series with an average of 22.50. In all of the 11 first-class games he appeared in on tour, he returned a mean figure of 16.27. Graveney took Edrich's opening slot for the final Test in Sydney and his 111 runs in this game hoisted his aggregate to 132 and his average to 44: poor figures to top the England averages. Even the ever-reliable all-rounder Trevor Bailey outscored the specialist batsmen Graveney, Compton, Hutton and Edrich in Tests. Only three M.C.C. batsmen reached 1000 runs on the tour: Hutton, May and Cowdrey. Of these, only the 24-year old Peter May and the 21-year old Colin Cowdrey notched centuries in the Test matches. Add this fact to the bowling statistic that George Statham and I - both 24 of age - took 46 of the 80 wickets to fall in the England/Australia Tests, 69 of the wickets to fall in the seven Tests played on both sides of the Tasman; and that Peter Loader - also 24 - took 41 first-class wickets on tour, and one has to accept the inescapable conclusion: the 1954/55 M.C.C. tour of Australasia was a young man's scene and youth was at the heart of our triumph. It was a series which ushered in a fresh generation of England batsmen and marked the beginning of outstanding careers for Cowdrey, May, Graveney and Statham.

England also owed much of its success with the ball to the strong support provided by the moving medium-pace of Bailey and the spin of Wardle and Appleyard. The mysteries of the Yorkshire spin twins were never completely solved by the Australian batsmen. The tall, apple-cheeked Bob 'Applecart' in Australia was too bouncy, too accurate and had too much variety for the Aussie batsmen. He was never 'collared'. A wonderful dual personality with the ball, he is an asset to any side, being quick enough to take the new ball or exploit a turning pitch. I hesitate to call Appleyard a spinner. He is more of a cutter of the ball, a factor which makes him all the more 'un-get-atable'.

The accurate subtleties of Wardle's orthodox spin complemented his over-the-wrist style of bowling, made him the best slow bowler of the series and, I believe, have now established him as the best spinner in the world on all types of wickets. Keith Andrew vouched for his unpredictability. That is a real commendation!

The ageing component of Hutton's team militated against it becoming a top-class, mobile fielding unit away from the close-in positions. Edrich, Hutton and Compton were safe catchers, and the presence of Cowdrey at slip greatly strengthened the behind-the-wicket cordon. Cowdrey's prehensile skills often saw him gather in batsmen's edges when the ball was past him at third slip - and then fooling the spectators by imitating Wally Hammond's trick of pocketing it before turning, as if about to chase it to the third-man boundary!

Hutton was criticised for tiring his fast bowlers by positioning them in the chasing positions in the outfield; the truth was that we were the only ones, young and mobile enough to do the retrieving! There is no doubt that Australia were a superior fielding team, and had we caught as well as the home side our margin of victory would have been greater than it was. Luckily, our fielding only broke down completely on one occasion - in the First Test in Brisbane - where we turfed twelve catches. In the aftermath of that disappointing innings loss, we had enough character, determination and work ethic to seal the chinks in our armour - at least until the final games of the tour in New Zealand, when the strain began to tell and we began to relax our focus on important basics.

In the all-important department of wicket-keeping, England had a real match-winner - Godfrey Evans - a.k.a. Godders. If there was one catch which decided the 1954/55 series, it was Evan's leg-side gloving of Neil Harvey on the final day of the Melbourne Test. When Benaud and Harvey took the field for Australia on that memorable morning, their side needed only 165 runs to win and had plenty of batting in reserve with eight wickets in hand. When, off my seventh ball from the Richmond end, Harvey moved across to the off-stump to glance a delivery which pitched on middle and leg, the resultant stroke looked to be heading for the boundary... when, out of nowhere, Godfrey Evans materialised to clasp the ball to his chest. Press photographs show the wicket-keeper taking the catch twice the distance of the return crease - more than eight feet - down the leg-side. The effect of that catch on the morale of the Aussie side was nothing short of dramatic. I claimed three wickets in the next half-hour and the Aussie batting collapsed like a house of cards. In 79 minutes and 12.3 overs the match was over, eight wickets falling to George Statham and me for 36 runs; and Godfrey Evans started it all! He started so many things - including a self-belief that we could win the series even after our disastrous start in Queensland. I shall never forget his war-cry: 'Come on lads, Attack with venom!'

The New Zealand segment of our tour proved something of an anti-climax. I do not write this in patronising vein. The Kiwis are bonny fighters; they excel on the rugby field as they have proved time and time again at Twickenham, the Wanderers, Lansdowne Road, Murrayfield and Cardiff Arms Park. Subsequent events have proved that they can give as good as they receive in the amphitheatre of world cricket. For a nation of four million weekend cricketers they do remarkably well against professional and semi-professional opponents. In Sutcliffe and Reid, the 'Land of the Long White Cloud' had two of the finest players in the world. The left-handed Sutcliffe was the epitome of elegance; he melted into his drives and pirouetted into his pulls and hooks, with nary an ungainly movement. He had the courage of a lion and stood up to the fastest bowling without flinching. John Reid, for his part, was all nuggety

defiance. Solid in defence, he hit with the power of a kicking mule and for many years held records for the number of sixes he has hit in a match or a single innings. As a bowler, he sometimes surprised with his nip off the pitch, but rarely exceeded medium-pace. He was completely disciplined in line and length and moved the ball appreciably off the seam.

The strength of the New Zealand bowling reposed in its ability to perform well in its own conditions. Thus pacemen like MacGibbon, Hayes and Blair might not aspire to extreme speed, but they could move the ball enough in the air and off the pitch to beat the bat with great regularity. And throughout the years, New Zealand's orthodox spinners have more than held their own against top batsmen around the globe. I think that the rest of the cricketing world has treated New Zealand shabbily. It deserves more international recognition and more Test series than it is presently awarded and the time is not far distant when it will receive its due.

The individual personalities in the team were the key factors in determining the success of the 1954/55 M.C.C. Tour of Australasia. If Hutton's 'Orsova Declaration of Intent' to Loader, McConnon, Tyson, Andrew and Wilson had left us with the mental resignation of being mere back-ups to the major players of the side, the team might never have recovered from the debacle of Brisbane. The fact that we did was due, in no small measure, to the determination of the Second Stringers to prove Hutton wrong. Andrew knew that he was only there as Evans's replacement in case of injury. Loader, however, adopted an anti-Hutton position which he expressed by bowling so well that he was never far from Test selection. As for me, I knew I was a wild card selection. My worst possible scenario was that I would return to England a virgin in Australian Tests, but infinitely more experienced. However, I was sure of one thing: if I did not succeed Down Under, it would not be for the want of trying - or the lack of intelligent application. This was the opportunity to live my Middleton 'bowling-along-the-balcony' dream and be part of a winning England team in Australia. My whole cricketing life had been fashioned to meet this challenge. I had played alongside and against Aussies in the northern leagues and county championship. I knew their competitiveness and could match it. What they dished out, they would receive back! If the Skipper wanted 110% commitment - I would give him 120%. If he needed an extra five overs, I would bowl 10 more! This was the only way to play in an Ashes Test - flat out! I knew no other. Guts cricket. They could knock me out, as they did in the Sydney Test - but they could not knock me out of the game. My father taught me to confront and oppose. When I was a squaddie doing my National Service, he once sent me along to a major shareholders' meeting of the Yorkshire Dyeing Company who employed him - with one share and a view to express!

Well, I did gain valuable experience from the tour. I learned and improved. At the Gabba, I learned by experience

OUR PIN-UP

FRANK TYSON
Northants and England

that express bowling needs reflex catching to match. I also discovered that cricket in Australia demands greater fitness and physical endurance. I upgraded my training schedule, and took advice from older heads than mine. Alf Gover, the former England fast bowler, was covering the tour for an English newspaper. Alf was the mentor of my winter tree-felling days of 1952/53. Each weekend I trained at his East Hill Indoor School in south-west London. He was aware of the fact that, at his nets and in league cricket, I bowled off a run which was much shorter than that which I employed in Brisbane. To economise on energy, he advised me to return to a briefer approach - and at the same time maintain my forward momentum in the delivery stride. I took up Alf's suggestion, increased my stamina and accuracy and maintained my speed. Success and wickets followed.

April 7th 1955.

Headwinds over the Atlantic delayed Pan Am flight 70's morning arrival in London by two hours. This was just the sort of ending to a four-day air trip home from Australia which I did not need. It necessitated a fourteen-hour transatlantic flight and a detour via Nova Scotia, where our plane landed and took off between snow drifts piled 10 feet high on either side of the runway. No wonder Trevor Bailey and I landed at London Airport ready to sleep 'for a fortnight'. By sheer luck we were spared too much media hassle. The national newspapers were on strike. Sleep, however, was the last item on the agenda. From the aircraft we were hurried through immigration and customs to a short press conference - then to a brief meeting with my mother and brother - before we were taken to a Nissen hut on the airfield to face the television cameras and B.B.C microphones.

The day became a blur as we were driven into London to lunch at a hotel which cost the equivalent of four week's tour pocket-money. Then I managed to grab a five-hour sleep before having to front up once more to another round-table television discussion of the tour with R.W.V. 'Cock' Robins, Peter May, Tom Graveney and a couple of the journalists who had accompanied the tour.

It was great to see my mother, brother David, the Kay family from Middleton and my Australian colleagues from Northampton, George Tribe and Ray Hogan - even George's son David had come along! Our victory in Australia had seemingly captured the national imagination and opened a lot of doors.

Compo, for instance, as promised, introduced me to his agent, Bagenal Harvey - the man who had set up his Brylcreem advertising deal. Bagenal at this stage was working for Hulton Press, but was about to set up on his own and act exclusively as an agent for eminent sportsmen, negotiating advertising contracts and providing financial expertise. He was the first of many. Trevor Bailey and Godders were already signed up to his 'stable'.

In my home town of Middleton, the Mayor, Councillor Wellens, established a Tyson Testimonial Fund which raised more than £200. In Northampton, the *Chronicle and Echo* - the local newspaper - opened a Shilling Fund as 'A Welcome Home Testimonial' to both Keith Andrew and me. Those were heady and confusing days. Certainly they were vastly different times to the - shall we say - 'low key' farewells of early September 1954!

In addition to the flattery handed out by those who were wise after the event, I was also given some fairly serious and sobering advice by those who were closer to cricket reality. The best counsel I received came from the mouth of the Skipper, Len Hutton, who captained Yorkshire against Northamptonshire at Northampton in the season after my Australian triumph. At the

Testimonial Presentation by the Mayor, Councillor Wellens, in Middleton.

time, the joke current in the county eleven was that the under-prepared Wantage Road pitches were so bad that cabbages could be planted in them.

'Frank,' said Len. 'Go back to Lancashire. If you continue playing on this wicket, you will be out of Test cricket in a few years.' He was right. I would probably have played until I was 35 at Lancashire, bowling in harness with Statham, and on pitches more sympathetic to pace bowling. In the fifties, however, it was not easy to change county allegiances. And although I canvassed for five years to have the Northampton wickets quickened up, I was unsuccessful. The

County Ground pitch remained a happy hunting ground for George Tribe, Jack Manning and Micky Allen - three slow left-arm bowlers - who each took most of their 100 wickets a season on it, year after year. Still, how can one instil cricket nous into administrators whose principal job qualifications are those of shoe-makers, furniture retailers and policemen: men who, after our contribution to the success of 1954/55 Australian tour, voted against a civic welcome for K.V. and I on the grounds that it was 'unwarranted and un-balanced'! These were the same people of whom I overhead one remark to a colleague after a Supporters' Club

The Royal Command Performance 1955. I am in between Mabel and Wilfred Pickles. On the left is Stanley Matthews next to 'George' Statham and far right is Tom Finney.

Welcome Home function on the stage of the Northampton Repertory Theatre: 'God, where do these professionals learn how to speak?' Not only had he not been to 'varsity' - but he had obviously not played too much cricket or bowled too many overs in Australia!

In the judgement of some cricket analysts and observers, the Bodyline Tour of 1932/33 - the cricket dispute which almost alienated a Commonwealth - was spawned by a fortuitous combination of events. They say that it was occasioned by a coincidence which put into the hands of an inflexible general, Jardine, a brutally effective tactic; and, in the persons of Larwood and Voce, at the same time furnished him with the two best enforcers of that tactic that the cricket world has seen.

Fifty years on, I look back on the events of the 1954/55 M.C.C. tour of Australia; and I wonder whether there is a parallel to be drawn between that series and the events of 22 years earlier. The England captain of 1954/55, Hutton, certainly did not resort to Bodyline tactics. Nonetheless, he had at his disposal an attack physically at the peak of their early-twenties powers, and well equipped to exploit the psychological flaws in their Australian opponents, who, like their predecessors of 1932, were running into a changing-of-the-guard period. Stripped of these advantages on their next visits to Australia, 'Gubby' Allen's team of 1936/37 and Peter May's side of 1958/59, both endowed with outstanding talents, found the three or four-match winning margins of the preceding series completely reversed.

These facts, when considered in the light of my personal successes in one tour- and my notable lack of success in the following rubber - stimulates the conceit that perhaps bowlers such as Larwood - and myself - were created with just one purpose in mind: to win the 1932/33 and 1954/55 series. After such accomplishments, and as the years recede and strength ebbs, one is left acutely aware of one's complete inability to repeat the achievements of one's youth. And there are few compensatory peaks in later life. Evelyn Waugh summed up the dilemma of achievement being swallowed up by advancing age when in an address to an author's club he said: 'There are many compensations in being an eighty-year-old writer.' Then adding after a long pause: 'I am just trying to think of one!'

In one respect I shall forever be indebted to the events of 1954/55 in Australia. At one Melbourne party during the second waterlogged match against Victoria, I met a girl, Ursula, who in the following year travelled to Europe with a group of young ladies on the 'Grand Tour'. At this time, my letters to and from Margaret had dwindled and eventually stopped. And when Urs arrived, I passed much of the social summer in her company - until finally she and her friend Gill joined me for the fortnight of the Scarborough Festival. There we decided that if, at the conclusion of the South African tour - for which I had been selected, we still felt the same about one another, we should become engaged. In South Africa I asked Godders to use his jewellery connections to have an engagement ring made. He obliged and I sent it to Urs. Six months later I followed the ring to Australia and Urs and I were married - after a year's absence the one from the other. After 47 years of marriage, I hope I can claim my family as at least an indirect legacy of the 1954/55 tour.

I try to console myself with the thought that I returned from Australia a better cricketer, an improved bowler and a more compassionate human being. But am I? I am sure there are many things which I could have done better - many things which I have left undone - people I could have loved more, helped more, cared for more. When I returned to my home town of Middleton I told the press: 'The spirit which brought back the Ashes to this country is eminently a North Country spirit. I am convinced it is the sort of thing that will win Test matches.' Have I lived up to this acknowledgement of my origins and proved myself worthy of the people who shaped my character: my family, the Kays, my *alma mater*, Middleton Queen Elizabeth Grammar School, my contemporaries at Durham University, my team-mates in the 1954/55 touring team and at North-ampton? I doubt it, and now, in some instances, it is too late to make good my sins of omission. A full eleven of my England contemporaries have now passed on. So I still strive. For me it will always be a case of: *Quand tu arrives en haut d'une montagne - continue a grimper.*

EXCLUSIVE: Mother's photo album of the sportsman of the week

Mrs. TYSON'S BOY

☆ Seven Australian wickets for 27 runs! No wonder Frank ("Typhoon") Tyson is the sportsman of the week, but here he is as his widowed mother sees him—the boy growing up.

As the four-year-old standing proudly outside his tent in the garden.

As the Boy Scout (right) on a trip to the Channel Islands at the age of 14

As the 15-year-old footballer (inside right) in the school team.

As the hockey player while studying for a B.A. degree at Durham University.

As the parson in a Queen Elizabeth Grammar School (Middleton) play.

As the soldier (Royal Signals) before he went into first-class cricket.

The Tour Party

Geoffrey Howard *(Lancs)* - Manager - nickname: The 'Ger.
George Duckworth *(Lancs)* - baggage man - nicknames: Ducky, The Admiral.
Harold Dalton *(Essex)* - physio - nickname: Woozer.
Len Hutton *(Yorks)* - Captain - nickname: Skipper.
Keith Andrew *(Northants)* - nicknames: KV., Gloves.
Bob Appleyard *(Yorks)* - nickname: Applecart.
Trevor Bailey *(Essex)* - nicknames: The Boil, Barnacle, Boiley.
Alec Bedser *(Surrey)* - nickname: Big Al.
Denis Compton *(Middlesex)* - nicknames: Compo, D.C.S.
Colin Cowdrey *(Kent)* - nickname: Kipper.
Bill Edrich *(Middlesex)* - nickname: W.J.
Godfrey Evans *(Kent)* nickname: Godders.
Tom Graveney *(Glos)* nickname: Long Tom.
Peter Loader *(Surrey)* - nicknames: Scrubs, P.J.
Peter May *(Surrey)* - nickname: P.B.H.
Jim McConnon *(Glamorgan)* - nickname: Big Jim.
Reg Simpson *(Notts)* - nicknames: Simmo, The Native.
Brian Statham *(Lancs)* - nicknames: Stat, George, The Greyhound, The Whippet.
Frank Tyson *(Northants)* - nicknames: Typhoon, Dingers.
Johnny Wardle *(Yorks)* - nickname: Johnny.
Vic Wilson *(Yorks)* - nickname: Vic.

The Tests

Australia v. England (1st Test)
Woolloongabba, Brisbane, on 26, 27, 29, 30 Nov, 1 Dec
AUSTRALIA WON BY AN INNINGS AND 154 RUNS
Australia 601 for 8 Dec (Harvey 162, Morris 153, Lindwall 64*, Hole 57)
England 190 (Bailey 88) & 257 (Edrich 88)

Australia v. England (2nd Test)
Sydney Cricket Ground, on 17, 18, 20, 21, 22 Dec
ENGLAND WON BY 38 RUNS
England 154 (Archer 3-12, Johnston 3-56) & 296 (May 104, Cowdrey 54)
Australia 228 (Tyson 4-45, Bailey 4-59) & 184 (Harvey 92*, Tyson 6-85)

Australia v. England (3rd Test)
Melbourne Cricket Ground, on 31 Dec, 1, 3, 4, 5 Jan
ENGLAND WON BY 128 RUNS
England 191 (Cowdrey 102, Archer 4-33) & 279 (May 91, Johnston 5-85)
Australia 231 (Statham 5-60) & 111 (Tyson 7-27)

Australia v. England (4th Test)
Adelaide Oval, on 28, 29, 31 Jan, 1, 2 Feb
ENGLAND WON BY FIVE WICKETS
Australia 323 (Maddocks 69) & 111
England 341 (Hutton 80, Cowdrey 79, Benaud 4-120) & 97 for 5

Australia v. England (5th Test)
Sydney Cricket Ground, on *25, 26, 28* Feb, 1, 2, 3 March
MATCH DRAWN
England 371 for 7 Dec (Graveney 111, Compton 84, Bailey 72)
Australia 221 (McDonald 72, Wardle 5-79) & 118 for 6

New Zealand v. England (1st Test)
Carisbrook, Dunedin, on 11, 12, *14, 15,* 16 March
ENGLAND WON BY EIGHT WICKETS
New Zealand 125 (Sutcliffe 74, Statham 4-24) & 132 (Tyson 4-16)
England 209 for 8 Dec (Reid 4-36) & 49 for 2

New Zealand v. England (2nd Test)
Eden Park, Auckland, on 25, 26, 28 March
ENGLAND WON BY AN INNINGS AND 20 RUNS
New Zealand 200 (Reid 73, Statham 4-28) & 26 (Appleyard 4-7)
England 246 (Hutton 53, Moir 5-62)

N.B. Dates in itallics indicate no play possible on that day
* indicates not out

Index

Index